The JIMI HENDRIX Companion

D0940874

The JIMI HENDRIX Companion

Three
Decades of
Commentary

Edited by
CHRIS POTASH

OMNIBUS PRESS
LONDON · NEW YORK · SYDNEY

Exclusive Distributors
Book Sales Limited,
8/9 Frith Street,
London W1V 5TZ, UK.

To the Music Trade Only:
Music Sales Limited,
8/9 Frith Street,
London W1V 5TZ, UK.

A catalogue record for this book is available from the British Library.

Visit Omnibus Press at http://www.musicsales.co.uk

This paper meets the requirements of ANSI/NISO Z39.48-1992 (Permanence of Paper).

To acoustic and electric
woman and man alike . . .
and well, EVERYBODY

Contents

PART TWO: CRITICS: BOLD AS . . . LOVE?

PART SEVEN: DIG

Acknowledgments

Denise Malek spent long hours in libraries and bookstores instinctively researching this project. She read every article in here at least twice, and in the end keyboarded a whole lot of them. Without her interest and input this collection would have been way less rich.

Thanks to Steve Roby, publisher of the Hendrix fanzine *Straight Ahead,* for meeting with me twice and providing insight into the "inner circle" of Hendrix fanatics—which includes Ken Voss (publisher of *Voodoo Child*) and Caesar Glebbeek (publisher of *UniVibes*), who also opened their archives to the project. Peter Knobler, former editor of *Crawdaddy,* took the time to refer an article, as did Jeff Campbell at Electric Lady Studios.

Here's to Reid A. Paige Associates for their *Selected Press Anthology 1967–70,* an unauthorized, unsubsidized, truly underground collection of early press clippings about Jimi. And speaking of underground, a plug is due the *Alternative Press Index,* compiled in Baltimore, which should be found, like the *Readers' Guide to Periodical Literature*, in any library (thanks, San Francisco Public) that fancies itself an adequate research facility.

Thanks too to Ray Yaros, for sending his stash of twenty-plus-year-old rock magazines; to Brendan McGowan and Linda Marousek-McGowan, our friends in Frisco, for their cooking and the use of their turntable; to Philly guitarist Andy Ferrence, for his '86 *Musician;* to Richard Kostelanetz, for getting me this gig; and, retroactively, to Richard Savage, Daisy Harris, and Paul Gallagher, good (-hearted) editors all.

Finally, thanks be to the authors, publishers, and reprint-rights staffs who responded to my permissions requests. Make no mistake—clearing permissions is definitely *not* the coolest part of compiling an anthology. Still, Real People such as Louise Boundas, editor in chief of *Stereo Review,* Mark Anderson at Cambridge University Press, Maggie (sp?) at *Melody Maker,* Hank McQueeney for *Creem* (on the stands again), authors Charles Keil and Steven G. Smith (see bibliography), and a few others were professional *and* personable—which proves that one does not exclude the other. (However, no thanks to *Art in America* and *The Village Voice.*) Furthermore, if I've used a piece without permission, it wasn't for lack of trying. I called here, there, and everywhere, time and time again. You few writers who've so far eluded my attempts, please contact me in care of the publisher so due credit can be granted before next printing.

Introduction

For sure, Jimi Hendrix will reign as master of electric-guitar sound and style at least through the end of this century. His facility with the modern instrument known commonly as the axe outshone all comers—and continues to do so. Yet it should be noted that from the fateful moment in '67 when *Melody Maker* editors set the above headline in 72-point type, pop culture started calling Jimi's shots. Indeed, through reportage, criticism, scholarship, and the two cents pitched in by plain ol' people who care, the zeitgeist continues to define (and perhaps confine) its prime movers.

In this book, I hope to document and illuminate the phenomenon of Jimi Hendrix as it was and is being played out, by arranging in revealing order newspaper, magazine, and journal articles that have made their claims on Hendrix. Including both "name" authors and lesser-known lights, my goal here is to create a charged pastiche of more and less complex verbal constellations that conducts *feeling*—much like Hendrix's approach to recording, layering sounds to build a heavy composition—as well as simply to collect some essential writings about Jimi into one volume.

Please note that pieces are reprinted as they appeared on the dates given, except for an added comma here or there, so you may notice alternating references to Band of Gypsies/Gypsys, "Foxy/Foxey Lady," *Are You Experienced* with *and* without the question mark, and other stylistic inconsistencies that in this context can be interesting. (The discography at the end of the *Companion* lists song titles as they "officially" appear on the original album/cassette covers.) British spellings and grammatical idiosyncrasies have been retained for flavour, and all epigraphs on part openings are Jimi's own words. Note that, throughout, three asterisks centered on a line (* * *) indicates a space break in the original text, while a centered ellipsis (. . .) indicates a missing (edited) block of text.

Now—let's get experienced.

* * *

In the beginning of his odyssey from sideman to front man and wild man to god, James Marshall Hendrix was like any other young buck coming up: into his music and into himself. As a deeply sensitive soul, though, he was more susceptible than most to the debilitating demands of the star-making machine—as you can tell from reading the hyped press reports gathered in part one, "The Experience." And what an experience. Of course Jimi wanted to hear and see everything—it was the sixties, after all—but at a saner pace maybe? The novelty of fame understandably waned as both British and U.S. press pressed him for precious time but then gave his middle name as "Maurice"; or called his virtuosic third album *Electric Landlady;* or had him bandmates with Keith Moon (this in Jimi's obituary). Such slips are mere typos, however, compared to the serious flak Hendrix took for his looks—"a cross between Bob Dylan and the Wild Man of Borneo: his hair is a foot long, uncombed and stabs the air in every direction around a heavily pimpled face" (*Ebony,* 5/68); his dynamism—"a high-strutting chicken going after a kernel of corn" (*Look,* 1/7/69); and, near the end of his experience, for resisting *Rolling Stone*'s politics—pro pop, pot, and the Panthers.

Ordered more or less chronologically, for effect, the pieces arranged in this first section show how far out of his way Jimi went for his music; how much he put up with, how much he spent, and how what was left was barely enough to sustain such a promising career and life.

It would have been poignant, convenient, and dramatic to close "The Experience" with Michael Lydon's sensitive *New York Times* obit. But the behind-the-scenes account of the funeral goings-on that immediately follows, while thematically messy, nevertheless portends the personal and political struggles that would dog Hendrix—the jockeying for favor and fortune, the infighting, the posthumous releases, the deliberately confused line between good business and good taste that was crossed again and again and again—even after he was gone. Hopefully the standard-bearing *Grove Dictionary* wraps up his accomplishments in honorary perspective. And check this out: Hendrix's *Grove* entry ends on the same page where *jazz* writer Nat Hentoff's begins.

Though Hendrix suffered the sting of censure ("Critics give me a pain in the neck"), it was in his character to have admired some of the rock criticism committed to type in his name. More than mere reporters, the groundswell of *writers* responding emotionally and creatively to the popular music of the sixties helped usher in the youth culture, of which Jimi was an active member. At their bold best, critics can—like Hendrix could—transcend the sensuous gulfs between mediums: as verbal artists, some are able to evoke sounds with words, or image vivid scenes; others can conjure moods; still others, complex feelings. Of course, there's always risk involved when creative minds meet. When egos engage, may the strongest vision prevail.

Of the two sections of criticism in the *Companion,* the first, "Critics: Bold as . . . Love?" is more balls-out evocative, while the latter, "Criticism (Slight Return)," takes a provocative cultural-historic angle with rather recent insights into the Hendrix legacy. Nevertheless, I consciously sought to construct parallel critical universes: where Bangs's postmortem interview jibes with Gogola's supernatural fantasy; where Goldman's SuperSpade haunts Baker's dream of revolution (Baker's piece, by the way, is the only one written specifically for this project); where O'Rourke fires up in Ellis's darkened bedroom while the siren song of Jimi's guitar calls all to glorious disorder. . . .

It was just before this brave new world came completely together that reality spoiled the scene, when an all-purple flower arrangement bearing a gift card that read "Have a good haze!" failed to secure from Gail Zappa permission to reprint Frank's *Life* magazine article "The Oracle Has It All Psyched Out" (6/28/68), wherein Jimi's music is described as "extremely symbolic." Damn.

Tempered by an attitude of healthy remove from its subject, music *journalism* is more objective than its passionate cousin, criticism. Which isn't to say it need be one-dimensional. On the contrary, the easy authority that informs the pieces in "Straight Ahead" provides for ready understanding of concrete ideas and complex relationships. Don Menn runs down JH's favorite guitar moves; Gene Santoro gives good background on an important tool in Jimi's craft, Electric Lady Studios; S. L. Duff sees The Man through Monkees' eyes; and Bill Milkowski presents testimony from jazz-scene heavies about Hendrix's place in that sainted idiom's pantheon. The journalism here is solid as can be, even if angle and tone betray a writer's emotional attachment to the once-removed subject. Quite naturally, the straightest dope about Jimi Hendrix occurs in the music-trade magazines: *Guitar Player, Guitar World, Down Beat,* etc.

* * *

Even further removed from the subject-in-the-world—in that the class-room is worlds apart from the barroom or the concert hall—scholars may proffer postulates that appear to head down the slippery slopes of logic toward severe subjectivity. Again, not a bad or boring thing. Hendrix was one hundred percent committed to ideas that pushed the envelopes of common knowledge and sense: in his playing (Goertzel), in his recording (Clarke), in his desire to explore his roots (Gilroy, Floyd). In fact, the sanc-tity of the Ivory Tower is not unlike that of the recording studio, where, finally free from the discomfiting gaze of an audience, Hendrix lost him-self in his work to find himself in his playing.

The lessons offered under the heading "Have You Ever Been (to University)" may not always be easy to follow, but repeated readings will eventually reveal some right-on ideas. Thank the academy for Sheila Whiteley's article on "psychedelic coding" in Hendrix's music. Any seri-ous fan should make an attempt to tackle this one-of-a-kind work.

* * *

You might say Hendrix's fifteen minutes of fame were amply augmented by voluminous sustain. *I* just did, and it felt real nice.

For disciples of a guitar god, it seems the playing would be the thing, what fans would hold on to as the axe master's legacy. But the various views/reviews reprinted in "1983 . . . (and Beyond)" suggest it is as much Hendrix's determined approach to artful self-expression that other musi-cians—as well as singers, dancers, composers, et al.—continue to cherish.

"Jimi did not just cross over, he took over, and stood alone at the top," said *Soul* magazine in April 1977. Luckily, some of those who came to watch brought their muses along. Thus we have Hendrix-inspired black rock and white noise; Black Flag and white boys; new music and fusion jazz; choreography and . . . like that. "If 60s Were 90s" by Beautiful People put Hendrix samples to an acid house/trance beat. Kronos Quartet covered "Purple Haze." The Chili Peppers's Flea has a Hendrix tattoo cov-ering part of his arm.

Jimi even predicted Lollapalooza: "I'd like to play some festivals, but I wish they would break up the events a bit more for the audience. There's no reason why these huge crowds should not be entertained by side attractions as well. They should make them like three-ring circuses, booths, movies—even some knights jostling . . . and Freak Shows!" (*Melody Maker,* 5/9/70). Ah, "Freak Shows." And imagine how Jimi'd do on *MTV Unplugged.*

* * *

The final reprint in the *Companion* is a throwback—a memorial, if you will—to the days when pop criticism could be hopeful, too. Another tribute to the over-understood sixties? No, the year is 1970, and Jimi is gone, and the sixties are gone, and yet hope—hope remains alive; more insistent, really, than ever. From a counterculture newspaper in Bellingham, Washington, not more than 100 miles north of Seattle ("if you travel by . . . dragonfly"), comes a cautionary cry: Hendrix was *not* a god. He was a man: caring, strong, sensitive, sensual—and now gone. Time to remember him and move on. Jimi had one life; you have one life; have a life. If Jimi lived large, was larger than life, then so can/are we. That's how I read it, anyway.

Hail King Jimi, sure. He played guitar like a prince. But he was a Voodoo Child, and he never lost his common touch.

Chris Potash
JIM THORPE, PENNSYLVANIA
JANUARY 1996

PART ONE

The
Experience

I had very strange feelings that I was here for something and I was going to get a chance to be heard. I got the guitar together 'cause that was all I had.

CHRIS WELCH

FROM "CAUGHT IN THE ACT"

Melody Maker, 31 December 1966

Jimi Hendrix, a fantastic American guitarist, blew the minds of the star-packed crowd who went to see him at Blaises Club, London, on Wednesday. Among those in the audience were Pete Townshend, Roger Daltrey, John Entwistle, Chas Chandler, and Jeff Beck. They heard Jimi's trio blast through some beautiful sounds like "Rock Me Baby," "Third Stones From The Sun," "Like A Rolling Stone," "Hey Joe," and even an unusual version of the Troggs' "Wild Thing." Jimi has great stage presence and an exceptional guitar technique which involved playing with his teeth on occasions and no hands at all on others! Jimi looks like becoming one of the big club names of '67.

KEITH ALTHAM

HENDRIX IS OUT OF THIS WORLD

New Musical Express, 15 April 1967

"Out of this world" is a much misapplied phrase; but when it's applied to that extraordinary guitarist Jimi Hendrix, it's appropriate. Looking as incredible as anything conceived by science fiction writer Isaac Asimov, whose work he endlessly devours, Jimi is composing some numbers of equally unearthly inspiration.

There is one titled "Remember," about a manic depressive, described as "raw nerves on record," another called "Teddy Bears Live For Ever" and a third concerning a visitor from another planet who decides that the human race is an unworthy animal to rule the earth and so destroys it, turning the world over to the chickens!

Hendrix is managed by Chas. Chandler, the ex-Animal, who has developed a kind of split personality to cope with the new image.

One moment will find him the good-natured ex–pop star wearing his Lord Kitchener uniform with gold braid, and the next immaculately attired in black suit and tie as Mr. Chandler, businessman—complaining resignedly about having to buy a £2,000 mixing tape-machine instead of the Lincoln Continental his heart desires. Both Chas. and his protégé share a newly acquired apartment off Edgware Road, where, together with newly acquired publicist Chris Williams, I found myself last Friday surveying a room dominated by a psychedelic painting (bought by Chas. while under the "affluence of inkahol" in New York). It depicted a bleeding eye letting droplets fall on a naked woman.

There was a brass scuttle from which projected a number of empty wine bottles—relics of some bygone happening, a book about vampires, the inevitable blind eye of the TV set, and an award for the Animals' best group record, "House Of The Rising Sun," on the mantelpiece, together with a model cannon.

The rest of the Chandler war souvenirs collection is yet to be installed, and the floor was covered with LPs and singles from Solomon Burke to the Beatles.

I was played tracks for the new LP by Jimi, and after one prolonged electrical neurosis, there was a mind-shattering instrumental from the three musicians who comprise the Experience.

As the last decibel faded into infinity, Chris produced an exercise in self-control by observing: "They play so well together, don't they?"

Hendrix, together with drummer Mitch Mitchell, who looks like a young Peter Cook, and bass player Noel Redding, are something new in musical and visual dimensions.

Jimi is a musical perfectionist who does not expect everyone to understand, and believes even those who come only to stand and gawp, may eventually catch on.

On a tour which boasts contradictions in musical terms like Engelbert and Jimi, he has come to terms with himself.

"Most will come to see the Walkers," said Jimi. "Those who come to hear Engelbert sing 'Release Me' may not dig me, but that's not tragic.

"We'll play for ourselves—we've done it before, where the audience stands about with their mouths open and you wait ten minutes before they clap."

Originally "Purple Haze," his current NME Chart entry, was written about a dream Jimi had that he was able to walk about under the sea. Had the lyric been changed to make it more commercial? And was he as satisfied as with the original version?

Fighting

"Well . . ." said Jimi, and there was a significant pause, "I'm constantly fighting with myself over this kind of thing—but I'd never release a record I didn't like.

"You've got to gentle people along for awhile until they are clued in on the scene.

"I worry about my music—you worry about anything that you've built your whole life around.

"It's good to be able to cut loose occasionally—we were in Holland doing a TV show last week, and the equipment was the best ever.

"They said play as loud as you like, and we were really grooving when this little fairy comes running in and yells, 'Stop! Stop! Stop!—the ceiling in the studio below is falling down.' And it was, too—plaster and all," added Jimi with enthusiasm.

"I'm getting so worried that my hair is falling out in patches," he sighed, tugging at a tuft in a hedge of hair which looks as if it could withstand a clip from a combine harvester.

Trend setter

Jimi has noted that since he adopted his bush-look that a number of other stars have been following suit—Gary Leeds is the latest bristling addition on the tour.

"I just thought it was a groovy style," grinned Jimi. "Now everyone is running around with these damn curls. Most of 'em are perms—but there's nothing wrong with perms—I used to get my hair straightened back on the block."

There has been a hold-up in Jimi's first LP because of the switch to the Track label, and tapes have been damaged in the transferring of studios.

"We're calling it 'Are You Experienced,'" affirmed Jimi.

I smiled and noted.

"There's nothing wrong with that!" emphasized Jimi.

Full of new ideas, Jimi came up with another on recording techniques.

"Sometimes when I'm playing I make noises in my throat—almost subconsciously," said Jimi. "Jazz men like Erroll Garner do it a lot as they improvise. I'm going to get a little radio mike, hang it round my neck and record them—maybe I'll incorporate some throat sounds on a disc."

Beck flip

Among Jimi's favourite singles at present is the flip side of the new Jeff Beck record, a number called "Bolero."

"Beautiful guitar," commented Jimi.

We talked of Mitch's new green suede boots—and how Mitch thinks high heels are coming back.

"Y'know what I'd really like to do in the act?" said Mitch, his eyes alight with the gleam of inspiration. "I'd like to pour paraffin all over my drums while the guy from Premier is sitting in the audience.

"Then, at the end of the act, I'd set fire to 'em, and up they go in flames—just to see his face."

That was the night Jimi's guitar accidentally caught fire on stage, and "the fireman rushes in from the pouring rain—very strange!"

DAWN JAMES
WILD, MAN!
Rave, August 1967

Jimi Hendrix, way-out pop star. Is there anything he knows is wrong and never does?

"I play it by ear, man. There's one thing I never do, clean my teeth with hair spray!"

Laughter filled the flat in Upper Berkeley Street as Mr. Hendrix's road manager, his drummer and a friend appreciated his wit. Here was something of the Proby pageantry, the followers who stand a little behind and laugh and admire. But Jimi Hendrix claims he doesn't need people.

"I guess I could do without them. In fact, sometimes I'd rather be alone. I like to think. Yes, gee man, I'm a thinker. I can really get lost thinking about my music. But then I think so much I have to get out among people again. I hear music in my head all the time. Sometimes it makes my brain throb and the room starts to turn. I feel I'm going mad. So I go to the clubs and get plastered. Man, I get real paralytic. But it saves me."

His is rather a twilight world. Music is life to him, but because of music he adopts strange values and unorthodox escapes. He gets up when the sun is setting, and breathes in the smoke-caked air of basement beat bistros. His friends are musicians. His hopes are married to music.

"It's all I really care for. My ambitions are tied up with it. Even my girlfriends are part of it because I meet them where there is music, and they are part of the scene I associate with music." He doesn't have a steady girl.

"I don't meet any girls I could be serious about," he said, and rolled his eyes, and shrugged.

"Sure I'd like to meet a real nice girl, one I could talk to like she was a fellow. But I've had so many girls and they're all the same. The ones I meet look good and make you feel like a man, but you can't talk to them. I get cross with them because they just talk gossip. I get sad about all the girls I see walking on the street when I'm in a taxi-cab, because I'll never meet them, and perhaps one of them is the right girl for me."

He has had three hit records. What does he think he has to offer pop and what has pop to offer him back?

"I've got a lot to offer pop," he said. "I care so much about my work. I record stuff I believe is great. Pop has less to offer me back because it is run by people who only talk about what is commercial."

Jimi talks freely but he isn't easy to reach. A shutter comes down and a facade puts you off just as you close in. He has lived a hard, full life. His parents were separated and his mother died when he was a small child. He went to live with an uncle and aunt.

"So? Lots of kids have it tough," he said, casually, but added, "I ran away from home a couple of times because I was so miserable. When my dad found out I'd gone he went pretty mad with worry. But then I don't really care about other people's feelings."

When did Jimi return home?

"When I realized my dad was upset. Not that I cared, but well, he is my dad."

Jimi has super manners. When he asks you out he says, "Would you do me the honour of dating me tonight?" When he leaves a room you are in, he says, "Excuse me for a moment please." When he meets you he shakes hands and says, "Nice seeing you."

Somewhere deep down beneath the raving recording star there is a lot of old-world charm.

He says he doesn't know himself well. "I can't say what makes me happy or sad. It has to happen before I know. It doesn't happen the same each time either. I must say that people being rude about me doesn't ever bother me now. The only time I get uneasy is when I know that pop critics and writers are waiting for me to fail so they can jump all over me. This is how pop is. You have a hit record and, gee, they love you! But you have one failure and they kill you. It's like a tight rope.

"I get kinda tense before a show. I like to be left alone to think. My road manager tries to keep the dressing room free from people then. If people come in I find a corner somewhere else. I have to think myself into my act. I can't just turn on."

How is he affected by other people's music?

"Again I can't define it. A blues or a sad melody can make me real happy. I am affected by sounds though. They can change my mood."

He has no religion.

"Religion is all the same—Catholic, Protestant, Jewish, it's just a lot of reasonable commercial quotes that sell because they're somewhere between very good and very bad, and people can easily hang on to that. It gives them something to believe in."

I asked him if he likes his looks.

"I've learned to live with them. The hair is rather wild, but it grows that way, and I look awful with it short and neat. The clothes aren't deliberate. I pick up what I feel like wearing when I dress. They represent my mood."

I looked at the scarlet and purple and orange. Was he in a gay mood? He shook his head. "Gee no, I'm quite melancholy today," he said. It would be hard on the eye balls if one caught him when he was wild with joy!

CHRIS WELCH

WHO SAYS JIMI HENDRIX CAN'T SING? (HE DOES!)

Melody Maker, 15 April 1967

Jimi Hendrix can't sing! "Oo sez so?" outraged Hendrix fans will demand, at this startling statement. But before Melody Maker readers who dig the sounds of "Purple Haze," "Hey Joe" and enjoy the stage act of Jimi, Noel Redding and Mitch Mitchell reach for their red ink ballpoints and search frantically for the address of Mailbag, it should be understood the statement comes from—Jimi Hendrix.

Jimi, who came to Britain from America last year under the aegis of ex-Animal Chas Chandler, who is now his manager, brought tremendous excitement to the group world with a hard-hitting sound with its roots in blues and Bob Dylan laced with freak-out showmanship.

The music is loud, deafening . . . but it has a lot of soul and invention. In the terminology of the hippy, it's valid.

Jimi is a happy, uncomplicated person, who gets his kicks from playing and has the American affinity for showmanship which Britishers find hard to adopt naturally, or even understand.

If Eric Clapton appeared on a pop show biting a flaming guitar with his teeth, he would be regarded as a traitor by thousands of dedicated fans. But says Jimi: "I regard myself as a guitarist and entertainer," and that doesn't stop him from creating something original and remaining true to his musical beliefs.

I met Jimi at his bright and airy apartment at the top of a modern block near Marble Arch. He was listening excitedly to acetates of tracks from his forthcoming LP.

Burnt-out

He smoked endless cigarettes and crouched on a low stool dressed in flowery, violently coloured shirt and trousers in a sparsely furnished room. The screen of a TV set was covered in soot and hadn't been used for weeks. The hi-fi equipment was bright and new and in constant use.

"I can't read a note of music," grinned Jimi, fingering the burnt-out wreck of his guitar which burst into flames on the opening night of his tour with the Walker Brothers.

How was the tour going? "The bosses of the tour are giving us hell," he revealed pleasantly. "The organisers don't give us a chance to tune up before we go on stage. They say we are obscene and vulgar, but we play our act as we have always played it everywhere else, and there have never been complaints before.

"We refuse to change our act, and the result is my amplifier sometimes gets cut off at the funniest times.

"I wonder why? But I don't let them hang me up. I play to the people and I don't think our actions are obscene. We just get excited by the music, and carried away.

"The thing that surprises me about the tour is the Walker Brothers. I expect them to sing all pretty songs, but they have a good variety of numbers. Cat Stevens is great too, and Engelbert Humperdinck is very, very professional. He knows exactly what he is doing.

"It's really funny playing for this tour. I don't know if it's like it on all tours but just before I go on I turn round and find a guitar string is broken, or I find my guitar is all out of tune after I just tuned it. I kinda don't know what to say about that. They just don't give a damn about us. But they are not getting rid of us unless we are officially thrown off the tour."

Where did Jimi find his first hit number—"Hey Joe"—and had he heard the many other versions?

"'Hey Joe' is a traditional song and it's about 100 years old. Lots of people have done different arrangements of it, and Timmy Rose was the first to do it slowly. I like it played slowly. There are probably 1,000 versions of it fast by the Byrds, Standelles, Love and others."

The style of the Experience seems very well formed. Was it exported from New York?

"No, the style was formed here in England. When I first came over I was having little plays together with Mitch and Noel. Noel can play really fast bass, and Mitch—well he is one of the best drummers. He can do anything."

Who were Jimi's influences? "Well, I like a lot of guitar players, but I don't copy. I like Eric Clapton and some of the things Jeff Beck does and that cat Vic Briggs. I was really surprised to find so many blues guitar players here. They mostly play the same style but you can sure tell the differences. Pete Townshend is very different. He's ridiculous."

Where is Jimi happiest playing? "I like playing clubs, but I don't want to play them for the rest of my life. We are satisfied with what we are doing at the moment, because it's playing the way we feel. I just want to make the music acceptable. It's free form.

"I just wish I could sing really nice, but I know I can't sing. I just feel the words out. I just try all right to hit a pretty note, but it's hard. I'm more of an entertainer and performer than a singer."

JIMI A HIT IN SWEDEN—REFUSED HOTEL ROOM

Melody Maker, 3 June 1967

Jimi Hendrix Experience broke all box office records at Stockholm's Tivoli Gardens last week. They drew 18,000 people, the largest crowd ever.

But they were refused a second night's stay at their hotel in the city. The management of the hotel—where they had already spent one night—refused to let them stay another claiming their booking was for one night only. They tried 30 hotels in Stockholm but none would take them and they were forced to fly on to Copenhagen earlier than scheduled.

Said Jimi: "It seems that people in Scandinavia just aren't ready for the way we look. The kids are great and the concerts have been much more successful than we could have expected for a first visit."

In Helsinki, the group were refused admission to two clubs after their concerts.

NORRIE DRUMMOND
BAD SHOWS BRING JIMI DOWN
New Musical Express, 10 June 1967

James Maurice Hendrix, day-dreamer, drifter and guitarist extraordinaire peered round the door of his London flat and recognising me released the bolt and invited me inside. He pulled on a shirt and a pair of trousers, woke up his manager Chas. Chandler and put a copy of "Sgt. Peppers Lonely Hearts' Club Band" on the record player.

The flat, which Jimi Hendrix shares with his manager, is tastefully furnished with long couches, leather armchairs, a teak coffee table, original paintings and the latest hi-fi equipment.

Jimi wasn't really in the best of spirits when I met him. The previous evening his concert at London's Saville Theatre had been plagued with amplifier problems and it was still worrying him.

"Man, it really brings me down when these amps don't work," he said lighting his first cigarette of the day, "and they were new ones, too."

Manager Chandler entered the room bearing cups of coffee. "Despite the troubles it was still a great show," enthused Chas, "but you should have seen them in Sweden."

Broke record

Jimi and his group had just returned from a tour of Sweden and Germany and Chas informed me that at one date in Sweden the group had almost doubled the previous record, set by the Beach Boys. "We'll definitely be going back there when we come back from America in July," he said.

I asked Jimi how he felt about returning to his native America after a highly successful year in Britain.

"I don't really think we'll achieve as much success there as we have done here," he said. "We have been told that we'll do well but I'm not sure that we will be accepted as readily there.

"In America people are much more narrow-minded than they are in Britain. If they do like us—great! If not—too bad! In the States the disc-jockeys stopped playing 'Hey Joe' because people complained about the lyrics."

Before he arrived in Britain Jimi travelled all over the United States. "I was a drifter. Sometimes I worked, sometimes I didn't."

He feels that he could—if he was forced to—return to that type of life. "We play the type of music we want to play. At the moment the public likes it—but their tastes change. Then I would like to produce someone else's records. But whatever happens just happens. Who knows?"

Many people have the impression that Jimi Hendrix is moody and introverted but he is not. Certainly compared to many other pop artistes he is quiet, but once he starts talking about something which interests him—mainly music obviously—he rambles on at great length.

"I know that people think I'm moody," he admitted, "but that's only because I'm thinking of music most of the time. If I suddenly clam up it's because I've just hit on an idea."

I asked what his main ambition in life is. "Oh," he sighed thought-fully, "that changes a hundred times a day. I really just want to continue playing and recording what gives me pleasure. What we play is straight from us. I don't ever want to have to bow to commercialism."

MASSIVE U.S. CAMPAIGN TO PUSH HENDRIX
New Musical Express, 18 March 1967

A massive campaign hailing Jimi Hendrix as "the greatest talent since the Rolling Stones" is being launched in America. This is the immediate outcome of a deal signed in Los Angeles on Tuesday—by the Hendrix Experience's co-manager, Mike Jeffrey—which gives American distribution of Jimi's recordings to the powerful Warner-Reprise company.

Initial fee paid to Hendrix for his signature is reported to be "in excess of 50,000 dollars." Mo Austin, president of Warner-Reprise, described it as the highest fee the company has ever paid for a new artist.

A spokesman for the company announced that meetings are now in progress between Jeffrey and Austin with a view to inaugurating a vast U.S. publicity campaign on Hendrix. He added: "We shall introduce a completely new conception in promotion which should put Jimi right at the top in a very short time."

Warner-Reprise is expected to rush-release Jimi's "Purple Haze," being issued in Britain next Thursday (23rd) as the first single on the new Track label—formed by the Who's co-managers Kit Lambert and Chris Stamp, in association with Polydor Records.

THE VOICE OF EXPERIENCE
Newsweek, 9 October 1967

With their hair frizzled to a frenzy they seem to be singing their way through an electrocution. And, indeed, their instruments, two guitars and a drum, throb with electric power—pull the master switch, and the "Jimi Hendrix Experience" would undergo a stagewide blackout. But this nasty-looking trio with its triptych of smirking simian faces is not merely a curiosity of the electronic age; it is a hard-driving, funky group in the soul style of Ray Charles and Little Richard that is musical to the tips of its technology.

Its lead-guitarist-singer-composer Jimi Hendrix has just been voted the world's top pop musician by the annual Melody Maker Readers' Poll in England. The group's first album, "Are You Experienced," is in the top ten in both Britain and the U.S. But more important, its curious blend of avant-garde electronic oscillations with soul sounds and its penchant for violence have already made the Experience something of a legend and the most interesting, if frightening, new figures to hop on the pop turntable since the nasty old Rolling Stones.

"Mau-Mau"

The group plays "accidental" music, not in the spirit of John Cage, but of three men inadvertently stumbling down a flight of stairs. "Once I was playing away and there was a short circuit and the guitar went up in flames," says Hendrix, whose musical immolations illuminated the recent Monterey Pop Festival. "It went over pretty well, so for three times after that I sprayed lighter fluid on it and then stamped out the burning pieces. When we played in the Hollywood Bowl, they were waiting for us with fire extinguishers." Sometimes the hirsute Hendrix, called "Mau-Mau" by one British paper, simply smashes his instrument to bits. That too, he explains, grew out of an accident: "One time I was rolling around the stage and I fell off into the crowd. I tried to get back but the crowd was pressing in so I threw the guitar back, I didn't mean to break it, but when you throw a guitar, it breaks."

In one sense the "Experience's" destruction is inevitable rather than accidental, the surfacing of a violent streak that has always run through rock 'n' roll, the spontaneous and impulsive violence of the young. "I kiss and caress my drums, I love them so much," says Londoner Mitch Mitchell, 22, who, with guitarist Noel Redding, 21, another Britisher, add Anglo rhythms and harmonies to Hendrix's strictly American blues style. "But if you can't get the right thing from them, destroy them. Once I couldn't get what I wanted out of the amplifier, so I kicked it and kicked it." Why all the violence? "We just try not to bore ourselves," says the 21-year-old Hendrix, "and hope the audience likes it."

Sometimes they like it too much, swarming on stage in droves. On the group's American tour this summer, the Daughters of the American Revolution in San Francisco blocked their appearance with the Monkees on the ground that the "Experience" was "too erotic." The group refused to soften their act, quit and packed houses on their own up and down the West Coast. Their album jumped from a cliff-hanging 100th to No. 12. They were made.

Frets and whines

Hendrix supplies the eroticism, making love to his guitar with the fervor and imagination of Chuck Berry and Casanova. "Sometimes I jump on the guitar," Hendrix told *Newsweek*'s Kevin P. Buckley, "sometimes I grind the strings up against the frets. The more it grinds the more it whines. Sometimes I rub up against the amplifier. Sometimes I sit on it. Sometimes I play the guitar with my teeth, or I'll be playing along and I'll feel like playing with my elbow. I can't remember all the things I do."

Hendrix learned his showmanship when he left his native Seattle at 16 and started traveling the Nashville-Memphis circuit, backing blues stars like Little Richard, the Isley Brothers and Joe Jackson. In 1965, he led a group of his own into Greenwich Village, playing in the low-ceilinged places he still likes best. Chas Chandler of the Animals heard him there a year ago and spirited him to London. Since then, it has been a bittersweet mixture of sweat and success. "We're constantly working," says Hendrix. "This isn't as easy as it looks."

But, of course, there are compensations. On the group's next U.S. tour Mitchell and Redding will drive a Rolls-Royce with Union Jack and Stars and Stripes affixed, and Hendrix can dream of the day when he will be free to control his own life. "In five years I want to write some plays," he says. "And some books. I want to sit on an island—my island—and listen to my beard grow. And then I'll come back and start all over again as a bee—a king bee."

ALAN WALSH

"I FELT WE WERE IN DANGER OF BECOMING THE U.S. DAVE DEE"

Melody Maker, 20 July 1968

The electrified hair has been shortened somewhat, but it was unmistakably still Jimi Hendrix. He loped into his manager's Gerrard Street office, grinned slyly, shook hands all round, fastened onto the latest copy of MM, accepted a stick of chewing gum and settled comfortably into an office armchair.

Magical Jimi, purveyor of excitement and mind-expanding music, was back in town, if only briefly. "I'm flying back to New York tonight," he said. "I left some recordings there that will make our next single and an album, no, a *double* album, and I've got to listen to them again and re-mix several of them."

Hendrix flew back to Britain from the States specially for the MM's Woburn Festival of Music ("It was really only a jam, we hadn't played for so long," he said) and was also due to visit Majorca ("It'd better be a gig or I'm not going") but we managed to pin him down long enough to catch up with the world of the man of Experience.

And, the immediate world, as far as Jimi, one of the most ferocious-looking yet benign of men, was the group's next single.

He hopes to have it ready for release within the next two weeks—a welcome piece of news for Experience fans who've had to wait a long time since their last album, "Axis: Bold As Love."

But the delay has been deliberate. They felt the group was becoming too pop orientated. "People were starting to take us for granted, abuse us. It was that what-cornflakes-for-breakfast scene. Pop slavery, really."

Tired

"I felt we were in danger of becoming the American version of Dave Dee—nothing wrong with that, but it's just not our scene.

"We decided we had to end that scene and get into our own thing. I was

The Experience
15

tired of the attitude of fans that they've bought you a house and a car and now expect you to work the way they want you to for the rest of your life.

"But we couldn't just say 'Screw them,' because they have their rights, too, so we decided the best way was to just cool the recording scene until we were ready with something that we wanted everyone to hear. I want people to hear us, what we're doin' now and try to appreciate what we're at."

What Jimi, Mitch and Noel want everyone to hear are the tracks they have recorded at a New York studio. "It's the 12 Track Record Plant, a new studio. It's new and we're all learning at the same time."

The tracks include three from which the new single will be chosen. One is titled "Crosstown Traffic," another is "House Burning Down," either of which could be the single.

The Experience have also recorded enough material for a double album. It will probably be called "The Electric Lady Land," which will have a total of about 17 pieces rather than numbers on two albums. "All the tracks are very personal . . . they're us."

Picture

"That's why we want to get them out as soon as possible, because this is how we are . . . now! I want them to be heard before we change." The album will kick off with a 90-second "sound painting" which Jimi said is an attempt to give a sound picture of the heavens.

"It's different from what we've ever done before. I know it's the thing people will jump on to criticise so we're putting it right at the beginning to get it over with."

The track is called "And The Gods Make Love"—it's typifying what happens when the gods make love "or whatever they spend their time on," said Jimi.

"The album is so personal because apart from some help from a few people like Stevie Winwood and Buddy Miles of the Electric Flag, it's all done by us. We wrote the songs, recorded and produced it.

"I don't say it's great, but it's the Experience. It has a rough, hard feel on some of the tracks. Some of the things on it are hungry."

It's a source of discontent among certain Experience fans that the group spend so much time these days in America. But Jimi doesn't agree.

"I'm American," he says simply. "I want people there to see me. I also wanted to see whether we could make it back in the States. I dig Britain, but I haven't really got a home anywhere.

"The earth's my home. I've never had a house here. I don't want to put down roots in case I get restless and want to move on. I'll only get into the house thing when I'm certain I won't want to move again.

"The other reason for working in the States is that we make 20 times more money there. And there's no harm in that . . . we have to eat like everyone else. America is so large, too; when you work regularly in Britain, you end up going back to the same places. That doesn't happen in America."

He doesn't feel it is ironic that he had to come to England to get success in America. He says that England was first because that's where his managers Chas Chandler and Mike Jeffrey thought it would be best to start. "I want to be known everywhere," he said.

Lucky

Jimi is, however, a native-born American, though he doesn't, he says, identify closely with that country's problems. "I just want to do what I'm doing without getting involved in racial or political matters. I know I'm lucky that I can do that . . . lots of people can't."

He does, however, have an awareness of the problems and wish to help.

He sent a cheque for 5,000 dollars to the Martin Luther King memorial fund because he thought that this was the best way he could help. He was busy working and thought vaguely that active participation could do the cause harm rather than good in an inverted way, because of his pop music connection.

He expressed regret at the news that the Cream had decided to break up at the end of the year. But he expressed no fears about his own group doing the same.

"We were lucky. When we started, we were thrown together, but we managed to create a personal scene, as well as a musical appreciation.

"But if someone did leave, there'd be no hang-ups, it would be amicable. Because it's like a family. If Noel or Mitch quit I'd wish him well because it'd be like a brother going on to better things. I'd be pleased for him. The only hard feelings would be in the minds of the selfish fans.

"I'd like to see Mitch and Noel getting into the things that make them happy. Noel is on the English pop and hard rock scene and is writing some good songs these days. Mitch is becoming a little monster on the drums. He's involved in his Elvin Jones thing.

"He's the one I'd worry about losing. He's becoming so heavy behind me that he frightens me!"

HENDRIX BUSTED IN TORONTO
Rolling Stone, 31 May 1969

TORONTO—Jimi Hendrix is now experienced, in the worst way. He was busted May 3rd at Toronto International Airport for allegedly "illegally possessing narcotics."

The bust, made by the Royal Canadian Mounted Police, reportedly uncovered several ounces of a chemical substance in a flight bag being carried by Hendrix.

One Toronto radio station (CFRB) reported that the chemical was in fact heroin—but even the Mounties do not yet make that claim. At last report, their laboratory was still at work analyzing the alleged stash.

The singer/guitarist, now in the fifth week of a two-month concert tour of the U.S. and Canada with his Jimi Hendrix Experience, would say nothing to the press beyond "no comment. I'm innocent and my lawyers will prove it."

Hendrix and his troupe—drummer Mitch Mitchell, guitarist Noel Redding, and five other men—were going through the customs check when an inspector found six small packages inside a glass bottle at the top of Hendrix' bag.

According to sources at the scene, the Mounties—who were waiting for Hendrix to step off his plane from Detroit—were at first unable to make any positive identification of the substance; nevertheless, they kept the stunned Hendrix detained while they called a mobile police laboratory unit to the airport. After a delay of nearly four hours (the bust took place around 1:30 P.M.) the Mounties took him downtown to police headquarters. Hendrix was finally released on $10,000 bail posted by a Toronto attorney.

At his arraignment before Magistrate Fred Hayes two days later, a June 19 date was set for a preliminary hearing. Youthful Hendrix admirers filled the staid old courtroom as Hendrix entered wearing a pink shirt open to the waist, an Apache-style headband, a multi-colored scarf around his neck, and beads. His manner was dead serious. When the magistrate called his name—James Marshall Hendrix of New York—he rose and leveled a venomous look at the bench, his lips slightly pursed, which said, without need for words, *fuck off.*

There was no demand for a guilty/not guilty plea. A few words were exchanged, the hearing date set, and in three minutes, Hendrix was on his way out the door.

He is continuing his tour. Hendrix went directly from police head-quarters to the Maple Leaf Gardens to appear before a full house of 12,000 in this Lake Ontario port city—just after the bust and questioning.

He walked onstage and said: "I want you to forget what happened yesterday and tomorrow and today. Tonight we're going to create a whole new world." This may be part of his usual rap, but the arrest gave it special impact. Unfortunately—understandably—however, it was not one of Hendrix' best evenings.

He played well, but it never quite got off the ground. The effect was rather like watching a bullfighter who's so good that no bull really challenges him, and therefore there is no danger, and therefore no suspense. Hendrix was just *too* cool.

The next night, in concert at Syracuse, New York, Hendrix improvised a verse or two of new lyrics for a new song. The words came out something like "*. . . and I was in this room / full of light and a thousand mirrors . . .*"

Those hours of interrogation by the Mounties had apparently taken their toll.

His June hearing date will also allow him to appear, as scheduled, at a Vancouver, B.C., concert on May 22nd. The Jimi Hendrix Experience is also slated for performances at the Northern California Folk Rock Festival in Santa Clara, Calif., on May 24–25th, and a stop in Hawaii before he returns to fight the dope charge.

Hendrix is being represented by the Toronto lawyer as well as by his own attorney, Steve Weiss. There is talk that the defense—logically—will claim Hendrix to be the victim of a plant.

Louis Goldblatt, who operates Celebrity Limousine Service and drove Hendrix around Toronto during his stay, says the singer was obviously surprised when customs inspectors found the purported stash. He describes how Hendrix stepped back, leaned against the railing and shook his head in amazement as if he couldn't believe it. Goldblatt naturally enough will not divulge conversations that took place later as he chauffeured Hendrix around, but does recount that Hendrix' attitude was *holy jesus, how did this happen?*

"He was," in Goldblatt's words, "genuinely dumbfounded by the whole affair."

Goldblatt met Hendrix just as he deplaned, and he witnessed the entire incident. He—and other observers—note that the Royal Canadian Mounties behaved unusually throughout. For one thing, the Mounties (who wear regular blue police uniforms these days, incidentally, and are the chief enforcers of narcotics laws in Canada) customarily do not wait at the airport to make dope busts, as they did in Hendrix' case.

Another item is that all the inquiry and searching at the airport was done right out in the open at the customs gate. The more usual procedure is for officers and those being detained to retire from public view, in respect for the privacy of the accused. But Hendrix and company were forced to stand for hours under the gaze of scores of onlookers at the cake-shaped airport building—rent-a-car girls, cigar stand operators, porters, cab drivers and travelers—while the feds poked through their belongings.

The whole business seemed a bit too pat to Goldblatt, who's seen many (similar) cases. "You should see some of the things that have been left behind in my car for pop people," Goldblatt says. "It's really incredible."

This is most often done as a token of love, but sometimes for spite. And if somebody was out to "get" Hendrix by laying a surprise stash on him—in his suitcase, more precisely, then phoning ahead to tip off the Mounties—there was plenty of time that this might have been accomplished, from the time he left off the suitcase at Detroit to when it arrived back in his hands at Toronto.

Whatever the case, the Mounties do not typically lie in wait at the airport, ready to pounce. Toronto authorities have been getting tough on the free-living hippie community of Yorkeville, more or less Toronto's version of the Haight-Ashbury, in recent months, and there is the possibility that Hendrix may have been caught in the squeeze.

The populace of Toronto are a very conservative lot, and tend to look with suspicion upon anybody who looks and dresses a little different from themselves. Hendrix looks a lot different. Make an example of this freaky, frizzy-haired psychedelic spade (if you go by this reasoning) and maybe you can scare the freaks out of Yorkeville.

The 26-year-old Hendrix has no previous police record and has traveled extensively on concert tours in recent years throughout Europe, Canada, and the U.S. without incident.

He was named Performer of the Year by this publication for "creativity, electricity and balls above and beyond the call of duty" in 1968. His *Electric Landlady* was named American and British Rock and Roll Album of the Year, as well. He was chosen Best Performer because: "Blues players, jazz players, rock players—all were agreed that Hendrix' improvisations transcended category and constituted music as imaginative and alive as rock and roll has known. Jimi, more than any other player, has extended the voice of amplified guitar to an incredible new range of emotive sounds."

With Hendrix at the airport, besides Redding and Mitchell, were Jerry Stickles, tour manager; Arthur Johnson, New York-based accountant; Abe Jacob, San Francisco sound engineer; Ron Terry and Red Ruffino, promoters, and Burt McCann, merchandiser of concert programs.

If the substance in question does turn out to be heroin and Hendrix is found guilty, it's a mandatory jail sentence with possibility of getting off by paying a fine or getting a suspended sentence. In Canada, the minimum dope stretch is a year's suspended sentence—and this for *possession* of grass. Dealing grass or holding anything stronger is punishable by at least a few months in the slammer.

There is the added possibility that by the time of Hendrix' June 19th hearing, the Canadian feds will have tacked charges of trafficking and transporting across the border onto the possession rap. And if he's convicted on all three of these, the penalties could be that much stiffer.

The best guess is that a conviction would put Hendrix behind bars for from two to seven years. Canadian courts don't screw around. A dealer was convicted of bringing $250,000 worth of grass in from Africa just the week before Hendrix was busted, and sentenced to 14 years.

In the face of this kind of justice, the likelihood that Hendrix would lose his right to travel outside the United States would be an incidental consideration.

The only light note in any of this has to do with the head of the judge who will hear Hendrix' case. It will be topped by an English-style 17th-century powdered wig.

HENDRIX' ONE-YEAR RETIREMENT PLAN
Rolling Stone, 17 May 1969

LONDON—Jimi Hendrix may do a Bob Dylan and go into seclusion for a year. He told a reporter for the New Musical Express (a pop paper) here that it was time to take a rest.

The Experience has been working steadily for three solid years, Hendrix pointed out, "and there comes a time when you have to get away from it all.

"What I want to do is rest completely for one year. Completely. I'll have to. Maybe something'll happen and I'll break my own rules, but I'll have to try. It's the physical and emotional toll I have to think of," said Hendrix.

This came with full assurances that Hendrix and the Experience would stick together. Bassist Noel Redding plans to perform with his new band, the Fat Mattress, and Mitch Mitchell might take another gig now and then.

But the Experience has no intention of disbanding.

SHEILA WELLER

"I DON'T WANT TO BE A CLOWN ANY MORE..."

Rolling Stone, 15 November 1969

Records, film, press and gossip are collectively ambitious in creating the image of a rock superstar. With Jimi Hendrix—as with Janis Joplin, Mick Jagger and Jim Morrison—mythology is particularly lavish.

Unfortunately, it is also often irreversible—even when it's ill-founded or after the performer himself has gone through changes.

Several weeks ago, Life magazine described Jimi as "a rock demigod" and devoted several color pages to kaleidoscopic projection of his face. Well, why not? The fisheye-lens shot on his first album cover shows him in arrogant distortion: on the second album, he becomes Buddha. Lest anyone forget, Leacock-Pennebaker's *Monterey Pop* has immortalized his pyromaniacal affair with the guitar. Rock-media bedroom talk makes him King Stud of the groupies. Stories circulate that he is rude to audiences, stands up writers, hangs up photographers, that he doesn't talk.

What Jimi's really all about—and where his music is going—is an altogether different thing.

For most of the summer and early fall, Jimi rented a big Georgian-style home in Liberty, New York—one of Woodstock's verdant "suburbs"—for the purpose of housing an eclectic family of musicians: Black Memphis blues guitarists; "new music" and jazz avant gardists; "Experience" member Mitch Mitchell; and—closest to Jimi and most influential—Juma Lewis, a multi-talented ex-progressive jazzman who is now the leader of Woodstock's Aboriginal Music Society.

The hilltop compound—replete with wooded acreage and two horses— was intended for a peaceful, productive musical growth period. But hassles did come, sometimes sending Jimi off on sanity-preserving vacations in Algeria and Morocco; local police were anxious to nab "big-time hippies" on anything from dope to speeding; the house was often hectic with hangers-on; pressure mounted from Jimi's commercial reps to stay within the well-hyped image and not go too far afield experimentally.

But with it all, growth, exchange and—finally—unity was achieved among Jimi and the musicians, whose work-in-progress was evidenced in occasional public appearances in the New York area (at the Woodstock/Bethel Festival, Harlem's Apollo Theater, Greenwich Village's Salvation discotheque, and ABC's Dick Cavett Show) and has been recorded for Reprise on an LP which will be released in January. The name of the album, *Gypsies, Suns and Rainbows*, epitomizes the new Hendrix feeling.

With close friends of Jimi, I drove up to Liberty on a quiet September weekend. The mélange of musicians and girls had departed. In a few weeks, Jimi himself was to give up the house, woods and horses for less idyllic prospects: a Manhattan loft and a November hearing on the narcotics-possession charge he was slapped with in Toronto, May 3rd.

Photographs have a funny way of betraying his essentially fragile face and body. He is lean. Almost slight. Eating chocolate chip cookies on the living room couch in this big house—furnished straight and comfortable—he seems boyish and vulnerable.

He offers questions with an unjustified fear of his own articulateness that is charming—but occasionally painful. "Do you, uh—where do you live in the city?" "What kind of music do you li—— would you care to listen to?" He is self-effacing almost to a fault: "Do you ever go to the Fillmore? No?—that was a silly question, sorry." "I'm sorry, am I mumbling? Tell me when I'm mumbling. Damn . . . I always mumble."

It becomes uncomfortable, so one says: "Jimi, don't keep putting yourself down. There's everybody else to do that for you." He attaches to that statement, repeats it slowly, whips out the embossed Moroccan notebook in which he jots lyrics at all hours of day and night, and scribbles something down.

Fingering through his record collection (extensive and catholic: e.g., Marlene Dietrich, David Peel and the Lower East Side, Schoenberg, Wes Montgomery), he pulls out *Blind Faith*; *Crosby, Stills and Nash*; and *John Wesley Harding*. The Dylan plays first. Jimi's face lights: "I love Dylan. I only met him once, about three years ago, back at the Kettle of Fish [a folk-rock era hangout] on MacDougal Street. That was before I went to England. I think both of us were pretty drunk at the time, so he probably doesn't remember it."

In the middle of a track, Jimi gets up, plugs in his guitar, and—with eyes closed and his supple body curved gently over the instrument—picks up on "Frankie Lee and Judas Priest," riding the rest of the song home with a near-religious intensity.

He talks intently to Juma and his girl. He cherishes real friends and will do anything for them. They, in turn, feel protective toward him. "Poor Jimi," one says. "Everyone's trying to hold him up for something. Those busts . . . Even the highway patrol exploits him. They know his car; they stop him on the road between New York and Woodstock and harass him. Then they have something to gloat about for the rest of the day. Once a cop stopped *me* on the highway and started bragging: 'Hey, I just stopped Jimi Hendrix for the second time today.'"

On the bookcase is a photograph of a fifties Coasters-type R&B group: processed hair, metallic-threaded silk-lapel suits, shiny shoes. The thin kid on the far left in a high-conked pompadour, grinning over an electric guitar: is it—? "That's okay," Jimi smiles at the impending laughter. "I don't try to cover up the past; I'm not ashamed of it." But he is genuinely humble about the present. For example, he'd been wanting for some time to jam with jazz and "new music" avantgardists, but worried that such musicians didn't take him seriously enough to ever consider playing with him. "Tell me, honestly," he asked a friend, "what do those guys think of me? Do they think I'm jiving?"

We are listening now to the tape of such a session, the previous night's jam: Jimi on electric guitar, avantgarde pianist Michael Ephron on clavichord, Juma on congas and flute. A beautiful fusion of disparate elements, disjunct and unified at alternating seconds. Now chaotic, now coming together. "Cosmic music," they call it. Ego-free music. Not the sort of stuff the waxlords make many bucks off. Not the kind of sound guaranteed to extend the popularity of a rock superstar.

"I don't want to be a clown anymore. I don't want to be a 'rock and roll star,'" Jimi says, emphatically. The forces of contention are never addressed but their pervasiveness has taken its toll on Jimi's stamina and peace of mind. Trying to remain a growing artist when a business empire has nuzzled you to its bosom takes a toughness, a shrewdness. For those who have a hardness of conviction but not of temperament it isn't a question of selling out but of dying, artistically and spiritually. Refusing to die yet ill-equipped to fight dirty, many sensitive but commercially lionized artists withdrew. I watch Jimi quietly digging the pictures of faraway people and places in a book, *The Epic of Man* ("South America . . . wow, that's a whole different world. Have you ever been there?") and I wonder just where he will be and what he will be doing five years from now.

We crowd into Jimi's metal-fleck silver Stingray ("I want to paint it over—maybe black") for a sunrise drive to the waterfalls. ("I wish I could bring my guitar—and plug it in down there.") The talk is of puppies, daybreak, other innocentia. We climb down the rocks to the icy brook, then suddenly discover the car keys are missing. Everyone shuffles through shoulder pouches and wallets. "Hey, don't worry," Jimi says. "They'll turn up. No use being hassled about it now." Jimi's taking pictures and writing poetry. "I want to write songs about tranquillity, about beautiful things," he says.

Back at the house, he pads around, emptying ashtrays, putting things in order. "I'm like a clucking old grandmother," he smiles. "I've just gotta straighten things out a little." It's 7 AM and he has to be at the recording studio in Manhattan at 4 in the afternoon. Everyone's exhausted.

After a few hours of sleep, Jimi floats into the kitchen looking like a fuzzy lamb unmercifully awakened and underfed. He passes up the spread of eggs, pork chops, crescent rolls and tea; breakfast, instead, is a Theragran and a swig of tequila in milk. "Jimi, you never eat . . ." Juma's girl worries aloud.

We pile into the car for the two-hour drive into Manhattan. Passing two Afro-haired guys in an Aston-Martin, Jimi turns and flashes a broad grin, extending his fingers in a peace salute. We turn up the radio on Stevie Wonder's "My Cherie Amour"; groove on Neil Diamond, Jackie DeShannon, the Turtles. Everything is everything: We're playing with a puppy, grateful for clear skies, clear road, clear AM station. What more could a carload of travelers in an inconspicuous blue Avis ask?

We pull into a roadside stop. No giggly bell-bottomed young girls in sight, Jimi gets out and brings back chocolate milk and ice cream for everyone. Truckers pay no attention. Middle-aged couples glare disdainfully.

The talk is of the session. They'll record at a studio on West 44th Street, then go somewhere else to mix it—maybe Bell Sound of A&R—because Jimi says the recording studio they're going to "has bad equipment . . . likes to take advantage of so-called longhair musicians."

Downtown traffic on the West Side Highway is light at rush hour. The fortresses of upper Riverside Drive are handsome in the sun, but the air has lost its freshness. Getting off the highway at 45th Street, it's 4:45. The session, costing $200 an hour, was booked to begin at 4:00. But delay couldn't be helped; no hassle. A carful of teenagers alongside us has the radio turned up loud on "If Six Was Nine"—the cut being used as part of advertisement for *Easy Rider*. I ask Jimi if he's seen the film; he doesn't answer.

Turning around, I find him stretched out on the back seat, legs curled up embryonically, hands clasped under his cheek. Sleeping soundly.

JIMI HENDRIX BLASTS THE OLD YEAR OUT WITH "SPACE ROCK"

The New York Times, 1 January 1970

Jimi Hendrix, a New Year's Eve noisemaker if ever there was one, played to a capacity crowd last night at the Fillmore East.

The guitarist and singer plays what has been called "space rock." His playing is so loud, so fluid and so rife with electronic distortions that it resembles that of no other currently popular performer.

Mr. Hendrix is less a tune weaver than a soundsmith. His bank of six amplifiers is turned up full blast. He seems as if he were molding a living sculpture of sound, rather than fulfilling the normal role of the entertainer. He grimaces, writhes and occasionally destroys guitars and sets them on fire as part of his act.

In short, he seems to be more concerned with creating an environment of intense sound and personal fury than he is with performing a particular composition. Perhaps because of this, his original compositions seldom rise above the mediocre. More important than the form of the song is the amount of aural and personal pyrotechnics he can cram into it. Only when he plays blues songs, which have a fairly rigid structure, does the identity of the composition matter very much.

Consequently, Jimi Hendrix playing a Jimi Hendrix song is one of the least-understandable performers to someone who is not a full-blown rock follower. He really is a piece of the underground scenery, and has to be appreciated as such. For this two-night series, Mr. Hendrix was backed by Buddy Miles, drums, and Billy Cox, bass, in an informal jam group he called a Band of Gypsies.

Sharing the bill were the Voices of East Harlem. This group of about 20 young people gave a skilled and tremendously exuberant performance of soul and gospel-derived songs.

JOHN BURKS
THE END OF A BEGINNING MAYBE

Rolling Stone, 19 March 1970

It was a New York winter day, frozen and gray and violently blustery. Indoors, out of the fearful cold, people seemed somehow gentler toward one another—strange in New York City—as if it was enough to battle the elements, no need to battle each other.

Inside his manager's neo-turn-of-the-century apartment, on a sofa near the radiant fireplace, sat Jimi Hendrix, in a gentle, almost reticent frame of mind. The light snow had begun to fall. You could see that through the narrow slits where the curtain allowed the merest sliver of daylight and streetscene to penetrate into the gloomy dark room.

On the same sofa, and on a richly upholstered chair next to it, sat the members of Jimi Hendrix' new band. He had broken up the old Experience (Noel Redding on bass, Mitch Mitchell, drums) at some indeterminate point during the Fall. He had been living and jamming with an all-purpose crew of musicians—everything from older black gentlemen from the South who played blues guitar, to a band of avant garde jazz/space musicians under the general leadership of a flute player named Juma—and talking about coming up with something new.

That avant garde/blues/rock and roll experiment faltered at some point along the way, and Hendrix announced a new band with the same instrumentation as the old Experience: it would have Hendrix singing and guitaring, Buddy Miles on drums and vocals, and Billy Cox, an old army buddy of Jimi's, on bass. The new band was called the Band of Gypsies.

By various accounts, they sounded pretty tough. The sound was not much different from the Experience; and, yes, they were still working up their repertoire; and there *were* early complaints about Buddy Miles' lengthy stretches of singing. But when they played Fillmore East, they dazzled everybody, including Bill Graham, who said he thought they had played perhaps the best set he had ever heard in his hall.

Off to a great start— And then, just like that, Hendrix dropped the Band of Gypsies. Or shelved them, anyway.

Now he had a new band to which he was going to devote his principal energies, as his number one thing. He had decided, through his publicity agent, that the time had come to rap about changes he was going through, about his new band, and about anything else that came up.

First, the news: the other two cats in his band are Mitch Mitchell and Noel Redding, from the original Experience. The Experience is back together again, and everybody's pals, and no hard feelings. Considering the attrition rate among rock and roll bands during the past year, this has approximately the news value of a trial separation between Dick & Liz. But this was the big news Hendrix' press agent was eager to Get Across, so this is what we started on, as Michael Jeffreys, Jimi's manager, brought on wine and booze.

The original plan (as described) was a rap with Hendrix. The actual circumstances brought together half a dozen people to rap in the flicker of a fireplace, on a day when Hendrix seemed just happy to listen to the others.

Then, too, there's the matter of Jimi's own personal terms of communication. To some question—precisely what it was cannot be recalled—Hendrix answered: "Start with a shovel, wind up with a spoon." A beautiful punch line. Does anybody know the joke?

Conversation went slowly at first—throughout, for that matter—and to goose it, I brought up the issue of the Black Panthers. One thing that's been written of Hendrix over recent months is that he's forming closer ties with black militant groups, possibly the Black Panthers . . .

That was about as far as I got before Hendrix laughed aloud. "I heard about that too. In *Rolling Stone*. Tell me all about it." He opened his eyes wide and grinned.

We thought the reporter who wrote our story had gotten his information straight from Hendrix.

"The thing is," said Mitch Mitchell, in his precise British accent, "we got the White Tigers."

All three of the Experience laughed privately among themselves. It was a private joke.

So it's not true about Jimi and the Panthers?

"No, man," he said. "Listen: Everybody has wars within themselves. We form different things and it comes out to be war against other people and so forth and so on."

Jimi Hendrix does not aim for one color or group. He digs all colors and all peoples. He wants that known.

Does that mean he doesn't relate personally to the Panthers?

"It isn't that I don't relate to them . . ." he said, and then trailed off in contemplation.

Does he mean he doesn't feel part of what they're doing?

"I naturally feel part of what they're doing. In certain respects. But everybody has their own way of doing things. They get justified as they justify others, in their attempts to get personal freedom. That's all it is."

Hendrix is with them, then?

"Yeah. But not the aggression or violence or whatever you want to call it. I'm not for guerrilla warfare."

Mitchell hunched up his shoulders monkey-like and said, "Gor-*illas*?"

Hendrix, grinning and looking at the floor: "I got a pet monkey called Charlie Chan." They all fell out laughing, the Panther issue forgotten. Hendrix grabbed his knees, leaning low to gaze at the burning logs.

Otis Redding, according to black business associates, had been planning an all-black recording enterprise. Studios and production and publicity and distribution. The whole thing, from the songwriter to the customer. Otis had been heavily involved in the planning at the time of his death. One of his goals was to bring older stars who'd slipped some back onto the charts. Men like Fats Domino and Chuck Berry and others. But Otis had died and nobody had picked up his plan. Did this sound appealing to Hendrix? He is one of the most likely black musicians to front such an organization, in terms of income and prestige.

Jimi objected to the idea on the grounds that it was restricted to one race. "It's the same thing as being Catholic or something," he began, then dropped it.

When Hendrix had been in court recently in Toronto on a dope bust that had taken place months earlier, he had told the court that he had "outgrown dope." What a perfect thing to say! That's what all the good-guy reformed "dope abusers" who come around lecturing high school kids and women's clubs always say. They saw the light. They saw that dope was wasting their precious talents. They saw that they didn't need dope. They *outgrew* it. Hendrix told the court he had outgrown dope, and immediately, on the strength of years of brainwashing, they reevaluated him. If he'd outgrown dope—this young fellow with his hair neatly cut, attired in sports jacket and slacks—then he must be a decent chap. Hendrix was acquitted.

Now he sat, crosslegged, in the quiet old splendor of this Manhattan livingroom, wearing all the familiar Jimi Hendrix costumery, a V-neck satin shirt of green, monumental wristwatch, jeweled pendant at his neck, violet bell-bottoms and pink boots.

Had this familiar visage turned his head away from dope? Outgrown it?

"At least," laughed Hendrix softly, "stop it from growing."

General mirth, accompanied by side-of-the-mouth muttering among all three of the Experience. More mirth. Laughter. Snickers.

Had he outgrown it?

Long pause, deep look on Jimi's face. "I don't know. I'm too . . ." He has said this seriously. All of a sudden he flashed his little-boy grin. "I'm too . . . *wrecked* right now . . ." This was Hendrix the comedian. This side of Jimi is the one people love. He does it all with slip-second timing, a shrug, an eye cast downward, a slightly over-accented word. It's the essence of his charm, and figures, in many ways, in the way he makes music. "I'll have to check into it," he added, getting serious again. About dope. "Oh yes, it's true, it's true. I don't take as much. That's what I was trying to tell them."

He didn't know much—nothing, in fact—about John and Yoko's peace festival in Toronto, but said he'd feel comfortable going back up there now, despite the bust. And anyway, he doesn't like to worry about things that happened in the past. "My *hangup* is getting hung up with things that happened in the past. I try not to."

Life has gotten less hectic for Hendrix during the winter. He'd moved away from the house with all those musicians. "I was trying to save more time for *myself*," he explained. "Where I could do more writing."

What kind of writing?

"Mostly it's cartoon-type material. I make up this one cat who's funny. He goes through these strange scenes, you know. You put it in music, I guess. Just like you put blues in music."

Was this something like writing long compositions?

"Pieces, I guess that's what you call it. Yeah, like pieces behind each other. Like movements, whatever you call it. I been writing some of those."

It would be simpler for Jimi if he knew how to write music, instead of having to remember it as it comes to him. He's been meaning to learn how to read music for a long time now. He needs it to express the larger concepts he's carrying in his head.

"Yeah, I was into writing cartoons, basically. You listen to it and you get such funny flashbacks." This dialogue comes through a lot better in Jimi's own gauzed and sinewy voice, with all the hesitation and musical jangles that come through in his speech, just like when he sings. "The music goes along *with* the story. Just like 'Foxey Lady.' I mean, *some*thing like that. The music and the words go together."

How does he write his music? What methods does he follow?

"Most of the time I can't get it on the guitar, you know? Most of the time I'm just laying around day-dreaming and hearing all this music. And you can't, if you go to the guitar and try to play it, it spoils the whole thing, you know?—I just can't play guitar that well, to *get* all this music together."

He repeated his desire to learn to write music for all the different instruments. He's thinking about getting down something *big*, that's for sure. Some day.

One result of his informal education in music is that most of the Experience's songs have taken shape inside the recording studio. "Foxey Lady" did. Hendrix came in with the lyrics, and among the three of them, they developed the musical line and the bottom and drum parts and the whole structure of it. This partly explained why Hendrix was back with the Experience—because they could really *work* together that way—

despite the rumors of bad, bad feelings within the group. (Noel Redding had said, some while back, that he would never be part of a Hendrix group again. Now that was forgotten. He and Mitchell said there had only been two major fights in the three years of the Experience, and all they came to was a lot of shouting.)

Redding: "Actually, the reason we work everything out in the studio is so everything will get as live and as *actual* as possible."

Hendrix: "It's like 'Voodoo Child.' Somebody was filming us as we were doing that. It was basically for the filming, we thought. We weren't thinking about what we were playing. We did it like three times."

Mitchell: "There's like a riff and we were just doing that . . ."

Hendrix: "Yeah, right, as they were filming us . . ."

Mitchell: "We were just doing it for the camera."

Hendrix: "It was like, 'Okay, boys, look like you're recording.' It was in the studio and they *were* recording it, you know, really. So it was one-two-three and then we went into 'Voodoo Child.'"

Hendrix invented the words as he went along, and the whole thing was improvised on the spot. It stuck. That's one of the versions on the album.

If there are any definite plans concerning the release of the next Hendrix LP, nobody was prepared to describe them. Hundreds of hours of studio time have yielded hundreds of hours of music which could possibly be included. On top of that, there are dozens of tapes of live performances by the Experience, by the Band of Gypsies, and by the Experience augmented with Juma and his avant garde ensemble (the latter taken at Woodstock). Hendrix is inclined to think that he would not include stuff by both the Gypsies and the Experience on the same LP. His immediate thought seems focused on two different singles. One would be by the Gypsies, entitled "Sky Blues Today."

The LP, however, will not consist of individual tracks like singles, but will be one continuous, sustained work. All three, Redding, Mitchell and Hendrix, absolutely do not want singles released "out of context" from the LP, the way "Crosstown Traffic" was pulled out of *Electric Ladyland* for release. They all feel this was a mistake on Reprise's part. A musical mistake; its sales are beside the point.

For the new album, they're planning on releasing a sort of "introductory" single, which might have one of the album's songs for its basic line, plus references to a lot of other things on the larger work. They're working, as usual, with engineer Eddie Kramer and longtime Hendrix associate Chas. Chandler as producer.

On *Electric Ladyland,* Hendrix was listed as producer. What did that mean, exactly? What had his role been?

"I don't know, really," Hendrix said, quite directly. "I haven't found out yet. 'Cause I heard it, and I think it's cloudy. The sound is very, you know, dusty."

Then that hazy, cloudy sound was unintentional?

"It got lost," he explained briefly, "in the cutting. Because we went on tour right before it was finished."

It was reported that Hendrix had been rehearsing the Band of Gypsies up to 18 hours a day. He laughed when asked about this. They *did* play 12 and 14 hours *some* days, he admitted, but it wasn't rehearsal, it was jamming for fun. They were grooving behind it. He still digs playing with Cox and Miles, and they're still friends. Hendrix repeated this a number of times.

What happened to the Gypsies was that Hendrix had walked offstage, right at the start of a major appearance, and hadn't appeared with them since. This was at the January Moratorium benefit at Madison Square Garden. They had barely begun when he stopped, dropped his axe, said into the microphone, "We're not quite getting it together," and walked off. This was precisely one month after Bill Graham had given them his ultimate accolade. I asked Jimi what had happened to blow the Gypsies apart.

"Maybe," he began, "I just started noticing the guitar for a change. It's like the end of a beginning maybe or something. I figure that Madison Square Garden is like the end of a big long fairy tale. Which is great. I think it's like the best ending I could possibly have come up with.

"The Band of Gypsies was outasite as far as I'm concerned. It was just . . . going through *head* changes is what it was, I really couldn't tell—I don't know: I was very tired. You know, sometimes there's a lot of things that add up in your head about this and that and they might hit you at a very peculiar time, which happened to be at the peace rally, you know? And here I'd been fighting the biggest war I ever fought. In my life. Inside, you know? And like that wasn't the place to do it."

But anyway, what came of it is that the Experience was going to be his main concern.

"We're in the process of, you know, getting our own thing together now again. Like we'll have time scheduled in a way so there'll be time on the side to play with your friends. That's why like I'll be jamming with Billy and Buddy and probably recording, too, on the side."

Would there be any new musical direction for the re-constituted Experience?

"Well," Hendrix grinned at Mitchell and Redding, "I'll try to make it more of an up." They all nodded. "We're going to go out somewhere into the hills and woodshed or whatever you call it, to get some new songs and arrangements and stuff together. So we'll have something new to offer, whether it's *different* or not."

Their first gig will be in mid-April at the Forum in Los Angeles. In mid-March they'll sequester themselves somewhere in England for that one-month workout.

Precisely how Hendrix and his management managed to patch up the bad feelings that reportedly undid the Experience in the first place was not mine to discover. But Mitchell and Redding said they were quite happy with the new schedule, which allows them time for themselves and their own projects. Redding is presently completing his second LP with Fat Mattress and may record further with them. But he'll not take them on the road again. At present, Mitchell is touring with Jack Bruce, Larry Coryell, and Mike Kandel, a sort of super-jam band. He'll do a lot of this playing in the future.

Mitchell was talking about other musicians he digs. He is particularly captivated by Tony Williams' drumming because it's so entirely original to Williams.

But when you ask the Experience about their influences, they're all quick to say they got where they are without picking up much from anybody. They grant major similarities between the way avant garde jazzmen like Cecil Taylor and Albert Ayler play and the sound of the Experience in full flight. To Jimi, it has a lot to do with the drumming. "That's where it *all* comes from, is the drumming," he says.

Mitchell: "Actually, in this group, the drummer and the bass player's roles are very much reversed. Because Noel is like such a good time-keeper that I don't have to be there with the drums. The bass and drum roles can be switched around at any particular time, at any particular moment."

Again, the undeniable parallel with contemporary jazz.

It's revealing to hear Hendrix talk about jamming in London last year with Roland Kirk, jazz's amazing blind multihorn player. Jimi was in awe of Roland, afraid that he would play something that would get in Roland's way. You can tell, by the way he speaks of Kirk, that Hendrix regards him as some kind of Master Musician. As it worked out, Jimi played what he normally plays, Roland played what *he* normally plays, and they fit like hand in glove. As Hendrix tells it, "Boy—that Roland Kirk!" says Jimi, pursing his lips. It is a fond memory.

A fond hope for Hendrix is that one day he'll form a band with Steve

Winwood. Simplest might be for Winwood to join the Experience. But any way at all, Hendrix would love to be performing with him on a regular basis.

Interestingly, while Hendrix retains his fondness for Dylan—including *Nashville Skyline,* from which Jimi intends to record "that one about the drifter"—none of the Experience are especially admiring of the Band. Hendrix allowed as how the Band definitely have it together enough to take you on *their* trip, if that's where you want to go. Mitch Mitchell asked with a small smile if the Band didn't all have pipes and mustaches.

Afterward, Hendrix stood out on East 37th, shivering as the night and the ice descended. The chill air had picked him up. This was not like part of the formal interview trip, so he could just rap. He had been amazed to see the stuff written about him and the Panthers, he said, because that wasn't where he was at at all.

A younger black cat stepped up and said, "Hiya, Jimi!"

Hendrix shook his hand and said, "How are you, man?"

It was not certain whether this was an acquaintance of Jimi's, but the other cat plunged right into it. "I saw your picture in the *Voice,* man," he said. "With Devon."

"At the Moratorium," said Hendrix.

"That was far-out."

"Yeah," said Hendrix. His long black limousine pulled up to the curb.

"How's it going with the band, man?"

"That's what we were just talking about. It's going to be groovy."

"You got any records coming out soon?"

"Yeah, I think pretty soon. That's where we're going now. Gonna listen to some tapes and do some mixing."

"Far-out."

He gave Hendrix another handshake and a slap alongside the shoulder and told him that the next time he played the city, man, he'd be there, and he'd dig talking again. Then he turned and walked down the sidewalk puffing great clouds of breath/steam into the darkening five-degree air.

Hendrix smiled wistfully, dropped the last reassurance that it was going to be "the best arrangement for all of us, I guess, you know?" The comeback of the Experience.

Another smile, another handshake, and he disappeared into the limousine, behind the steamed-over car windows. The limousine expelled a huge cloud of exhaust. No one was willing to let the long car break into traffic, and it was still waiting to get away from the curb, in the same place, when I turned the corner, walking.

Two and a half weeks later, I received a phone call from Hendrix' publicity person, suggesting that Jimi had a lot more to say. Too late, too late. The story as written was already laid out in the newspaper. But was there any important news? Well, yes, there was. As it turned out, Noel Redding decided to take a tour with Jeff Beck, so Hendrix would be using Billy Cox—his bassist with the Band of Gypsies—in his place. Otherwise, everything was pretty much the same. Redding would likely return to the group later. So it was still actually the Experience, and could I adjust the story I'd written accordingly?

ROY HOLLINGWORTH
HENDRIX TODAY
Melody Maker, 5 September 1970

Jimi Hendrix, the man with the misleading reputation that had mothers locking away young daughters when he was in town, is talking again.

After six months of hiding in corners, crawling into cracks when people were around, and generally locking himself away from the world, our Jimi is back in business, and his mind is six months pregnant with ideas.

For Jimi the first long trip has come to an end. It's time to go back home, feed himself until he's fat again, and then set out on trip number two, which will be a longer trip, an intrepid exploration, and for Jimi a new experience.

"It's all turned full circle; I'm back right now to where I started. I've given this era of music everything. I still sound the same, my music's the same, and I can't think of anything new to add to it in its present state," Jimi told me as he sat tending an English cold in a lavish London Park Lane hotel.

"When the last American tour finished earlier this year, I just wanted to go away a while, and forget everything. I wanted to just do recording, and see if I could write something.

"Then I started thinking. Thinking about the future. Thinking that this era of music—sparked off by the Beatles—had come to an end. Something new has got to come, and Jimi Hendrix will be there.

"I want a big band. I don't mean three harps and 14 violins. I mean a big band full of competent musicians that I can conduct and write for. And with the music we will paint pictures of earth and space, so that the listener can be taken somewhere.

"It's going to be something that will open up a new sense in people's minds. They are getting their minds ready now. Like me they are going back home, getting fat, and making themselves ready for the next trip.

"You see music is so important. I don't any longer dig the pop and politics crap. That's old fashioned. It was somebody's personal opinion. But politics is old hat. Anyone can go round shaking babies by the hand, and kissing the mothers, and saying that it was groovy. But you see you can't do this in music. Music doesn't lie. I agree it can be misinterpreted, but it cannot lie.

"When there are vast changes in the way the world goes, it's usually something like art and music that changes it. Music is going to change the world next time."

Jimi couldn't fully explain what his new music would be like, but he put forth his visions of how the next music form would be born.

"We are going to stand still for a while, and gather everything we've learned musically in the last 30 years, and we are going to blend all the ideas that worked into a new form of classical music. It's going to take some doing to figure out all the things that worked, but it's going to be done.

"I dig Strauss and Wagner—those cats are good, and I think that they are going to form the background of my music. Floating in the sky above it will be the blues—I've still got plenty of blues—and then there will be Western sky music, and sweet opium music (you'll have to bring your own opium) and these will be mixed together to form one.

"You know the drug scene came to a big head. It was opening up things in people's minds, giving them things that they just couldn't handle. Well music can do that you know, and you don't need any drugs.

"The term 'blowing someone's mind' is valid. People like you to blow their minds, but then we are going to give them something that will blow their mind, and while it's blown there will be something there to fill the gap. It's going to be a complete form of music. It will be really druggy music. Yes, I agree it could be something on similar lines to what Pink Floyd are tackling. They don't know it you know, but people like Pink Floyd are the mad scientists of this day and age.

"While I was doing my vanishing act in the States I got this feeling that I was completely blown-out of England. I thought they had forgotten me over here. I'd given them everything I'd got, I thought maybe they didn't want me anymore, because they had a nice set of bands. Maybe they were saying, Oh we've had Hendrix, yeah he was okay. I really thought I was completely through here."

About his future big band Jimi had talked a lot. But he was also eager to talk about thoughts on the three-piece outfit, which he believed could go on forever.

"It was fun, it was the greatest fun. It was good, exciting and I enjoyed it. But the main thing that used to bug me was that people wanted too many visual things from me.

"I never wanted it to be so much of a visual thing. When I didn't do it, people thought I was being moody, but I can only freak when I feel like doing so. I can't do it just for the sake of it. I wanted the music to get across, so that people could just sit back and close their eyes, and know exactly what was going on, without caring a damn what we were doing while we were on stage."

Could Jimi give any indication when he would start to form the big band?

"I don't know, but it won't be very long. Isle of Wight might be the last, or second to the last. But if the kids really enjoyed it, then it might carry on a little longer. But I will only carry on that way if I am useful, you know you have got to have a purpose in life."

His hair is a little tamer now. Did he feel he was a tamer person, a changing person? "No I don't think so, although I feel as though I get little sparks of matureness every now and then.

"I think of tunes, I think of riffs. I can hum them. Then there's another melody that comes into my head, and then a bass melody, and then another one. On guitar I just can't get them out. I think I'm a better guitarist than I was. I've learned a lot. But I've got to learn more about music, because there's a lot in this hair of mine that's got to get out.

"With the bigger band I don't want to be playing as much guitar, I want other musicians to play my stuff. I want to be a good writer. I still can't figure out what direction my writing is going at the moment, but it'll find a way.

"I won't be doing many live gigs, because I'm going to develop the sound, and then put a film out with it. It's so exciting, it's going to be an audio/visual thing that you sit down and plug in to, and really take in through your ears and eyes.

"I'm happy, it's gonna be good."

"I could sit up here all night and say thank you, thank you, thank you, you know . . . I just want to grab you, man, and just umm kiss you, but, dig, I just can't do that . . . so what I want to do, I'm going to sacrifice something right here that I really love . . . don't think I'm silly doing this, 'cause I don't think I'm losing my mind—last night, ooo whew, but, wait, wait, today I think every-thing is all right, you know, so I'm not losing my mind. This is just for every-body here, this is the only way I can do it, okay? . . . Don't get mad, don't get mad, no."

—*Jimi Hendrix*, before he burned his guitar at the
Monterey Pop Festival, June 1967

"Rock Star Jimi Hendrix Dead at 27"—that's what the papers said. Sad enough and true. Jimi Hendrix is dead, he was 27, and he was a star, as brightly gorgeous a star as ever graced rock 'n' roll music.

And yet, and yet. Twenty-seven is very young to die, even for a blues singer, and Jimi Hendrix was more than a star. He was a genius black musician, a guitarist, singer, and composer of brilliantly dramatic power. He spoke in gestures as big as he could imagine and create; his willingness for adventure knew no bounds. He was wild, passionate, and abrasive, yet all his work was imbued with his personal gentleness. He was an artist extravagantly generous with his beauty.

My words do not do him justice; his own do. "I want to hear and see everything, I want to hear and see everything." "Stone free, to do as I please." "Excuse me while I kiss the sky." It does not do to read them; they must be heard as he sang them, his voice urgent, earnest and humor-ous over his quirky rhythms while his awesomely inventive guitar splashed sound in dazzling hues.

It will be years before we know enough to know how fine an artist he was.

* * *

Jimi Hendrix was a blues man, perhaps the greatest of his generation. Like his predecessors in that noble line, Robert Johnson, Sonny Boy Williamson, Otis Redding and all the rest, he was a man, proud and boldly sexual; a musician, a dedicated innovator who immeasurably widened the range of the electric guitar and a dreamer, alternately dazzled and plagued by visions he could not help but pursue.

Some say the blues are declining. The evidence is that they are the most vital art form in the world today. Each decade has brought new syntheses, each generation new leaders. Jazz has never strayed far from its blues roots, and the blues mainstream, after successfully negotiating the move from Southern country to Northern city in the forties, took over electric music in the fifties.

Rock 'n' roll was, as everybody knew at the time, blues with a beat, created by men whose potency had wider scope than sex alone. "I'm a MAN," sang Bo Diddley, "spell it M, A, N," announcing the end of the days of black boyhood, while Chuck Berry in his zoot suit, eyes burning with liberated anger, dared to take on Beethoven. White kids, first country boys like Carl Perkins, then high school teen-agers like Bob Dylan, responded with their own blues. Then gospel singers began to sing the blues and that got called soul music. They even started "reelin' and rockin'" in England.

Jimi Hendrix was heir to all those traditions. The first music that tuned him on was Muddy Waters; he heard the Hit Parade and the Top 40 in his Seattle high school. He was in the Air Force like Johnny Cash, and he toured with the first gospel rocker, Little Richard, and also with Ike Turner, who long before that had inspired Chuck Berry in St. Louis and even before that had signed B. B. King to his first contract in Memphis.

The black show biz world, however, had an automatic ceiling which Jimi could not accept. His friends, who are still playing the same anonymous honky tonks, advised caution, but Jimi split for New York to break the big time. Greenwich Village with its interracial underground of artists and heads was more congenial than bleak Harlem, where competition was cruel for the smallest gigs. Challenged by the freedom of Bob Dylan's imagery, he began to write his own songs, though at first he didn't dare sing them. When, in 1966, he was invited to England, where experimental black musicians have been given gratifying welcome since Duke Ellington's first visit in 1933, he accepted at once.

In six months he and his Experience (bassist Noel Redding and drummer Keith Moon) had conquered the English pop scene. Monterey in June 1967, was his triumphant return home. A psychedelic hootchie-kootchie man, suave in red and orange, he was magnificent, at the very edge of the believable and totally real.

His first American tour that summer (part of it on a bill below the

Monkees) was not exactly a failure, but the second the following winter was a complete success. A year after the Monterey Pop Festival, Jimi was the superstar of rock, second only to the inactive Beatles, Rolling Stones, and Dylan. A dazzling stage performer, he also made masterful records: "Are You Experienced," a no-holds-barred debut; "Axis: Bold as Love," a mellow second, and "Electric Ladyland," both bluesy and surreal.

* * *

Stardom is never an easy life, and rock stardom in the late 1960s was as tough as any created by stage or screen. A lot of people wanted pieces of Jimi for their scrapbooks. He was arrested and tried for possession of drugs in Toronto in 1969, but was acquitted. He was at the center of an energy vortex as powerful as the music he created. The Experience faltered and broke up. Jimi experimented with several groups of musicians to get something new that worked. A few performances (one recorded) as the Band of Gypsies were the result; they were good but not good enough. Last spring The Experience came together again. At times it was brilliant, yet it too was often close to breaking up again. He and the group were resting from a European tour when he died. Friends say he had a troubled and unhappy summer.

The records are left, as well as, luckily, two superb films of him onstage—at Monterey and at Woodstock where, with a surgical and demonic precision, he gave "The Star-Spangled Banner" what it deserves.

I met him twice as a reporter; both times he was open and friendly. I would like to think his death accidental; if it was not, it is hard to guess the strains he was under. I just wish Jimi Hendrix were alive and making music today.

JOHN MORTHLAND
HENDRIX IS BURIED IN HOME TOWN
Rolling Stone, 29 October 1970

It had been very hot and sunny the last few days in Seattle, most unusual for this time of year. But on Thursday, October 1st, the sun didn't quite make it all the way out.

Down in the coffee shop of the Hilton Hotel, right by the airport, Jimi Hendrix's friends and associates were slowly gathering for breakfast. At the Hendrix family's house in south Seattle, the family was getting ready. They would all meet at Dunlap Baptist Church on Ranier Avenue South, where Jimi's funeral was to be held.

Nearly two weeks after his death in London, Jimi Hendrix was back in Seattle, his hometown, to be buried. The results of the inquest had been relayed from London; it was an "open verdict" in every sense of the word, but at this time nobody was really concerned with how he died anyhow. The reality of the present situation—Jimi's funeral—said all that seemed to be said.

The funeral was to begin at the church at 1 PM. The Hendrix family had requested a small, private funeral for friends and relatives only. A pool reporter and pool photographer were allowed inside the church, but that was all. Rope barriers had been strung along either side of the walkway leading up to the church door, and press and onlookers stayed behind it.

The Seattle longhair community was most respectful of the family's wishes. They stood quietly behind the ropes and watched as people walked into the church. They had also come to pay tribute to Jimi, for no other reason, and they provided none of the problems with crowd control that Seattle police had prepared for, just in case.

The church itself was very simple, even dull. A small building, the chapel had no stained glass windows. At the front were the pulpit, the coffin, and a floral arrangement dominated by a large and striking guitar.

Dunlap Baptist Church is attended by Janie, Jimi's nine-year-old sister. The Hendrix family had determined funeral arrangements, and chose to do it very traditionally. Participants were the Rev. Harold Blackburn, Mrs. Freddie Maye Gautier, a close friend of the family, who read the eulogy, and Patronella Wright, another family friend, who sang three beautiful spirituals backed by a gospel piano.

In her eulogy, Mrs. Gautier read from Jimi's own works: "Electric Church" and "Angel." The latter is the last song Hendrix wrote and recorded at Electric Lady, his New York studios, before he left for Europe in August to play the Isle of Wight. It is an ominous song, even more so in the context in which it was read.

At the end of the short service, the people filed by the open casket and out of the church.

Then the pallbearers—Dave Anderson, James Thomas, Steve Phillips, Herbert Price, Eddy Howard, and Danny Howell—came out, bearing the coffin. With the exception of Price, who was Jimi's chauffeur and valet in Hawaii this summer when a film was being made, all were friends from Jimi's childhood.

From the church, the procession of perhaps 100 cars made the 20-minute drive to Greenwood Cemetery, in nearby Renton, where, after a few more words from Rev. Blackburn and a chorus of "When the Saints Go Marchin' In," Jimi Hendrix, age 27, was returned to the earth.

(Hendrix's birthdate on all his press biographies was listed as November 27th, 1945, when, in fact, he was born on November 27th, 1942, and was 27, not 24, when he died.)

* * *

It had been a hectic week in Seattle prior to the funeral. The ceremony itself had been put back a few times because the autopsy in London had been put back. Funeral arrangements—handled primarily by Michael Jeffery, Jimi's manager, through his father, James Allan Hendrix—had been sometimes chaotic, an endless series of meetings and phone calls with Seattle officials.

Initially, there was talk of a huge rock and roll memorial service and jam. That was scotched quickly, partly due to lack of time to organize such an event, partly because the city of Seattle freaked at the idea. "If we can't do it right, we won't do it at all," Jimi's father said, and that settled that.

"It was never a really special thing when Jimi played Seattle," promoter Tom Hulett said Thursday as we were driving away from the cemetery. "The press never played it up like the return of the hometown boy, it wasn't like a special gig for Jimi, and the kids didn't really relate him to Seattle. When the press last week heard about the possibility of a big memorial concert, I think they started getting scared of something like another Woodstock. That was certainly one of the things."

Hulett had promoted Jimi's four Seattle gigs, as well as other West Coast dates. As one of Jimi's closest friends in Seattle, he had been game to organize the memorial concert were it ever a real possibility. He did get together the gathering and jam session for friends and family that took place after the funeral.

Included in the funeral arrangements were all the people who called that week at the Hilton Hotel, where the Hendrix staff was staying, and who just *had* to go to the funeral.

Meanwhile, Jeffery himself had come under much criticism after Jimi's death, and, while he insisted he didn't want to "bad-rap" anyone, he felt compelled to answer charges against him. That meant mostly to answer Eric Burdon, as well as Buddy Miles.

Miles felt Jeffery had cheated him financially when he was a member of the Band of Gypsys, and, from that, he inferred that Jimi had been cheated too. Jeffery produced papers that bluntly disproved Buddy's charges, and the rest of their dispute centered around basic personality conflicts. The bad feelings between them had all but subsided by Thursday, out of respect for Jimi, and Thursday night the drummer said he wanted nothing but to forget the whole unpleasant affair.

Burdon was something else. He had gone on BBC television shortly after Jimi's death and made some statements that appalled Jeffery and most everyone else. He claimed that Jimi had "made his exit when he wanted to"; that he "used a drug to phase himself out of this life and go someplace else."

He also said that he had a poem which Jimi had written just before he died—it was not presented at the inquest, and he could not be prosecuted for withholding evidence—and added that Jimi was ". . . handing me a legacy to continue the work of bringing the audio-visual medium together." His first project, he says, will be a film called *The Truth About Jimi Hendrix,* and he further plans to use the poem as the climax of the film.

Burdon never showed for the funeral.

He was in San Francisco the next weekend, though, appearing with his new group, War. He said that he didn't go to the funeral because Jimi had told him before that he hated Seattle, and Eric thought it improper to bury him there. He also says now that if he ever described the poem as a "suicide note"—which he did—he meant it figuratively.

Burdon also claims Jeffery, his former manager, took him to the cleaners. Jeffery, however, says it was Yameta, a Bahamian management firm, that is unable to account for the money that Burdon says is missing, and that he, Jeffery, lost out as well. Jeffery also says that he offered to jointly sue Yameta with Burdon, but Burdon turned around and filed suit against him instead. The outcome of that will be determined by New York courts.

As concerns Hendrix, though—for the constant inference, never stated outright, is that Jeffery was bilking Hendrix—his money all went straight to an independent New York accountant (who also handles finances for Barbra Streisand and Dustin Hoffman), and Jeffery produced more papers to show that he never takes a cent until the accountant pays *himself* a standard manager's fee, out of Jimi's earnings, per the contract agreement. Such papers are pretty hard to argue with.

All of this seemed pretty irrelevant to Jimi's friends and fellow musicians, who started arriving at the Hilton in Seattle in large numbers Tuesday, and continued coming in right up to the day of the funeral.

Noel Redding and Mitch Mitchell—the other two-thirds of the Jimi

Hendrix Experience—got in from England Tuesday night, along with roadies Jerry Stickles and the perpetually cheerful Eric Barret.

"Look at the beauty in his music and lyrics; what more can you say?" asks Redding.

"I think people are trying to make it like some kind of Judy Garland syndrome. It's getting too fucking theatrical," said Mitchell. "All I hope for is the man is in peace at last. All he ever wanted to do was play his guitar, he just wanted to play music which says, 'Here, I've got this energy, and go and do what you want, but direct it somewhere.'"

"Last week I was looking at a film script Jimi was working on, and in the margin he had written, 'Don't raise me up; I am but a messenger.' That's definitely the direction he was going in," Jeffery said. "He realized the power of soul, as one of his own songs said. He was an up, one of the highest people I've ever known, and he was getting more and more spiritual. To my mind, his music was the music of the new religion.

"His stage image halted him, though, and that was frustrating for him. That old ghost from the past—the humping the guitar, the 'Foxey Lady' stuff. Because that wasn't the true Jimi Hendrix, that ballsy, raunchy image. And as he was becoming more and more spiritual, he wanted more to fling that image off and just play his music."

Johnny Winter and his manager, Steve Paul, arrived. Paul's New York club, The Scene, was one of Jimi's favorite places; he spent many evenings there jamming with whoever wanted to get up on the stage with him. John Hammond Jr. slipped in quietly with Al Aronowitz, the New York music writer whose column in the *Post* has included some of the most lucid words about Jimi and his art. Miles Davis checked into another hotel downtown, and came to the funeral Thursday. He said afterwards that Jimi's were the only albums he listens to at home. Buddy Miles and his whole band were at the Holiday Inn.

Abe Jacob, who did the sound on two Hendrix tours, arrived. "He was the easiest person in the business to do sound for," Jacob said. "He was loud, but he was so careful himself with the sound."

Chuck Wein, who had filmed Hendrix in Hawaii several months earlier, discussed the movie. "Jimi was extraordinarily sensitive; he could talk to someone just a minute and know right where their heads were at. He was aware of the whole planet, and his relation to it," Chuck said. "The movie will surprise a lot of people; it shows a side of Jimi that few really knew at all." It's called *Rainbow Bridge,* and Chuck is still editing. It will still be released, as a tribute.

And late Wednesday night, Eddie Kramer, the dapper chief engineer at Hendrix's Electric Lady Studios, arrived. He has spent as much time in a recording studio with Jimi as anyone—and Hendrix spent hours upon hours in studios—and Thursday morning he was talking about the spate of Hendrix albums that will undoubtedly be released now.

"I'm certain there's all kinds of unscrupulous people in the business, who shall remain nameless, that will release tapes of Jimi now. We'll just have to try to do our best with Warner Brothers to stop it. The thing is, these people will put them out on the basis that any Jimi Hendrix music is good music.

"And that's not true! I know it and Jimi knew it. He had to have everything just perfect by his standards, and he never did that same thing twice. He'd lay down tracks, and every time he put his guitar over it, and played it different. Sometimes he'd take tapes home and listen to them all night, and the next day he'd come in and do it entirely different. You should have seen him—he'd be down there grimacing and straining, trying to get it to come out of the guitar the way he heard it in his head. If you could ever transcribe the sound in a man's head directly onto the tape . . . Whew!" he said.

Jimi left behind, according to Kramer, about two albums worth of studio cuts, and a superb live album recorded at Royal Albert Hall. They will be released soon. There's lots more Hendrix tapes that few will ever hear, however; if they can't cut what's already cut, Jimi's associates feel, it wouldn't be fair to his memory to release them.

* * *

The gathering that followed the funeral was described by many as a wake, and it was certainly closer in spirit to Jimi Hendrix than what had preceded it that day. The musical tribute was held in the Food Circus building of the Seattle Center, directly below the Space Needle left over from the World's Fair. Hulett had arranged for music, there was food and the atmosphere was much lighter.

The only hitch came when the program director from KOL-FM, there by Hulett's special invitation, called his station to say he'd be late for work because he was down at the Food Circus with the Hendrix family, Mitch and Noel, George Harrison and so forth. Besides the fact that he named some personalities who weren't there (George wasn't), it went out over the air and Hulett spent much of the rest of the afternoon telling the hundreds who gathered outside that the Hendrix family preferred it remain a private gathering for friends and relatives. He was understandably upset that he was put in this position (the location had been kept secret to avoid just such a scene), but, again, the kids understood, and cooperated.

Inside, the Buddy Miles Express played a full set. From there it turned into a free-wheeling jam, started off by Miles, Redding, Winter and Hammond. Pretty soon Mitchell took over on drums, the two guitarists fell out, and it was like that for the rest of the afternoon, with the musicians stepping in and out or trading axes. Jimi's young cousin, Eddie Hall, displayed a fast and fluid blues guitar, and the music went on into the early evening.

JOHN PICCARELLA
The New Grove Dictionary of American Music, 1986

Hendrix, Jimi [James Marshall] (*b* Seattle, WA, 27 Nov 1942; *d* London, England, 18 Sept 1970). Rock guitarist, singer, and songwriter. He taught himself guitar while growing up in Seattle. As he was left-handed he learned to play the instrument upside down and continued to do so throughout his life; his unorthodox technique included the use of the right thumb to form unusual fingering patterns for some chords. From 1958 to 1960 he played in a high-school band, the Rocking Kings, which performed songs popularized by such groups as the Coasters; he was strongly influenced during this period by the electric guitar solos of Charlie Christian. He left high school during his senior year and joined the US Army paratroopers; while stationed in Fort Campbell, Kentucky, he visited Nashville, where he listened to country-blues performers. With another paratrooper, Billy Cox, he formed a group called the Casuals, then, on his discharge from the army in 1961, went to Nashville and joined another band, the Imperials; while he was there he met Steve Cropper, a guitarist with Booker T. and the MGs, and with him recorded a demonstration tape. In 1962 he moved to Vancouver and joined Billy Taylor and the Vancouvers.

In 1963 Hendrix was engaged as a backing guitarist by Little Richard, and in the course of a tour of the South he met the blues guitarist Albert King, who taught him the technique of "bending" notes; in Los Angeles he played on his first recording, Rosa Parks's *My Diary*, which was produced by Arthur Lee. He later toured with Solomon Burke, Chuck Jackson, the Supremes, Ike and Tina Turner, Jackie Wilson, and B. B. King. In Chicago he visited the Chess recording studios, where he observed Muddy Waters and other blues musicians. In 1964 he moved to New York and was hired by the Isley Brothers, who encouraged his taste for flamboyant costumes and his exhibitionist performing routine, which included playing the guitar with his teeth, with one hand, behind his back, or between his legs. Late in 1964 he joined Curtis Knight's band and played on some of its recordings; he toured with Joey Dee and the Starlighters the following year, then played in King Curtis's band with guitarist Cornell Dupree and bass guitarist Chuck Rainey.

In late 1965 Hendrix moved downtown in New York to Greenwich Village, where he associated with a number of white folk-rock musicians. He formed a group, Jimmy James and the Blue Flames, with guitarist Randy Wolfe (*b* Los Angeles, 20 Feb 1951), who later became known as Randy California, a member of the group Spirit. They played blues, rock-and-roll, and songs by Dylan, and Hendrix began experimenting with feedback, fuzz, distortion of sound through high volume levels, and other electronic effects. He won the admiration of Dylan's guitarist Michael Bloomfield, John Hammond, Jr., who engaged him to play lead guitar in his group, members of the Rolling Stones, and Bryan "Chas" Chandler, a former member of the Animals. Chandler became Hendrix's manager and took him to England in 1966, where with bass guitarist Noel Redding (*b* Folkestone, England, 25 Dec 1945) and drummer Mitch Mitchell (*b* London, 9 July 1946) he formed the Jimi Hendrix Experience. The group released its first single, which consisted of *Hey Joe* and *Stone Free,* in December 1966, and became the opening act for the English rock trio Cream, whose guitarist Eric Clapton had been impressed by Hendrix's playing. Hendrix's outrageous showmanship (his handling of his guitar was overtly sexual and he sometimes brought his act to an end by setting fire to the instrument) and the unusual racial constitution of the group—a black American guitarist and singer leading a white rhythm section—gained much attention, and his innovative guitar techniques strongly affected other musicians.

Hendrix's first album, *Are you Experienced?* (1967), was notable for a number of unusual sound effects, which he had devised with his recording engineer, Eddie Kramer, and which they continued to explore; these included the building up of multiple tracks on four-track equipment, the manipulation of tape speeds, the mixing down of some material played backwards, the use of controlled feedback, phase shifting, Fuzz Face and Cry Baby sound-effects pedals, and special effects achieved through the manipulation of the tremolo arm and the toggle switch controlling the selection and combination of the pickups. The range of Hendrix's distinctive guitar sound is most strikingly represented in the songs *Purple Haze* and *I don't live today*.

In the summer of 1967 Hendrix and his group made their first American appearance at the Monterey (California) Pop Festival, where his performance was the highlight of the event. He then began a tour of the USA with the pop group the Monkees, but his performances proved controversial and the engagement was soon canceled, though not before he had gained enough publicity to advance considerably his rise to international success. His second album, *Axis: Bold as Love* (1968), is characterized by more self-consciously imagistic lyrics, more refined song structures, and complex, skillful arrangements that create soulful rhythm and melody from the multitracking of guitar parts. He continued to search for new equipment and effects, until his group and management became impatient with his costly, time-consuming experimentation. He also began to use hallucinogenic drugs. The double album *Electric Ladyland* (1968) contains some of his most highly developed psychedelic music, including a version of Dylan's *All along the watchtower* (no. 20, 1968) as well as some of his more extravagant soundscapes.

In early 1969 Hendrix and his group began a tour of the USA, but Hendrix continually changed his programs in the attempt to find a more sophisticated, black "electric church music." He was by this time involved in group improvisation with jazz musicians in New York and expressed an interest in playing with Miles Davis, whose fusion of jazz and rock music showed evidence of the influence of Hendrix's funky rhythms and colorful textures. In May 1969 he was arrested in Toronto for possession of heroin. During this period he supervised construction of his own recording studio, Electric Lady, in Greenwich Village. In the summer of 1969 he played at Woodstock with bass guitarist Billy Cox and drummer Buddy Miles; the group remained together for some time after the festival and recorded an album, *The Band of Gypsys,* which was issued early in 1970. The original Jimi Hendrix Experience was then re-formed, but Cox soon replaced Redding as bass guitarist. The group began to record at the completed Electric Lady studios in the summer of 1970; some of the material, in a new style influenced by soul music, was included on *The Cry of Love* and *Rainbow Bridge* in 1971, and some was completed by studio musicians and released later on *Crash Landing* (1975) and *Midnight Lightning* (1976). After Hendrix's death (from asphyxiation in his sleep when he had taken sleeping pills) Alan Douglas, who was left in custody of the substantial body of Hendrix's unreleased recordings, produced two albums: a collection of group improvisations called *Nine to the Universe* (1980), and a double album of numbers recorded at concert performances.

The sound that Hendrix created was unmistakable: typically it was loud, sustained, and full-textured, with much use of expressive timbral nuances, and though it had a basic toughness, his music generally avoided a rigid rock beat. Hendrix was not gifted with a naturally fine singing voice, but compensated for his shortcomings by developing an idiosyncratic and compelling vocal style, a form of heightened speech that had its roots in blues and soul. His revolutionary guitar technique and his innovative use of the recording studio as a compositional environment have had a greater impact on rock music than the work of any other musician. His songs and instrumental numbers are not easily separated from his individual style of performing them, and for that reason have been recorded by other musicians only occasionally.

Bibliography

D. Henderson: *'Scuse Me while I Kiss the Sky: The Life of Jimi Hendrix* (Toronto, Ont., 1981).

R. Denyer: *The Guitar Handbook* (London, 1982), 26.

J. Hopkins: *Hit and Run: The Jimi Hendrix Story* (New York, 1983).

PART TWO

Critics: Bold as ...Love?

*People make
sounds when they
clap. So we make
sounds back. I like
electric sounds,
feedback and so
forth, static.*

DAVID FLOOKE
WHITENOISE?
Crawdaddy, September 1967

The problem of foreground and background as well as the distinction between different forms of sense data is explored on the new and first Jimi Hendrix album. "Third Stone from the Sun." (The group plays a double-time, jogging accompaniment to a musique concrète background. I wish I could tell you more but I don't feel like it.)

Now, however, with renewed zeel, return us to the question at hand. What happens when you turn the gain control all the way up. The compression effect. Whereas before the ratio between noise and conventional information was great enough to virtually nullify the noise, the normal program material can be amplified no louder than it is due to the amplifiers' limitations, but the noise, which is lower in input intensity and has not as yet reached overload level, is brought up to a level which compares to that of the normal source.

Now let us labor beyond this to discover what Hendrix does with this compressed form. Going back to "Third Stone." The track begins with what appears to be a now-normal technically produced Omaha-type background. The background becomes foreground however when mixed with a "live-normal" musical section similar to the transitional part of "A Day in the Life." As the piece progresses and the normal line becomes less normal, that which we called the technical foreground slowly fuses with, becomes subordinate to, re-fuses with, dominates etc. the now-transfigured "normal."

What does this have to do with saxophones? It is difficult to say, but easy to comprehend. Would it offend you if I said that Jimi Hendrix has a saxophone fixation. 'Cause it seems as though all of his runs come from, to one degree or another, old hard-rock sax solos. If this is repulsive, try to realize that Hendrix has managed to liberate the spirit of the instrument from all of its bring-down sociological overtones. Saxophones aren't psychedelic at all. Saxophone music is. What more could you ask for?

For one thing, you could ask for white noise, or, more specifically, a bridge between "normal musical space and time" and "pure sound and silence." Hendrix definitely provides the major part of the bridge by allowing his music to develop in time from "saxophone in space" to "information barrage." If your amplifier blew up and fatally injured you at the end of the album, you might really make it.

Now into the eye of death, we might look for immortal nontemporal sound. Not, mind you, in the sense of the classics. Not music which survives for time immemorial, but sound which is timeless, formless and will be forgotten less than a second from whatever "now" you choose. Take Ad Reinhardt at the North Pole, for instance. This is pretty confusing. Pure blackness. Pure whiteness. No bridge between the two and even less to say. In the time between the point at which you realize this perceptually and the point at which you begin to try to explain it by twitching, vomiting or philosophizing, you may have been ——— (for want of a better term). Can this happen with sound? Can something which is extended in time be timeless?

The answer to the first question is a most definite yes. Push yourself off a cliff clutching empty Coke bottles. Blow the price of an album and take a trip to the airport on a busy night. Put firecrackers in your ears. The least harmful (but perhaps the least effective) is the airport trip. Jet noise is something that the Byrds knew about (not Lear jet but "kriiiiiii-iiiiiiiiiiiiiiiiiishhhhhhhhhhhhhhhhhhhhhhhh") but seem to have forgotten. Compare a bunch of jet engines warming up to the beginning of almost any Hendrix work or to the 30-second buildup before the 50-second fadeout on "A Day in the Life" (which doesn't quite make it along these lines). A progression from relatively articulated sound to pure, unarticulated threshold volume, rich, everything noise. Now, the articulated bridge which Hendrix provides may be better than the earlier stages of the jet noise in that it helps you to accomplish the transition between time-knowing and pressure-knowing. The jet, on the other hand, seems to have the upper hand (so far) on pressure. Perhaps the detonation of a nuclear device would help in the third position of a sequence beginning with 1) Hendrix leading to 2) jet noise, and culminating with 4) the finality of some kind of cosmic snap.

Alas, the industry lags behind.

JIM MILLER
JIMI HENDRIX: *AXIS: BOLD AS LOVE*
Rolling Stone, 6 April 1968

Jimi Hendrix sounds like a junk heap (Ben Calder crushed monolithic mobiles bulldozed), very heavy and metallic loud. Rock's first burlesque dancer, superman in drag, his music is schizophrenic. *Axis: Bold as Love* is the refinement of white noise into psychedelia, and (like Cream) it is not a timid happening; in the vortex of this apocalyptic transcendence stands Hendrix, beating off on his guitar and defiantly proclaiming, "If the mountains fell in the sea, let it be, it ain't me." Such cocky pop philosophy shall not go unrewarded.

"EXP" is Hendrix's white tornado advertisement aperitif (come-on), "My God Martha, it's a white tornado": "There ain't no life nowhere." The science fiction continues (Mose Allison) in "Up from the Skies," while "Spanish Castle Magic" transforms the Clovers; in fact, much of *Axis* demonstrates that Hendrix stands in relation to rhythm and blues of the fifties as the Who stand in relation to mainstream rock of the fifties—two useful transplants, indeed. "Ain't No Telling" is all Mitch Mitchell, who is by now definitely one of rock's most frantic drummers (from Moon to Baker). "If 6 Was 9" cracks foundations with banalized hippie lore ("wave my freak flag high"), while "She's So Fine" positively destroys walls. If "One Rainy Wish" repairs everything (like "May This Be Love"), pomp and circumstance ushers out "Bold as Love"—we all know that she by now *has* to be experienced.

Jimi Hendrix may be the Charlie Mingus of Rock, especially considering his fondness for reciting what might loosely be called poetry. But his songs too often are basically a bore, and the Experience also shares with Cream the problem of vocal ability. Fortunately both groups' instrumental excellence generally saves the day, and Hendrix on *Axis* demonstrates conclusively that he is one of rock's greatest guitar players in his mastery and exploration of every conceivable gimmick. Uneven in quality as it is, *Axis* nevertheless is the finest Voodoo album that any rock group has produced to date.

Jimi Hendrix, who never ceases to amaze the weirdest of people, has been doing a great deal of jamming here on the East Coast. During the month of March, he's played with everyone from Mike Bloomfield to Jim Morrison. The jam is probably the best source of new material and the only way to experiment freely with anything. Jimi bought a four-track stereo tape recorder recently and has been taping all his jam sessions for future reference.

Jim Morrison (another Sagittarian named James) had to be dragged off the stage when he sat or should I say fell in with Hendrix at the Scene recently. He gets drunk and can't control himself, knocking over mike stands and falling on his back a few times for show—they took him away after he tried to make love to Jimi's guitar while singing some beautiful blues thing he made up.

Jimi is using different musicians on some of the cuts of his forthcoming triple album, to be released whenever it's finished. I've already played harp on a number called "My Friend" (a funky blues) and made some barroom noises with Steve Stills and Kenny of the Fugs for the aforementioned.

Another song he's doing completely on his own is called "I Dreamed I Was a Mermaid in 1984." He plays bass, drums, lead and rhythm and whatever else he might need at the time.

He's been doing a super-human bit of touring all over the country, and may someday create his own universe just to get away from the inter-viewers and fans in this one. His writing is similar to Lennon's "I Am the Walrus" (if compared on a practical surrealistic level), but describes a more tangible obscurity than Dylan's or Lennon's.

He will also do Dylan's "All Along the Watchtower" in his typically explosive style and perform open-heart surgery on nearly every musician in the business in the long run.

Someday the U.F.O.s will find out about him.

Last time I saw Jimi Hendrix onstage, he was playing SuperSpade. His Afro-Annie hairdo looked like it was plugged into his Sunn amp. His country duds—emerald pants, purple shirt, iridescent vest—were drawn from rainbow vats. His music—ominously circling, coiling and striking home—had the motions of a great black snake. Tossing his left-handed guitar over his shoulder, between his thighs or into fast hand spins, Hendrix came on like a flashy Western gun slinger. (Sammy Davis would have *kwelled.*) "Flash" was just the word he chose later to nail his own image: "a big flash of weaving and bobbing and groping and maiming and attacking."

Hendrix is camping as a musical mugger, but his sound identifies him as an artist—rock's most resourceful noise sculptor. Mixing fuzz and feedback at *fortissimo* levels, he rears massive acoustic constructions that loom threateningly over his audience. The sound is of a tactile solidity that makes you want to reach out and run your hand around the bend in a blue note. Some of his pieces remind you of totems of scabrous rusty iron; some move like farm machines run amok; some suggest shiny brass columns and spheres breached to reveal an interior textured like a toadstool.

Hendrix should have welded some unforgettable assemblages that night at the Fillmore East; but he didn't have his electric mojo working. Every time he'd start to fuse one sound with another, his tandem two-hundred-watt amplifiers would blow another sort of fuse. Dancing upstage to make a fast adjustment on the speaker face, then coming down again in a slow split, he got into a *pas de deux* (or was it a *paso doble?*) with his equipment. So graceful were these face-saving vamps, he almost persuaded you that all this fancy footwork was part of the act. "Jimi Hendrix, ladies and gentlemen, in *The Dance of the Dying Amp.*" Finally, he announced in a voice wry with exasperation that he couldn't last much longer. Anxiety gripped the huge house. What would happen, we all thought, if this colossal noise symphonist were left standing there with nothing but the feeble plink of an unamplified guitar? Fortunately, he quit while he was still audible, and we filed out past the mobs waiting to get in for the second show.

After the show aborted, I went home and put *The Jimi Hendrix Experience* on the turntable. Tough, abrasive, brutally iterative, the uptake suggested the ironshod tracks of a bulldozer straining against a mountain of dirt. Hendrix's program for the country blues was rural electrification. The end products were Futurist symphonies of industrial noise. I felt I was back home in Pittsburgh, walking along the old South Side with its clangorous sheet-metal plants, raucous open-hearth furnaces, whirring power stations and hissing yard engines. This new factory music brought the evolution of the blues full circle. Those famous laments had begun as labor pains: the field hand working alone in a Sahara of cotton would cry out to raise his spirits or purge his pain. When these hollers were joined to the chants of laborers and prisoners, the manacled rhythms of work were broken by wild cries of release. Now a New Negro from the North had revived the primitive form by shouting ecstatically above the blind roar of the machine. That shout was an industrial arwhoolie.

Hendrix had grown up in Seattle, and as he told me later, "there was all kinda soul there, and Chinese, too." That was really the secret. He grew up in a time and place that knew nothing about the purity of tradition. Everything was mingling and mixing to produce new strains, new sounds, complex amalgams that meant many things. In the *Hendrix Experience* you could hear everything from country frailing[1] out of Nashville and dirty hollering from the Delta to the high-tension crackle of the Who and the surrealistic glossolalia of Bob Dylan. Yet some things were much better realized than others. Hendrix might make capital out of his image as SuperSpade, a mythical Black Man committing acts of violence before fascinated audiences of English and American teenies (his tour with the Monkees had to be terminated because the bookers were terrified of his debauching effect on the little ones). He could wink at the hipper soul brothers as he stood spotlighted between his hard-working rhythm section of pale English boys. (There's an inverted stereotype for you!) But Hendrix was the greatest living proof that today black is gray.

Apart from his lissome physical grace—a quality no white rock performer has ever displayed—Jimi Hendrix is essentially one with the white pop scene wherever it is most advanced, in London or Nashville or on the West Coast. Like the last generation of jazzmen, who transcended their Negro origins to become figures in the international music avant-garde, playing to almost exclusively white audiences, working with white sidemen, studying with white masters and consorting with white women, Hendrix's blackness is only skin deep. Nor is he simply American or English. Every time he starts to jam, he bends instinctively toward the East. His guitar becomes a sitar; his soundscape is enveloped in purple moiré. Listening to track after track in the cushioned cool of my living room, I began to sink into a familiar trance. There was, I realized drowsily, a glittering psychedelic thread running through even the coarsest burlap spun by Hendrix's infernal mills.

Having stepped over the threshold of appreciation, I entered a new zone of awareness of Jimi Hendrix. I recognized belatedly that he was the only thing live and moving on the current rock scene. Judging from what I had seen and heard at the Fillmore, he was in that ardent phase of the

---

1. Frailing: [dialectal for "flailing"] primitive American guitar technique antedating the blues.

creative cycle that transfigures a man and his work. Now was the time to get with Hendrix, to hear his story, to learn where he was going. I called his agent and she told me that I could see him at the Drake Hotel after he awoke (at 7 P.M.) and got his head together (round about midnight). At that hour the lobby of the Drake, all velvet panels and crystal sconces, with the antique furniture pushed to the walls, is practically deserted. Yet the music makers grind on in the hotel's sideshows. In the Drake Room, a brown leather retreat like the inside of a lady's handbag, Cy Walters is still driveling at the keyboard. In Shepheard's—El Cairo by Al Capp—young teams from the best colleges compete in a taut-muscled discathalon.

On the seventeenth floor, where Mr. Hendrix had his suite, the mood was Oriental pleasure dome. When I arrived, services were being held. Candles were burning in red glasses, incense was curling heavenward and mini-skirted cup-bearers were charging chalices with sparkling Lancer wine. Hendrix was flitting about like an emperor moth. Dressed in blue velvet bellbottoms, an open island shirt and no shoes, his famous fright wig at half-mast, he looked about half as big and as old as he did in his pictures. Far from being a cross between Genghis Khan and Anthony Quinn, Hendrix's offstage appearance is almost girlish. He's flirty, jivey, archly insinuating; he giggles, casts looks out of the corners of his eyes, and murmurs demure "Thank yous" after every compliment. Taxing questions he brushes aside with verbal shrugs: "I can't remember now"; "I don't know, man, it's really strange"; "I don't know too much about it." To familiar queries he responds with deft jabs. Question: What is the difference between the old blues and the new? Answer: Electricity. Question: What is your opinion of jazz? Answer: Jazz is "Blue Moon." Question: Did you receive an education in music? Answer: I tried to sign up for violin and harp, but they was always filled.

His family was not especially musical, though his father tapped and played the spoons. His first guitar he bought for $5 from a friend of his father's, sounding out the cat when he was drunk, and the next day "walking all the way 'cross town to git it." (He's always walking "'cross town" in his songs.) He tried to copy B. B. King, but he couldn't make the changes; so he started playing "honky-tonk." At the age of sixteen, he short-circuited his youth, enlisted in the army and began to haunt the servicemen's clubs looking for left-handed guitars (strung in reverse order). After doing fourteen months in the 101st Airborne, he landed in Nashville and there he learned his trade.

Joining a little group of "blues addicts," he played songs by Booker T. (Jones), Ted Taylor and Elmore James—all funky blues men. His little

Silvertone amp with its two twelve-inch speakers was always feeding back; so he wove the noise into the texture of his music, and thus was born the blitzy sound that is today his hallmark. Moving around the soul circuit, he played behind many headliners and spent an unforgettable year with rock's greatest prima donna, Little Richard. Once he and another boy in the band bought fancy shirts; Richard reprimanded them severely, hissing: "I'm the King of rock 'n' roll. I'm the only one that's allowed to be pretty."

Eventually the trail led to Greenwich Village and the Cafe Wha?, where he met Chas Chandler, a veteran rock bass player who urged Hendrix to make his bid in England. Picking up his now-famous sideman, Noel Redding (bass), and Mitch Mitchell (drums), at a try-out jam session in London, Hendrix broke through in a burst of notoriety, burning his guitar on the stage and making with the mayhem.

Having suffered the interviewer gladly for half an hour, Hendrix rose now to proffer enthusiastically a musician's finest hospitality: a taste of his new music. Settling me in a deep chair, he filled my glass, offered me a giant joint, clapped a pair of elephantine headphones on my ears and began to spin the tapes from which his next LP will be cut.

In the tight little world of the earphones, I heard thunderous sounds like salvos of howitzers. Hendrix leaned over and purred: "It's the gods making love." Then I began to cringe as the roar of a jet engine mounted in my ears—but something magical happened. The intimidating sound became an esthetic object; impulsively I thought, How beautiful are our noises! The tunes that followed spanned a wide spectrum of pop music. I recall a shouting, talking blues, backed with a heavy, raunchy beat; a long, exotically instrumented jam session, reminiscent of Roland Kirk (a blind jazz musician who plays simultaneously three weird instruments—manzello, stritch and flexaphone—and blows a whistle worn on a string around his neck). There was even an Anglican Chinese—call it Chinese Chippendale—rock number that was designed as a send-up of the square-toed Handelian anthems affected by the British groups.

All these songs I recall as one does the other pictures in a gallery that houses a masterpiece. For near the end of our séance, Hendrix unwound a tape which even in the rough cast stood forth as one of the two or three extended compositions that justify our hopes for art rock. I'll call the piece "Atlantis" because it raised a sunken continent in my mind; yet I know that this rock "La Mer" must have been composed by Hendrix out of recollections of his youth spent in a seaport near the Pacific.[2]

2. The piece was later released as "1983" in *Electric Ladyland*.

"Atlantis" is an impressionistic evocation of the sea and all its sounds. Its dominant theme is one of those plangent psychedelic melodies that sing of sensuous surrender, of upturned eyes and outspread limbs and head humming with cosmic vibrations. Around this unforgettable melody (played mellifluously on a backless guitar), Hendrix has composed a remarkable assemblage of oceanic motifs: lonely ship buoys (whose notes bend blue) are blended with exquisite wind chimes; throbbing ship motors become basso ostinatos for clusters of sonar pings. The sea collage is enriched with musical pastiche: a bolero rhythm shading into a military polonaise, a Krupa drum break dissolving into a flamenco bass solo. Toward the end, Hendrix sings in the entrancing voice of a siren, "Down and down and down and down and down and down we go"; and as he disappears into the vortex, the theme comes wailing up from the sea bottom. The final impression is of an empty sky pierced only by gull cries and the whine of a distant jet.

Hearing all these sounds under such conditions was an overwhelming experience. As I struggled to express my pleasure and admiration for his new music, one of Hendrix's female friends, who had been sketching him through the evening, turned to me and said firmly in words that sounded like a manifesto: "First we had a music that was all body; then we had a music that was all mind; now we have a music that is mind and body." Hendrix giggled and, flitting to the phonograph, dropped the needle on a record that almost blew me out of my seat. A brass chord, sustained, distended, thrusting into the room like the end of a girder, was snapped off savagely by a funky bass which in turn was transfixed by the most piercing, astringent, nerve-thrilling guitar sound I had ever heard. Instinctively, I looked up at Jimi Hendrix. He laughed and said, "No, man, that's not me. That's the guitar player I learned from. That's the King. That's right, Albert King." At 4 A.M., I just blinked. Man, I was zonked.

JIMI HENDRIX IN CONCERT: PAUL SAUVE ARENA [MONTREAL]

Logos, May 1968

HENDRIX—*ggggrrreeeeeeech*—MITCHELL—*fffzzzzzzeeeeeeps*—REDDING—*grork*—SCREAMING MOVING MANY—*chhhhhaannnk*—COPS RUN CHARGE—*jjjjuuuuuuuuurrrrrkkkssss*—JIMI SPIN BITE SCREW HEAVE—*bleep*—ELECTRIC FLYING AXE—*ssssgggggl*—JESUS—*ssblip*—WHADDASHOWMAN

FRANK KOFSKY
FROM "THE SCENE"
Jazz & Pop, December 1968

What sets Jimi Hendrix apart from all the imitative purveyors of *sexualité exotique*—the practitioners of "cock rock," I suppose my companion in critical crime Richard Goldstein would dub them—such as the Iron Butterfly and Deep Purple, is that Hendrix *can* play when he sets his mind to it. That is just what he has done, I would guess, for his third album, *Electric Ladyland*. In consequence, while all the psychedelic paraphernalia are still in evidence (he certainly likes to whiplash back and forth across stereo channels, doesn't he?), they now come through as integral parts of the music and not as gratuitous bits of freakery, tacked on to titillate the teeny-boppers. Along the same lines, Hendrix's solos on *Ladyland* strike me as more musical (they are certainly more extensive) and less preoccupied with gimmicky effects than those of his previous albums; they seem to spring (I trust that is the appropriate verb for this context) directly and organically out of the material and manifest greater continuity than his earlier improvisations. There are a number of fine tracks, but I was especially taken with "Come On" (suggestive of Ray Charles' "Let the Good Times Roll") and Hendrix's version of Bob Dylan's "All Along the Watchtower" (the introduction is splendid). There are a number of sitters-in—large parts of the album even have a jam session feeling—including Chris Wood and Stevie Winwood from Traffic, the Airplane's Jack Casady, drummer Buddy Miles, and Al Kooper on piano; but aside from a saxophone solo by Freddie Smith, none of the guests make much of a dent in the proceedings. (Neither, alas, does Hendrix's remarkable Elvin-inspired drummer Mitch Mitchell.) In the end, it is Hendrix's show, and it suits him to keep it that way. I don't think it was absolutely essential that we be given a long and sometimes monotonous double album to digest; but that, again, is a petty stricture about an overall solid achievement.

DOUGLAS PRINGLE
JIMI HENDRIX AT MAPLE LEAF GARDENS [TORONTO], MAY 1969
Arts Canada, August 1969

Jomo Hantrax woke up to the screaming sun. He washed his face and hands in the stream, erased, ate slowly, and erased again. Pain is total abstraction, and not easy to bear; then music filled his ears, and he left it all behind.

Jimi Hendrix swung out on stage, took up that incredible curved stance, knees bent, pelvis up; he made an unfelt effort at his usual rap on chicks and the Experience, but stopped at the bitter taste of it. Then got to the music; he called three songs, none appeared, then laid into the fourth, mostly guitar, words from the past that caught in his throat . . . so hard to smile. The music came as light through holes in the form, carrying a heavy restless passion. The Gardens, the airport, electric hum, somebody else's dream of making you pay what they say you owe.

His hair is so much shorter now, and tied back with a scarf, and the next record is dedicated to the Panthers. The music penetrating the life we share. "Art does not seek to describe but to enact. And if man is once more to possess intent in his life and to take up the responsibility implicit in his life, he has to comprehend his own process as intact, from outside, by way of his skin, in, and by his own powers of conversation, out again" (Charles Olson, *Human Universe*).

An attempt to verbalize the pain, to make things come clear: he announces a song improvised for the moment, about the real Jimi Hendrix. "We all know who Jimi Hendrix is . . . ," as if he hadn't already given that. "I grew up in a room full of mirrors / Couldn't see nothin' but myself / So I took my spirit, that is, my soul, and I smashed those mirrors . . . Pieces of glass stuck in my head . . ." Sagittarius: Illuminator of the Great City, horse, man, arrow. "When the windows all are broken / Windows really all a seer can own . . ." (The Grateful Dead). And few words after that.

Take this mask, she said, and I being in no wise unwilling, fled with the sun in my pocket; but just could not stay away. The guitar sang on, for over an hour, never losing the intensity. Mitch Mitchell and Noel Redding would come into it, then lose contact; they hardly seemed present at the highest points. Hendrix does it all anyway, with or without studio multi-tracking. The sound was rough, the rhythm unsteady, far from the composure of *Electric Ladyland*; but soared, higher, into the last song, "Voodoo Child," a fragment of identity, the blues. Black Music, opening into release, at least for the moment.

"And all the world was filled with voices of all kinds that cheered me, so I charged. I had the cup of water in one hand and in the other was the bow that turned into a spear as the bay and I swooped down, and the spear's head was sharp lightning. It stabbed the blue man's heart, and as it struck I could hear the thunder rolling, and many voices crying 'Un-hee!'

meaning I had killed. The flames died. The trees and grasses were not withered anymore and murmured happily together and every living being cried in gladness with whatever voice it had" (a vision of the Sioux holy man Black Elk, about 1860).

A shaman? We all watch the sun rise every morning.

P. J. O'ROURKE
I DON'T LIVE TODAY
Harry, 3 October 1970

At the coroner's inquest they said that Jimi Hendrix died after an overdose of barbiturates, of choking on his own vomit. That's a piece of karmic irony no artist deserves.

"Hey Joe" was playing on the stereo the first time I shot speed. And the music that followed was different than anything I'd ever heard. In fact, Jimi Hendrix was playing on the stereo through all the worst or most amazing part of my life—when I was a younger kid, tearing myself apart and trying to fuck myself to death. He was so intense—some kind of Edna St. Vincent Millay of the wah-wah pedal. I'm not old enough to remember when Great Bird Parker died, but Lenny Bruce said that for months after, on the walls and subway stations of New York, you'd read: "Bird Lives." It's the Man's culture. The situation. Art always deals with the situation. And the situation is intense. When you're too knocked out to get off by cutting up in the streets—then you're a worse nigger yet. There's no room in the situation for any bad niggers. If you let it get ahold of you and you got to let it loose, they'll shoot you in Chicago or burn you out at the Fillmore. There's this intense way to go out and it's quick, man, flash. Aeschylus knew all about it. You can Cassandra yourself to death and they'll sell your heat when you crash and burn.

What's to say when a Charlie Parker dies. It's not like some Kennedy. There's no gnashing of teeth in high school cafeterias across the nation. A personal thing, some ways. My friend Carliner has been three days listening to everything Hendrix recorded. He doesn't say what's on his mind. I suppose a whole lot more people know Hendrix and a whole lot better than just a few days ago. Kadi Kiiss waited tables at the Cafe Wha? in '66 when James Hendrix played there. "He was always very nice," she said, "and quiet. I wonder if he would remember me?" She was backstage at Atlanta when he played and took some pictures there. But we lost the film.

She didn't have the nerve to go and ask and, anyway, she's gone off to Sausalito somewhere.

In a bar in Columbus I used to come down from acid by "All Along the Watchtower" and a quart bottle of Stroh's. Not so long before Hendrix was dead, Constance Nowakowski had to write in here about seeing the kids shot at Kent. And she and I used to lie in bed together, across the street from that university, to the tune of "Foxey Lady." So in the fall of '67, Pete the Needle brought *Are You Experienced?* back from L.A. I sang "I Don't Live Today" over my lost girlfriend, who lives today with a truck driver in Oxford, Ohio. In 1968 I walked every day across the side of Tompkins Square humming "Manic Depression."

It can be said that he's really a part of something. But I must admit that he's part of something that's gone. That didn't bear the weight. Good-bye Jimi Hendrix and the bubble-burst drug culture, Summer of Love, and the Gothic Blimp Works, Family Dog, sugar cubes, acid rock and the I Ching. Hello again, Dwight David Eisenhower. Things do come full circle.

When Hendrix played "The Star-Spangled Banner" at the end of Woodstock, it was the best thing I'd heard since Billie Holiday. But it *did* sound like he was signing off.

RICK
HENDRIX
Berkeley Tribe, 2 October 1970

Jimi Hendrix could get more music out of an electric guitar than anyone else. He was the ultimate rock guitar player.

As a musician he was so good he could keep several melodies going at once. As a technician he got sounds from his instrument that no one else could. As an acrobat he could play guitar behind his back, with his teeth, or even while fucking it.

He was also a singer, composer, showman, sex symbol, and voodoo child. Millions were thrilled by his records and performances. He revolutionized rock music. He was a hero to the Youth of many nations.

But last Friday it all ended in a London hospital. Jim Hendrix was dead at age 24. A victim of junk.

"I can see how poor people, lonely people, someone without hope, might do smack," a brother told me. "But Hendrix had everything. Why Hendrix?"

I didn't have a ready answer but it's been on my mind since. And I think the hollowness of the Youth Culture is largely at fault. Like we haven't done much to break down alienation. We haven't truly become sisters and brothers.

The day after he died, a disc jockey on the radio called him "Brother Jimi Hendrix." But I'd never heard him referred to as "Brother" while he was still alive.

Jimi Hendrix was born and raised in Seattle. But he had to go across the country and, then, across the Atlantic to find acceptance for his music. Racism, cultural stagnation, the normal hassles of breaking into the "music industry" . . . Whatever the reason, Hendrix had to leave the U.S. and go to London before he achieved recognition of his talent.

With drummer Mitch Mitchell and bassist Noel Redding he formed the Jimi Hendrix Experience. They were the first of the super high energy bands—the epitome of acid rock. And the model for countless other bands and guitar players.

I saw the Experience on their first tour of the States. They played a free concert in the Panhandle of Golden Gate Park. Hendrix wasn't that famous yet, but you knew he would be soon.

He was absolutely beautiful! You couldn't just stand there—you had to move. The music had too much power and life in it.

Finally, after a long set, he quit playing. Stage managers started taking down the stage and the generator. But the people didn't quit dancing! We kept it up about an hour after the music stopped.

The next time I saw him it wasn't so good. He played Winterland for Bill Graham. The place was packed and everyone had set themselves down in neat, orderly rows. They were spectators who'd paid their $3 and were there to be ENTERTAINED.

All the energy was flowing in one direction. It went from Hendrix and the band to the audience, which greedily consumed it. Hendrix obviously felt the drain. He was snotty and condescending. The music was good but he wasn't enjoying himself like he had been in the park.

Hendrix was, by that time, a rock idol. The believers paid homage (money) to bask in his presence. They hoped some of the idol's music, soul, excitement, power, sex, or whatever would rub off on them.

The audience didn't realize they had the power themselves. The power to "recycle" the energy Hendrix was giving them. To tear down the performer/audience walls. To bring the performance together. To get the whole place high.

Sure, you can say the audience was being exploited—by Graham,

Hendrix, the managers, business agents, record companies, etc. And it's true. But Hendrix and the band were being bled of a lot more than money. They were the real losers.

The band was being cut off from their people, from their culture, from the basis for their music. Their "fans" were leeching their energy, their beauty, their music, everything they gave on stage. They were draining Jimi of all they professed to "love" about him. And they weren't giving him anything of themselves in return. Except maybe some money and some bullshit adulation.

Our revolutionary music, our new art form, is still part of the old show business hype. For this bullshit "star system" to continue, performers and audiences must be kept apart. The performers alone on a pedestal. The audience wishing they could be just like the performer, and BUYING (this is the key) the performer's artifacts. If they ever got together they might find they were all people. And the whole idol/worshipper relationship might crumble.

The people who run the "music industry" (and it's an industry in every sense) know this. A few months back, when Jimi was in Berkeley, some local people asked him to do a Black Panther benefit show. Jimi dug the idea. And his advisors did too—IF they could make a film of Hendrix relating to the radical community. They felt this would even further enhance the value of their "property"—Jimi Hendrix.

Without the shuck film, the managers weren't interested. And though Jimi wanted to, "contractual obligations" prevented him from doing the benefit. Despite being a big star, he wasn't free to perform how and when he wanted.

This system is so tightassed that even its privileged classes are put in a box. And no one was meant to live in a box.

With the whole glorification/capitalism trip, you can imagine how often a performer gets used. How many times "old friends" came around for money. How many times he got laid so people could brag to their friends that they'd balled Jimi Hendrix. Sure, it's nice to get laid, but it's even nicer to get LOVED.

But why did Hendrix take up smack? Traditionally, smack has affected the poor. It's been put into the Black community where poor people are glad to escape the daily degradation of slum life. But more and more we find people of all races and social classes trying to escape through smack. Loneliness, alienation, and despair make smack attractive to increasing numbers of young people. Even the famous. Even the rich. Even Jimi Hendrix.

This wouldn't be the case if our righteous Youth Nation was a reality. But so far it's only a slogan, only a dream. We're going to have to build it. And we're going to have to put a lot of love and warmth and concern in it.

Altamont should tell us something. Dylan's "retirement" (was he perhaps sick of being drained?) should tell us something. The death of Jimi Hendrix should tell us something. The Woodstock Nation isn't here yet—no matter what Abbie, or *Life,* or the movie, or the record company say. We aren't together. Not yet.

If we can't tear down the walls that divide us, if we can't start being more open and loving to our sisters and brothers, if we can't relate both to Hendrix and the 12-year-old teenybopper, if we can't stop smack . . . then the culture isn't worth much.

Goodbye Jimi. Thanks for the good times.

MORT A. CREDIT (LESTER BANGS)

DEATH MAY BE YOUR SANTA CLAUS: AN EXCLUSIVE, UP TO DATE INTERVIEW WITH JIMI HENDRIX

Creem, April 1976

Needless to say, it took us a lot of legwork, both on and off the astro-turf, to track Jimi down; he's been a pretty reclusive dude for about five years now. But finally, using every means and pulling every string at his disposal, one of our star reporters managed not only to locate Jimi, but rap with him for several light-years. What follows is a direct, verbatim transcription of a very spacy rap recorded in his plush and exceedingly far-out lair, with one of the titans of modern rock—the immortal Jimi Hendrix—Ed.

> MORT: Jimi, you used to sing a lot about astral planes, the cosmos and such when you were on earth. Now that you're out here, how does it stack up against what you originally envisioned?

> JIMI: *Well, I'll tell ya, Mort, it's not like the advertisements.* [Laughs] *But then, neither was I. Because see, a lot of people got the wrong idea about me.*

> Like who?

Me, for starters. I didn't know what the fuck I was doing, except I dug R&B and Dylan, and found out howta get all these weird sounds outa my axe. That's where things got confused, just a little bit. Like I'm jammin' my ass off one night onstage at the Fillmore, playin' some kinda dirt bike ride round the rings of Saturn, and I look out at the crowd and they're like one big pinball machine I'm lighting up, making 'em go buzz and tilt by playing "See See Rider" backwards or something I didn't know because my fingers were turning into celery stalks and I'm afraid to look at that, so I shut my eyes a second but there was some kinda Marvel Comic S&M Thor's Mistress flashing this whip and snorting at me in there so I open 'em up again fast as I can and now everybody in the audience is Bob Denver.

What? What do you mean?

I mean that every face out there looked identical, like Bob Denver on Gilligan's Island, *with the little hat and the ratty shirt and everything, and they were all staring up at me with that goofy Gilligan look like "What're we supposed to do now?" so I screamed out right in the middle of a chorus of another song I'd forgot anyway,* "I'm the Skipper and I want you to go get Marianne and bring her here to me! I want that bitch on her KNEES!" *It seemed to make sense in the context of the lyrics at the time.*

Well, it was a time of great experiment and innovation, after all.

I know I changed some things, not nearly as much as some people seem to give me credit for, but I coulda really CHANGED things, I think, if I knew then what I know now. But at the time the alternative was so irresistibly tempting, and I ended up takin' the easy way out with jive and shit. So like on the night I was tellin' ya about, screamin' my lungs out at Gilligan, I had no idea in hell what the fuck Noel and Mitch were doing, they coulda been on a Greyhound to Tucson, Arizona, for all I knew or cared. So I just tore up into a long high note, held it, tore it off and decided to get the hell out of there.

Now, no sooner do I get off the stage than who do I practically slam foreheads with but Bill Graham. Asshole's been standin' there on the side of the stage watchin' me this whole time. Now he just blocks my way, grabs my arm, stares deep into my eyes and says: "Jimi, why do you go out and play shit like that, when we both know you're capable of some of the best blues I've ever heard in my life, man."

Well, I hate to say it, but I just niggered out, played even more spaced than I was, because I didn't wanna hassle with the cat, I just wanted outa there. But if I'd been physically and psychologically capable of staying, man, I woulda said: "Because there are times when I strongly suspect, deep down inside, that I hate the fuckin' blues. Every broke-down nigger behind a mule he don't own can sing the blues. I only do blues because it's fun and easy to get into once in awhile, and because I know all them ofays don't think a music show by a black person is their money's worth unless they get to hear some.

Yeah, but what about cuts like "Red House" and "Voodoo Chile"? They were incredible songs, fantastically played!

They weren't exactly what you would call original compositions. They were good takes, especially the second "Voodoo Chile." The long ver-sion had a nice feel, but it was there to fill out a double album, and Winwood played the same damn solo he played in "Pearly Queen" and every other damn session he did for about three years. I played good blues on "Red House," but it got way more attention than it deserved, probably because it was so hard to get in America for a long time. I mean, "I Don't Live Today" is real blues, modern blues—it's what hap-pens when you drop a hydrogen bomb on the blues, which is what it deserves.

Listen. The blues is white music, and so was most "free jazz." All the musicians know it, everybody in the ghetto knows it because they be boppin' to James Brown and Stanley Turrentine, don't own Muddy Waters albums much less Robert Johnson, and 98% of 'em never heard of Albert Ayler. My music was at least 70% white. If I'd played what black people wanted to hear at that time I'da been spectacularly unsuc-cessful in the hip rock superstar world, and if I'd gone down to the Apollo Theatre and played what I played at the Fillmore I probably woulda been laughed off the stage. And knowing that has dogged my ass all the way to this moment. That and the fact that to a certain extent and in the interests of image, I had to shuck and jive because you know niggers is just sposed to be bad and fuck good wid big dicks an' be finger-poppin' all de time. I just added a little acid and feedback.

And hell, for all of that I didn't even get laid that much either, or at least not as much as I should. I mean, you would think with me bein' JIMI HENDRIX and all the big deal was made out of it, I'd be gettin' more pussy than Haile Selassie's whole harem and better quality than, I dunno, who's the hottest cunt you can think of?

Uhmmmm . . . Wilma Flintstone.

Thanks a lot. Like I coulda dug gettin' into some a that Julie Christie, you know, or maybe some a that Ursula Andress, you know, movie stars, continental flash class clits. Instead I get all these dopey bitches wanna read my Tarot and always gotta I Ching in the Bantam edition in their back jeans pocket ready to spring on you at any second and tell you just the exact state of the gobbledegook. Well, I got more gobblede-gook than I know what to do with already, as even a passing listen at my songs will tell you. You think I wrote all them fuckin' cosmic lyrics because I had the Universal Mind on tap? Hunh. I liked Star Trek, *but I ain't Paul Kantner. I got more out of it than Paul Kantner, who shoulda profited by my bad example. I just dropped this and snorted that, and pretty soon a lotta shit was swirling around my head. Same shit as hit everybody else, really, especially Dylan, who was as inspiring and as bad an influence on me as anybody. I started out sincere, but half the time I couldn't fuckin' think straight, so stuff I knew was sloppy-ass jive-time mumbo-jumbo come tumblin' out, and people jump up like whores for a blow of coke: "Oh wow, Jimi, far out . . ." And maybe that's where things started to really go wrong, when I saw that folks'd buy that jive as* profound, *well, I just spaced it all a-way.*

Are you saying you were a suicide?

I ain't saying nothing, man. Except maybe that no dead niggers are sui-cides. But it's got nothing to do with me now. 'Cause there ain't no race bullshit Out Here. Ain't no races—"Just us angels up heah, boss!" Maybe I'll come back—just once—and do a three-night stint of God's Trombones *as a rock opera, with Gil Scott-Heron and Stevie too. 'Cause I wanna lay some shit on Stevie—that cat is* off *and I don't care if he's blind, I don't care if his mama sent him to seven churches for each day of the week, he is flat* wrong, period. *I mean, nobody should know this "Heaven" shit better'n me. I allow myself as something of an expert on the subject. It's been nothin' but blowjobs 'n' soma since I*

*bailed out back in '70. Don't ever go ta Heaven, man, it's the shits.
Only reason not to split is Hell is worse, we went down there one week-
end on a binge and it's the dregs. Heaven is like total stardom with a
constant-touring clause, nothin' but arenas and hotels, but Hell is like
Baltimore. The whole Afterlife trip is rigged to the rimjobs, and like
New York cabaret cards it's one system you can't beat.*

I get a feeling you're pretty critical of your fellow musicians, dead and
living.

Your rap is . . . well . . . I honestly can't think of another question right
now.

That's okay, I'm on speed, I'll fill in. [Lights a cigarette, with compul-
sive urgency but steady hands.]

I get a feeling you're pretty critical of your fellow musicians, dead and
living.

*Yeah, but it's cool, see, because there's nobody I'm more ruthlessly criti-
cal of than myself. I was a good guitar player, no Django but I did
manage to come up with a few new riffs and a few new ideas about
how to finger or get some weird noises outa the thing. But there ain't
much percentage in ego-tripping when you're dead, so I gotta cop that
that was about it. The songs I wrote that had actual melodies, that you
could hum or have a real zinger cover, can be counted on the fingers of
one hand. "Angel" I'm still proud of, as a composition, and a couple
others. But the rest is mostly just metal riffs, with mostly jive lyrics that
I talked instead of sang. I got a lotta credit for introducing "advanced
technology" or whatever they're callin' it these days to rock, but the
thing that almost everybody missed was that once the distortion and
technology became a "required" part of the whole style and, like, insti-
tutionalized, then it was all over. Because technology is cold—so's technique, for that matter—and humans are hot. Or at least they should be.
Because the emotion behind the distortion is the whole thing. And what
we didn't realize was that all of us cultivating distortion so much was
just digging our graves, emotionally speaking. And literally too, I guess,
in some cases.*

*Because as time went I began to realize that what people craved was
just noise. Now, I took a lotta care with my own albums, the first three
anyway—they were very carefully produced, all that shit. They were
tight. But I was beginning to really, really wonder. Because when I listen*

to Are You Experienced?, *at least half of what I hear and remember is just this really crazed unhappy desperation and pissed-offness that can't make no sense out of nothing. It's there in the lyrics and in the music too. Because that was where I was at at the time. When I said, "Ain't no life nowhere," I meant it! Meanwhile I'm thinking do they expect me to bring the can of lighter fluid in my pocket onstage every night? Obviously something is wrong somewhere.*

Well, what was it about distortion that started bothering you so much?

Well, like Graham wants blues, so do the fans, but Graham don't want distortion and they do. He thinks that's shit, and blues is "real." Well, I don't know what the fuck is "real." I never exactly did. Like, do I play two chords or three or just fuck around with tremolo and feedback and make funny noises and burn my guitar and swallow the strings and cannibalize my sidemen and then stand there alone on the stage with the buttons poppin' off my shirt like Brock Peters singing "John Henry" and "Cotton Fields" back home and a selection of work songs personally recorded on Parchman by Alan Lomax? See, it seems to me when I look back that there was something larger that I always really, really wanted to do, but I could never quite get a firm grip on it.

On one level I'm really glad I got out when I did. Because it's like Kennedy, see, a legend—everybody can sit around saying, "Well, gee, nothin' happenin', but if Jimi was around now, he'd show us where it was all goin' next!" But they're wrong. I wouldn't have a fuckin' clue what to do now, if I was so unfortunate as to be "around." I'd probably be just like the rest of 'em, repeating my same shit over and over until everybody is as bored as I am and we mutually agree to call it quits and I'll go sit in the islands and listen to reggae or something. Or maybe, what would be even worse, I'd be one o' the ones that keeps grinding out the same old shit and doesn't know *it: "Yeah, Jimi, your new album* Toe Jam Asteroid *is the absolute* best *thing you've ever done!" "Yeah, like, dig, I'm hip, pops . . . just be cool." Yeah, that's how I'd cop out, come on as a real jive throwback spade wearing shades all the time, a little hat and cigarette smoke, the old Lonely Unapproachable Jazz Musician routine, sitting around in smoky clubs, sidewalk cafes, talk nothin' but bebop jive shit. "Yeah, cool, ah, that was a wiggy scene. Later." [He breaks up laughing.] The Thelonious Monk of the wah wah. Either that or just go hide and do session work.*

Become like Louie Shelton. Because I know I couldn't do what I started out to do and make it really cook.

And it ain't that I don't still got my chops. I do. Everybody's too fucking hung up on chops, though. I think the only studio album where I really burned all the way was my first one. And that's after practicing night and day, year after year, trying to learn it all and do it better, coming up hard and fast and paying dues and busting your chops and out to whip ass on everybody, when suddenly one day I discovered somehow that I could be fuckin' Segovia and if that some other weird component is missing, then I might as well be Louie Shelton.

What is that component?

I wish I knew. I know I lost it somewhere. I take consolation in the fact that just about everybody else came up same time as I did too. Maybe we all just got too high.

How do you feel about people like Eric Burdon and Buddy Miles, whom some observers have accused of cashing in on your name or their association with you, after your death?

Listen, once you kick out you tend to let a lotta bad shit just go under the bridge. Fuck it. I hope they copped a few extra bucks. Besides, nobody lives forever, and I'm gonna have to sit down and have a serious talk with poor old Eric whenever he gets up here, in lieu of busting his face open. It's actually amusing, and besides, he really didn't know any better. Buddy Miles is a different case—I'd be afraid of getting my ass kicked, but anybody racks up as many bad records as that cat's probably gonna end up on the first coal cart to Hell anyway, so hopefully I'll never chance to see his fat face again.

Ever see any of the others who kicked off close to the time you did, hanging around up here?

Nah. I hear about them once in awhile, but I don't hang out with 'em. You wouldn't either. Morrison—I heard all about him, although I didn't see it. He put up such a big stink how he wanted into Hell and wasn't gonna accept anything else and how if they put him Here instead he was gonna make 'em all wish he'd never died, and on and on. . . .

I identify with him on a certain level—we both came along at the right-wrong time, right to become figureheads, wrong in terms of longevity. We were like the test models for crap like Alice Cooper and David Bowie. We both got suckered, but I like to think he got suckered far worse than I did. He, like, had more complicity in his own destruction. I like to think I just got more confused, and basically confused musically as much as in life, until it was all too much of a mess and there was no way out. I let too damn many people intimidate me, for one thing, because I knew I was off but I never had the simple street-smarts to figure just maybe they were off too, maybe ten thousand times worse than me, so I just kind of ended up laying myself in everybody's hands. I mean, I was really an innocent, man. It's embarrassing in retrospect, and it wasn't comfortable then.

What about Janis?

I was hoping you weren't going to ask me that. Jeez, you fuckin' journalists, always after the next lurid headline. Well . . . she was pathetic there and she's pathetic here. It's not her fault, but she doesn't do anything, particularly, to try to improve it, either. That's all I got to say about that.

How do you feel about being a hot chart artist still, and record companies overdubbing other accompanists on your old tapes?

My records still selling is just like Jefferson Starship being more popular than Jefferson Airplane—quality has nothing to do with it, it's just people hanging onto things they know were good and represented something once, instead of taking a chance on a dubious unknown artist.

As far as the overdubbing goes, I feel almost as much indifference there. It sounds weird and egotistical for a dead guy to crow about how he was actually a one-man show, especially since his old sidemen really have no means of retorting, so obviously the smart position for me to have is no position. Why don't you go ask John Coltrane the same question, and see if connubial fidelity extends beyond the grave.

You seem pretty negative about the people who've followed you musically on earth, though.

Yeah. I am. Because they're cold. I may have played real dogshit some gigs, and cut some tracks that were too smooth for my taste. But I was loose. There was something bigger than me sweeping me along and it killed me in the end, but some pretty incredible music came out of it at times, too. My only regret is that I wonder how much of it, under those circumstances, was really my *music, when you get right down to it. If a fucking lightning bolt strikes you, and out of it you get a masterpiece, well, is it you or the lightning bolt? And in the final analysis it's just no contest. You know you lost control, you let the music and the life play you, and that's why you went under. But it really happened, it was real fire and real dues, and nothing can erase that. It should be pretty obvious by now that I consider my life and my art a failure, but it was an honest failure.*

What bugs me is these cats now—no bolt. And no them either! I don't mind people copping my riffs, but they're like a buncha fuckin' college students! Most of my riffs I copped off somebody else, but then I went on and played and forgot about it. I didn't sit around with seven candles burning in a shrine to Chuck Berry. So who even cares if cats like this Trower or that guy in Canada succeed or fail, what's the fucking difference? There is more happening in any bar on Friday night when the dance floor's full, than in all those cats' albums and concerts put together.

What's even worse is that they missed the biggest lick of all, the thing that was so discouraging to me—that I saw the end of it coming. I don't mean rock 'n' roll or popular music or even heavy metal—just the end of the particular experimental, technological branch we riffed out on and sawed through. There's got to be something else. Because one thing I learned while killing myself was that a hell of a lot of that shit was just sound and fury kicked up to disguise the fact that we were losing our emotions, or at least the ability to convey them. Most of Electric Ladyland *and the second album sound real cold to me now. I don't know what it sounded like to me then, because I was too spaced out to make any accurate judgment except that it had all the ingredients, I got some rocks off especially in things like "Voodoo Child (Slight Return)," the albums were relatively slick and I knew they would sell.*

I guess that's what I was trying to get at before when I talked about the missing component. I just forgot how to feel unless I was getting electric

shocks or something—and after awhile even electric shocks began to
feel all the same. And even saying it like that doesn't really explain it.
It's really THE great mystery, for everybody Out Here. And nobody's
come up with any solid answers yet. So when you get back, when you
publish this, if anybody comes up after that and tells you they got some
kind of a line on it, I don't care how thin it is, well, you'd be doing me
the biggest favor of my death if you'd pass it on back. I'd like that more
than anything in the . . . cosmos.

[He laughed again, briefly, then stared through us into some sort of distance. It was obviously time to go.]

DAVE MARSH
HENDRIX LP NOT ESSENTIAL
Rolling Stone, 16 November 1978

A couple of months ago, CBS News broadcast a Friday night special about the year 1968. But the network's representation of the pop music of that era served only to confirm my impression that they'll never catch on: according to this version, the dominant sound ten years ago was exemplified by *Hair.* There was barely a mention of anything that these aging ears recall as authentic. Somehow, though, late in the program, a snippet of reality did intrude, in the form of a segment of D. A. Pennebaker's *Monterey Pop,* a documentary of the first rock festival (which, incidentally, took place in 1967), featuring that memorable weekend's three most important artistic debuts: Janis Joplin, the Who and Jimi Hendrix.

On a program where the big news was the network's belated conclusion that government agents had at least partially stage-managed the riots at the Democratic Convention in Chicago that year (information that's at least five years old), these performers still felt like news and Jimi Hendrix was unquestionably the lead story. His careening, guitar-burning "Wild Thing" finale was an announcement that there was something Other in the world. It impressed me with a force stronger than reminiscence, for in many ways everyone else is still trying to catch up to what Hendrix had to offer.

A few days later, I attempted to explain what it was like to hear Hendrix for the first time to my fourteen-year-old friend Andre and one of his cronies. Andre is a good subject for such lore, it would seem: he plays drums in a Kiss-style rock band and knows about Jimi only because "Purple Haze" is a golden oldie. But the only evidence I had at hand was the new Warner Bros. anthology, *The Essential Jimi Hendrix,* which is so inadequate to the task that at the end of its first side I was informed that Hendrix was actually rather reminiscent of Mahogany Rush.

Was I crushed? Did I run out and buy a cassette of *Smash Hits?* You bet. After all, one of the reasons Jimi Hendrix was born was to teach teenagers that rock & roll holds secrets of greater dimension than Gene Simmons' tongue. To call a record that is insufficient *Essential* is absurd.

The blame belongs squarely on the shoulders of producer Alan Douglas, who programmed it. A couple of years ago, Douglas looked like a hero for uncovering a trove of unreleased Hendrix tapes. But he is apparently determined to do for Hendrix what Norman Petty did for Buddy Holly. Petty, you may recall, is the producer who added voices and instrumentation to unreleased tapes after Holly's death. Douglas did the same on a pair of Hendrix LPs, *Midnight Lightning* and *Crash Landing,* and on a couple of songs even added another guitarist.

The new retrospective never challenges the stereotype of Hendrix as a performer who is chiefly interesting as a technician—both with the guitar and in the studio. The selection includes psychedelic relics like "Third Stone from the Sun," but omits such emotionally powerful material as "I Don't Live Today," one of rock's few mature attempts to deal with death; "The Wind Cries Mary," Jimi's great Dylanesque love song; "Red House," the devastating twelve-bar blues that serves as a sort of historical climax to the bedeviled blues tradition founded by Robert Johnson; "Fire," which does something similar for soul clichés; or anything from *Band of Gypsys,* which is so progressive that it might have been made by a contemporary black rock band, such as the Commodores.

Douglas' album also lacks any perspective on Hendrix' most popular material. "Purple Haze" and "All Along the Watchtower" are included, but "Foxey Lady," an immediate bar-band classic, is missing, as are all of Hendrix' live recordings: the Monterey versions of "Wild Thing" and "Like a Rolling Stone," which are capsule definitions of rock & roll, the outrageous "Star-Spangled Banner" from Woodstock, much less anything from the Berkeley concert released as *Hendrix in the West.*

The latter omission is most surprising, since *The Essential Jimi Hendrix* is meant to replace all of the posthumous releases (with the exception of Douglas' own bastardized concoctions, of course). To this end, we are offered seven songs from three of those albums, constituting barely one-quarter of this set's running time. Clearly, Douglas has a greater ambition: to define Hendrix historically.

One wonders whether it's possible to get all of this great rock innovator's facets on two discs in the first place. But to accept this meager glimpse as essential, much less definitive, is impossible. More than anything, Jimi Hendrix remains fundamental listening because every moment of his music involved a redefinition of himself. That's what made him more than just a technician, or a momentary craze. And it is what keeps so much of his music fresh. More people ought to be familiar with his legacy, but this definitely isn't the way to find out about it.

CURTIS KNIGHT

HIS GUITAR WAS HIS AMULET

from Jimi Hendrix: The Spirit Lives On *(Nona Hatay)*, 1983

Jimi Hendrix was a messenger from another world. A genius guitarist sent from another place, another time, to give us a message of LOVE, PEACE, HOPE, and FREEDOM. I was fortunate to have known, loved, and been associated with him.

There was certain spiritual and scientific knowledge given to him. Jimi didn't get too specific, but he once told me that he had given some people instructions to construct a guitar that would emit certain colors of light as he struck the chords and notes. It was to be similar in effect to a light show, except that he wanted the colors of light to emanate from the guitar, so that he and his audience would be bathed in the colored lights corresponding with the music, changing subtly as he played. He spoke of changing music into colors a lot. The reason he never completed this project or any others in this vein was due to a lack of enthusiasm on the part of his management. They sidetracked his inventiveness to their own plans. This and additional pressures left him little time for experimentation and destroyed some of his zest for life.

Jimi spoke to me many times on subjects that I knew little of at that time. He spoke of how each of us must suffer in the struggle to reach spiritual maturity before we may live in the spiritual world. I didn't fully comprehend, but I was aware that Jimi Hendrix was no ordinary person. He was blessed with Superior Knowledge, yet as a mortal he was spirited away from the true path, so that only through his music was he able to walk in the light of spiritual truth. No small achievement, that.

His guitar was his amulet. Through the guitar and his special musical gift, he could attune with the great cosmic force. By listening to his music, we can attune ourselves to his vibration, a soul-healing, mind-expanding experience.

His writings are poetic, at time abstract; for some people, difficult to understand. To understand them you need to use your spiritual senses. Jimi's music can ignite in us a spark of light that can help us to develop that part of our nature that is too often locked away in our subconscious. That was his mission, to be a spark, helping to light the way of "all the sleeping people." To make us see things we have never seen before, the true essence of what is real.

He spoke about the Planet of Material Wisdom and said that help was now being offered to the world. Our world is in a constant state of change and turmoil. The saving factor will be if we are able to plug into that energy reaching out to us and so become more spiritually and mentally involved with life in a positive way.

I believe that Jimi exists in more than one place or time. He has returned to his Planet of Supreme Wisdom, leaving a part of his essence behind, in his music and spiritual energy link. An energy we can all tap into. It is my feeling that Jimi would want people to use that energy if they can. He always did give of himself, that was a special part of his nature. He wasn't just here today and gone tomorrow, he left us something important, both spiritually and musically.

The magic of Jimi Hendrix is still with us.

PART THREE

Straight Ahead

*A couple of years
ago all I wanted
was to be heard.
"Let me in" was
the thing. Now I'm
trying to figure out
the wisest way to
be heard.*

DON MENN
JIMI'S FAVORITE GUITAR TECHNIQUES
Guitar Player, September 1975

Trying to unscrew Jimi Hendrix' favorite techniques is as puzzling an undertaking as finding an adequate way to describe with words the difference between red and green. Mathematical equations may do that, but where are the *words* that encapsulate the perception of two very clearly differing realities? The problem is really even more complex. It's more like trying to verbalize the distinguishing qualities not of two colors but of every hue used in some wildly vibrant canvas.

We know that Jimi must have gone through certain procedures that always resulted in certain sounds. And it follows that since all those weird sounds were repeatable effects (most say he could conjure them at will), then it should be possible to list in tidy order the manipulations that led to each Hendrixian effect. After all, something causes something, and it ought to be easy to itemize what happens. So where are those one-through-ten lists that go with each item? Jimi never thought to write them down. Such an analytical logging was totally antithetical to his musical approach. He was too involved with creating new effects to chronologize the old. Nevertheless, there were a few highly noticeable movements that Jimi went through that seemed to have had some bearing on what sounds came out of his amplifiers. A few are sketched below, though they don't even represent the tip of the iceberg—scarcely a trickle down the side.

1. SHOWMANSHIP

Using tricks that go back a half century or more, Jimi revived and repopularized many of the old bluesmen's favorite high-stepping, up-staging show stoppers. He played his guitar behind his head or back, shoved the neck of his guitar between his knees. Most memorable of all, he played—actually played music—while holding the guitar to his mouth. It's not entirely a closed matter on how he used his mouth, or for that matter if he really used his teeth. Jess Hansen, a major Hendrix authority, says Jimi pushed forward with his front teeth, moving his chin from his chest outward. Eric Barrett, Jimi's equipment manager, while conceding that no one really knows, thinks Hendrix did just the opposite, i.e., plucked with his teeth, moving his chin towards his chest. Chuck Rainey, who played with Jimi, believes that Hendrix was not using his teeth at all, but picked with his tongue. Innumerable photographs give credence to all theories, and observers abound who swear by their own pet explanations. Jimi himself said the idea came to him "in a town in Tennessee. Down there you have to play with your teeth or else you get shot. There's a trail of broken teeth all over the stage." Did it leave his gums sore? He advised others against trying it, but said he would never do it if it hurt him. Towards the later part of his career, Jimi disregarded most of these maneuvers.

2. DESTRUCTION AS MUSIC

The sounds of a neck shredding or an amp flying apart; of a string popping, writhing, and melting away; of a dismembered pickup amplifying its own unraveling through a shattered speaker were sounds that Jimi did not invent but nevertheless used to a particularly "musical" degree. They fit in well with his more aggressive, raw finales. Peter Townshend of the Who was doing this before Jimi, and he picked it up in art school. "Auto-destruction" was an offshoot of "happenings" staged in the early Sixties. They were created by painters who used the everyday world not *for* a canvas, but *as* a canvas when they concocted events such as dropping a piano from a crane, filling the splintered wreck with hay, and then incinerating the whole mess. In the early part of his career, Jimi smashed many guitars, burned a few, and harpooned his speaker cabinets sometimes for show, sometimes out of frustration, and occasionally to create a raucous acoustical effect. It was all part of trying to get the most from his equipment, and when he could wring no more from it, he'd pound it out.

3. USING THE TREMOLO BAR

Jimi used the "whang" bar on his Stratocasters to wrench out numerous effects for which the device had not been originally designed. According to Mike Bloomfield, Jimi altered his tremolo bars to make them capable of changing a string's pitch by three steps. Eric Barrett says Jimi bent these bars by hand so that they would be close enough for him to use to lightly "bop" individual strings with the handle. He manipulated the bar in the usual way, with his picking hand, but also used less orthodox methods, vibrating it rapidly with his chording hand while tightening and loosening machine heads, or pounding on the guitar's neck, or playing around with the tone and volume controls.

4. HAVING A FIFTH "FINGER"

Jimi got his wrist vibrato in every way imaginable. Primarily he used a push-pull action (moving the string back and forth across the frets) while slightly shaking his wrist. Eric Barrett recalls Jimi's incredible strength— he could bend the first string on a bass all the way to the top. Jimi also used his thumb extensively for chording. It was long enough to extend all the way around the neck and cover from low to high E strings. Jimi used his thumb mainly on the bottom three strings. For example, Mike Bloomfield describes how Hendrix "would play an E-minor triad on top, but use his thumb to play a D on the bottom strings." He would use his thumb going *along* (not always across), so that beginning on the third fret on the bottom three strings he might play at one time a G, D-flat, and another G. He used his little finger for runs and chords, but he would often hook it behind the neck of the guitar when using his thumb.

5. SLIDING TECHNIQUES

Though Jimi did not use a metal cylinder or glass bottleneck for slide, Jimmy Stewart remembers seeing him use his ring for slide effects. He would also grab the microphone stand and run it up and down the fretboard, for bold, searing slide effects. For more raw, less defined sounds, he used his amp cabinets and his elbow (wiping the strings up and down).

Eric Barrett thinks that Jimi usually held his pick with his thumb and first finger. But Jimi seems to have performed occasional sleight-of-hand. Film footage of him playing clearly shows the pick vanishing as he begins strumming the instrument open-handed. Many guitarists do this, and like them, Jimi may have palmed his pick either in his hand or grasped it with his fingers or thumb. Conceivably he could have devised some way to hold it secure with the band of his ring or even put tape somewhere to stick it on, though films don't substantiate this idea.

7. EFFECTIVE RETUNING

Jimi used to frequently change the tuning of his instrument midway through a selection. Aside from his fanatical attention to intonation, he did this intentionally to achieve wobbly on-off pitch variations. While cranking away at the machine heads his line to the audience used to be, "Oh well, only cowboys stay in tune, anyway." The only indication available that he may have used open tunings comes from Chuck Rainey, who distinctly recalls that in the King Curtis days Jimi used to tune to an open chord. Beyond this memory, Chuck could not recall the tuning, nor could anyone else when asked to come up with a specific case indicating that Jimi played open tunings after he became more famous.

8. UTILIZING THE CONTROLS

The combinations are endless, but Jimi controlled his volume and tone almost exclusively from the body of the guitar (all amp controls were full on). This allowed him the usual range of possibilities, but he turned his left-handedness to advantage. With a right-handed guitar turned upside down, the controls were above the strings. Therefore, he could pick the guitar and at the same time move the tone and volume controls with the heel of his hand, to ooze in and out of a tone, or get a smooth, "rock" diminuendo. In conjunction with other instrument parts, he also fooled with his toggle switch to achieve everything from a howling-wind effect to machine gun blats (Jess Hansen says Jimi would get a harmonic, flip the pickup switch, mess with the amp dials, shut the stand-by on and off and come up with the gunfire). Jimi also used to set his Stratocaster toggle switch in a little notch that can be found between the first and second pickups, to catch both. This created a twangy sound such as is heard on

"Little Wing," "Wait Until Tomorrow," and "House Burning Down." Hendrix also took out the back of his Stratocaster so that he could pull the strings and springs to get various "sprongy" sounds.

9. PLAYING THE NECK

Jimi used the back of his guitar's neck nearly as much as the front. He would tap it lightly with the back of his knuckles up and down to bring out harmonics, or jar the instrument into setting up other vibrations that could be reprocessed and permutated. Tapping or tugging the neck, he could be gentle or merciless. Eric Barrett says Hendrix used to even grasp the neck and shake it back and forth to get a wild vibrato that was not possible either by hand or with the tremolo bar. In fact, Jimi used to wrench the neck back and forth so hard that it would sometimes come completely loose, leaving limp strings (and probably intonation problems that only someone like Jimi could deal with).

10. APPLYING ELECTRONICS

No one could unravel this with words or charts—probably not even Jimi. Obviously, years of experimentation with body placements, an extraordinary sense of equipment characteristics, a childlike willingness to play with possibilities that sounded "bad," an extraordinary intuitiveness and capacity to work on his feet with whatever started happening in his equipment, combined to help Jimi develop his unparalleled electrical inventiveness. As far as anyone knows, Hendrix did not have a textbook knowledge of equipment, though most who knew him insist that he could duplicate any sound he used on record. A few tricks included getting feedback on two strings, then tapping the guitar with his ring, which set off a commotion that sounded like a five-alarm fire. He also often bumped his instrument with his hip to get a booming sound. He had his techniques so refined as to be able to get feedback going on a two- or three-string chord, coax and develop and alter that, all the while playing lead on the other strings. The facility is what made many musicians listening to his LP's wonder where the second or third guitar players with the group were, and why they weren't photographed on the album cover. It was inconceivable, at the time, to arrive at the actual conclusion—that there was only one guitar player.

* * *

These are only some of the many and varied techniques that helped Jimi achieve the sounds he needed for self-expression. In the hands of lesser musicians, these are mere gimmicks; in the hands of a Jimi Hendrix, however, they are valuable tools of his craft—as necessary to him as properly trimmed nails are to Segovia or the right-hand mute is to Atkins.

S. L. DUFF
JIMI AND THE MONKEES
Guitar World, March 1988

Life, and especially the music business, is full of strange juxtapositions. Take, for example, the 1967 tour which featured two diametrically polarized extremes of sixties rock music—the Monkees and the Jimi Hendrix Experience. But truth is always stranger than fiction, and yes indeed, the Last Train to Clarksville made a pretty historic stop in Electric Ladyland.

This may be hard for Hendrix devotees to swallow, but the Monkees headlined the tour. Given the success of their weekly series and their carefully assembled, hit-packed lp's, the pre-fab four were one of the hottest tickets in showbiz in the summer of '67. The Monkees had only done a handful of concert appearances when they decided to knock off their first national tour that summer. They were touring behind their second chart-busting lp, *More of the Monkees,* and were set to play 30 cities in 40 days across the US. As with most headliners of that stature, they had more than a little say in who their opening act would be.

Mickey Dolenz had been the first Monkee to become a Hendrix fan, and it was his enthusiasm that led to the Experience's opening slot. Dolenz, who is currently working on the screenplay for the proposed upcoming Monkee movie, recalls stumbling across Jimi quite by accident in Manhattan. "I first saw him in New York at a club called the Cafe Au Go Go. He was playing with John Hammond, as Hammond's guitar player. I was just invited down by somebody, and they said, 'Let's go see John Hammond, there's this guitar player who plays with his teeth.' And, sure enough, there he was. I said, 'That's fantastic,' and didn't think too much more about it until a few months later when I was at the Monterey Pop Festival, and suddenly they say, 'Here's the Jimi Hendrix Experience.' And out they came, and I said, 'There's that guy who plays with his teeth!'"

Fellow Monkee Peter Tork was with Dolenz at Monterey, and although he ended up being closest to Hendrix, Tork had reservations at first. Peter remembers: "Jimi followed the Who onto the stage at Monterey Pop, and there were these two destructo rock groups, and I said, ya know, *c'mon.* I saw Jimi flame out on his guitar, but that was just done. What's the big deal? But Mickey picked up on it."

Though now running a successful video production/distribution company, Pacific Arts, and no longer touring with the Monkees, original guitarist Michael Nesmith was also deeply affected by Hendrix. Nesmith heard him for the first time at a dinner party in London, and therein lies a tale: "I was having dinner in London with John Lennon, Eric Clapton and a group of people," remembers Nesmith. "In the middle of dinner, John produced this portable tape player and requested that the restaurant turn down the piped-in music, and then proceeded to play 'Hey Joe' on his recorder, saying, 'You guys gotta check this out.'" How did Clapton, also hearing Hendrix for the first time, respond? "Everyone was reverential. Hendrix had taken off on his own, and had done it in such an artistic and creative way. Like everybody said, 'Gee, if we could really play music like that, we would!'"

Given the Monkees' fondness for Hendrix' music, he seemed a natural for the opening spot on the big tour, which was ultimately both acts' first American jaunt. "I suggested that he would make a great opening act—very colorful, very theatrical," says Dolenz. "The producers, being rather liberal-minded—we all were—thought that it'd be a great idea. They approached Hendrix' people, and they jumped on it."

The tour began in North Carolina, and while the Monkees were in awe of Hendrix—they all went down early every night to catch his set—their audience felt differently. "It was a bit embarrassing," Dolenz admits. "'Cause we went early to watch his set all the time, which, to be honest, we never did for any other opening act. It must have been a bit difficult for Hendrix with the kids yelling 'We want the Monkees!' and 'Where's Davy?' over 'Foxy Lady.' It was bizarre in retrospect, to say the least."

"Poor Jimi, they booed him off the stage," Tork regrets, adding a bit of explanation. "The Monkees were designed to bring rock to the next level below where it was standing. So you had kids who were 16, 17 and 18 years old who liked rock, the Monkees were designed to bring 13-, 14- and 15-year-olds into the fold, and not to scare the living daylights out of Mama. The Monkees were in the derrière garde of music, and Jimi was in the avant garde." (Tork shouldn't be too hard on his band; their current lp, *Pool It,* has already topped 200,000 in sales.)

In 1967, sound systems and monitors were still in live music's future. Nesmith used three Vox Super Beatles, not miked, which amped his guitar. Vocals were blasted through primitive horns. The Monkees' guitarist was amazed at how full and huge Hendrix sounded. "Jimi was just playing through one Marshall stack at the time," he recalls. "I'd just never heard anything like it. You never heard any power like that in your life. There was something he could do with a guitar and that whole set-up that was just different."

The Experience and the Monkees all travelled on the tour jet together. Tork struck up a friendship with the young guitarist. "We got high together. We had, I think, a DC6, with this lounge in back. There were some reporters on the plane, so we would leave the reporters in the front and go into the back and smoke it up!" Tork has fond memories of Jimi. "Jimi was the most accessible, gentle and self-deprecating man I think I ever met. Certainly he had the most of those qualities in anybody as talented as he was. He talked about struggling to generate that vibrato. He said, 'I'm just beginning to get it, you know, where you sort of twist the hand instead of shake it. Yeah, and you sort of bounce the weight of the neck against it.' A-ha! So I scurried back to my guitar and started bouncing the weight. He would just drop a word in your lap; if you indicated interest, he would help."

As one can imagine, there were strange moments. Nesmith remembers one sleepless night on the road when he saw the strangest vision. "We were in North Carolina when he joined up with the tour. We would typically go in and take over a wing of a hotel. The police would come and block off the wing, and generally stand guard down the hallway, maybe just three or four of them stationed there, because we would always attract a large number of people to the hotel. The hallway was lined with probably five or six on either side of these stereotypical southern police with the big beer belly, and different color blue shirts, and a very southern kind of redneck attitude. I'd just come out of my room, guess it was about one or two in the morning. I was just standing there in the hallway for no particular reason, just couldn't sleep or something. A door opened, and there was this kind of eerie blue-red light that came in from it because of the exit sign over it. Hendrix appeared in silhouette, with this light in back of him, and of course his hair was out to here, and he had on what has become his famous ribbon shirt. And he took a step forward, and it was like it was choreographed. Noel and Mitch both came up on either side of him, and they made this perfect trio; it looked like the cover of *Axis*. They started walking down, and none of those guys was very big, and all those cops were like 6'5", and Hendrix just started walking down the hall with these pinwheels in his eyes. And to see him walk under the nose of these cops and these guys lookin' at him going by was something to see. They didn't know what in the world had landed, they figured it was a spacecraft outside or something. It was really pretty spectacular, wall-to-wall hair brushing against the pot bellies of these cops. Jimi was in absolute control. He had such a command of himself and of circumstances."

Hendrix' days as an opening act were numbered. He only played between five to seven dates with the Monkees. (No one can remember exactly who replaced him on tour, but it was probably either the 5th Dimension or Lulu.) Shortly after his Monkee dates began, "Purple Haze" was making headway on the US charts. "He broke his record on tour, obviously," says Dolenz. "I think Bill Graham, or some New York promoter, approached him and said, 'Listen, you can headline with this record now for your own crowd,' and offered him some headlining gigs. He asked to be released from the tour, and we said, 'Yes, of course.'"

The Monkees kept in touch with Hendrix after the tour. They often socialized when in the same cities, and Tork can even claim to have been the bassist at jams with Hendrix and Buddy Miles. The last Monkee to see Hendrix alive was Michael Nesmith. "The last time I saw him, I was in London a week before he died, actually, I think, just a few days before he died, and he had come to a party that I'd given. We spent most of the time just talking and doing a lot of reminiscing. Of course, by that time he was 'Jimi Hendrix.' I was surprised to see him in somewhat of a funk. He was not happy with the way his music had developed. He felt stultified somehow. He felt that what he was doing didn't have the substance that it once had. I'm not sure that he even realized how much substance that it ever had. We were standing outside alone in a lobby and I felt a great deal of compassion for him. As he stood there, his eyes kind of drifted off, and I could see him trying to come to terms with some devil or something in his own head. And he said, 'You know, I think I'm gonna start an r&b band. I gotta do something. I think I'm gonna work with some horns and put together something like Otis does, 'cause that's really where it's at.' I put my arm around him and I said, 'Jimi, don't you understand, man, you invented psychedelic music. You *invented* it. Nobody ever played this before you came along. Why are you going through this crisis of self-confidence right now?' And he didn't say anything, he didn't respond to that at all, but it was a very extraordinary moment in my life, and I think in his as well. He nodded kind of in agreement to that, but in a very humble way. And I went off to Amsterdam, and got the call two days later that he was dead."

Tork was obviously greatly saddened by Jimi's death, and attributes it to what he calls EPDS—Early Pop Death Syndrome. He explains: "Art is escapism. Drugs is escapism. The reason for escapism is that you do not have a sense of yourself as being genuinely valuable in a practical, well-grounded way. . . . If you don't believe you are worth saving, then you are worth drugging to death. It's one thing to smoke some dope and have a little drink, it's another thing to take so much of one kind of dope or another that when you cough you don't have enough instinct left to turn your head so that you don't choke on your own phlegm. You're so drugged out that normal interferences become life-threatening."

Nesmith concurs, adding that additional drug intake and displeasure with his music finally took their toll on Jimi Hendrix. "I never saw him do any drugs, period, but it was common knowledge that he was heavy into psychedelics—LSD and mushrooms and peyote and so forth—and it just continued to deteriorate over a period of time, until I found him in London in this extraordinary state of mind where he was no longer happy with this music that once had just made him sail."

GENE SANTORO
THE HOUSE THAT JIMI BUILT
Guitar World, September 1985

In 1968, when Jimi Hendrix, with his manager Mike Jeffrey, bought the Generation Club on West 8th Street off Sixth Avenue in the heart of Greenwich Village, he had no idea what he was getting into. According to Jim Marron, who worked closely with Hendrix and Jeffrey as president of Electric Lady Inc. from 1968 to 1972, when they laid out their $50,000 for the site they fully intended to make it into another club; after all, even before it was the Generation Club the location had housed the old Village Barn, a big-band dance venue owned at one point by Rudy Vallee.

However, Marron explains, "I had a feasibility study done for Mike and Jimi," and the staggering results of that study led them to reconsider their direction. In 1968 alone, it seems Hendrix spent the staggering sum of $300,000 for studio time, due largely to his practice of block-booking the Record Plant in New York so that he could shoot into the studio with friends and fellow jammers direct from venues like the Scene or Ungano's. The study concluded that it would be cheaper and more effective, in the long run, for Jimi to own his own studio—and thus was born Electric Lady. A Sunday morning phone call from Marron to architect John

Storyk—who had just finished the night before, drawing up the plans for the club Hendrix and company had commissioned him to design—marked the first in what would become a long series of changes of direction.

First, a little background. At that time, there were few independent recording studios of any real significance: the Record Plant in LA and NY, A&R in NY and a handful of others were pretty much it. The studios owned by the record companies themselves, which had traditionally done most of the recording of pop and classical musicians alike, had proven themselves unable to cope with the demands of rock music and musicians in the mid-sixties. They didn't know how to record the music well enough to suit the musicians, and they didn't have the kind of environment where the musicians could relax as well as work. With the exception of the Record Plant, the indies were technician-oriented affairs with hanging wires and baffle boards aplenty. Electric Lady was a pivotal design that changed the face of the modern recording studio. "I want it *comfortable*," is what both Marron and Storyk recall Hendrix emphasizing; what he meant was no more dangling cables, dirty and broken toilets, non-existent lounges.

"None of us knew what we were doing because no one had ever done it before," Storyk says candidly, and so not knowing quite where to start they started at the beginning, in June of 1969, by projecting a budget of $350,000 to build the studio complex. (By the time of its completion in 1970, the actual cost of building Electric Lady totalled at somewhere over $1 million.) "It was funded hand-to-mouth as the earnings came in," explains Marron, pointing out that the initial plan was to finance construction entirely from the profits of Hendrix' highly successful *Electric Ladyland* lp. That didn't work out; before the building was actually finished, Warner Bros. had kicked in $300,000 in advance of Jimi's earnings, and Mike Jeffrey had sunk in an unspecified amount of his own money as well.

In addition, Marron recalls, "Jimi would go out and do a colosseum date, in San Diego, say, and come back with $100,000 in his pocket. So he'd peel off $50,000, hand it to me, and say, 'Okay, start it up again.' And so I'd get the crews back in—we had to use ponytail carpenters to get it done, because of the way construction would start and stop—and we'd go until the money ran out again."

Nor were financial pressures the only problems facing the builders of Electric Lady. Storyk's unconventional design, prompted by Hendrix' desires, called for gently curving walls of solid concrete. "Make the walls round" is how Storyk remembers Jimi's directive. Structurally, the masonry construction was meant to help buffet the studio against the waves of sound emanating from the subway tunnel next door on one side and the movie theater on the other. "Actually," says Storyk, "the theater was more of a problem."

Work was proceeding when in late 1968, the crews struck water. "As soon as we cut through the floors," recalls Eddie Kramer, "the whole bloody place was flooded." John Storyk continues, "No one knew about the creek [Minetta Creek]; no one even knew it was there. It wasn't exactly a stream, because it was just all over the place, and it flooded us out." Work stopped for nearly three months while Storyk raced back to the drawing board— literally—to resolve the design problems he had thought solved. "The creek really screwed us up," he admits. "It screwed up all the initial solutions we had worked out for the soundproofing."

It was early 1970 before construction was resumed. Nor was that the end of Minetta Creek's interference with Electric Lady; in 1977 it flooded the studio again, and to prevent a repeat performance there are three types of pumps—electrical, mechanical and manual—always either working or at the ready to divert the constantly sluicing water.

Studio A was the first part of Electric Lady to be completed, and it was the only studio in the complex that Jimi ever got to record in. Kramer, Marron and Storyk all agree that, as Storyk succinctly puts it, "Studio A is still valid." The design concepts that it employed, though unusual for the time, have since been incorporated into many other studio designs. "The thing is, it's basically a very tall room with lots of mass," explains Storyk, "which gives you more isolation and a chance to create more appealing solutions to design problems."

Among the most striking of those solutions is the beautiful floating ceiling that hovers over Studio A like an oddly weightless cement cloud. The combination of masonry walls, 20-foot-high ceiling and underground water created a distinctive sonic personality in the studio. Current owner Allan Selby says, "A lot of groups think that the water running below makes the sound, especially for the bass, unique here." Eddie Kramer points out, "Jimi always wanted to record where there was water, so it was appropriate, in a way." While Storyk himself is reluctant to attribute so much of the studio's sound quality to the underground creek, he willingly agrees that it plays its part in the overall makeup.

From the outset, as you would expect with Jimi Hendrix, Studio A was intended to be state-of-the-art. "Just get me the best" is what Kramer and Storyk both recall Jimi saying any time Electric Lady was discussed. With Phil Ramone and Bob Hansen as technical and acoustical consultants, chief engineer Kramer oversaw the development of the facilities.

"Basically, what I wanted to do was to keep the room as live as possible," he explains, "and what they [Storyk and Marron] wanted to do was to make it more or less like the traditional, acoustically dead studio. What we came up with was a compromise."

(As Storyk tells it, "Eddie ripped the damn thing apart twice.")

Kramer continues: "It got to be a little deader because there was some flutter echo and some strange humps in the bottom end that we had to take care of—that's why we built those big screens. But it was never really finished, for me, as an acoustic design. It happened to turn out to be a great sounding room; the rhythm section sound in there is *still* magnificent. And in those days it was far and away the best studio around."

In addition to its unique physical characteristics, Electric Lady was designed to be more advanced electronically than any other studio of the period. "It was the first 24-track studio around," asserts Kramer with obvious pride. "The console was prepared for 24 tracks; I even had the machines wired for it, so when 24-tracks came in it was an easy stop to convert. When Jimi was alive, though, we had a 16-track operation." (Today Studio A, B, and C are equipped with 48-track consoles, with 56-input capability.) Studio A was the only working area completed before Jimi died, but he began using it intensively during the spring and summer of 1970 to lay down tracks for the projected double album he tentatively called *First Rays Of The New Rising Sun.*

It's hard to miss the curving mural that stretches from the entrance foyer down the length of the complex to Studio B. Designed and painted by Lance Jost, who worked in the same loft on Fourth Avenue that Jimi used for rehearsal space, the 50-foot canvas captures the feel of the psychedelic era at its spaciest. "Jimi *hated* the mural," insist Storyk and Marron, and Kramer agrees: "I guess it's weathered—or withered—the test of time. But that was purely Mike Jeffrey's idea, not Jimi's." Still, Allan Selby notes that "I get calls from musicians all over the country telling me that if I took the mural down they'd never set foot in here again—it's that important to them."

After thirteen months of sweat and hassle, Electric Lady was formally opened on August 27, 1970—the very day Hendrix was leaving America for what would turn out to be the last time. As president of Electric Lady, Jim Marron arranged times and police escorts so that Jimi could attend the opening and party and still make his flight on time. Less than a month later he was dead, and Electric Lady, without its built-in client, was in financial trouble. "No one wanted to use it at first," explains Marron, "because it was like going into Jimi's living room after he was dead—it was *his* studio, after all." As fate would have it, another black musical prodigy named Stevie Wonder just happened to need a studio to hunker down in. Wonder wanted to renegotiate his contract with Motown Records before releasing any more material, but he wasn't able to act until his twenty-first birthday. So for over a year he block-booked Electric Lady, working round-the-clock Hendrix-style with engineers Bob Margouleff and Malcolm Cecil, while he stockpiled music in the can. "That saved Electric Lady," says Marron, and Storyk adds, "Stevie really likes big rooms, so he loved Studio A." When Wonder released *Music Of My Mind* and *Talking Book* in 1972, Electric Lady suddenly became *the* place musicians wanted to record; and since then, of course, luminaries like the Rolling Stones, Hall & Oates, the Clash, Foreigner, Billy Idol, Roy Buchanan, the Cars and Dan Hartman have used its consistently updated facilities. Not a mausoleum by any means, Electric Lady studio is a living monument to the vision of the musician who built it.

BILL MILKOWSKI
JIMI HENDRIX: THE JAZZ CONNECTION
Down Beat, October 1982

Don't bother looking under "H" for the name of Jimi Hendrix in any current jazz encyclopedia or text on the market. You won't find it. Authors and archivists over the years have slighted Hendrix in the jazz history books, failing to recognize any contribution that Jimi may have made to the music (although *Down Beat* readers did vote him into the Hall of Fame in 1970). Yet Hendrix was clearly at the forefront of a movement that gradually brought about the ultimate cross-pollination of rock and jazz.

Miles Davis is generally credited with originating so-called fusion music in 1970 with his landmark LP, *Bitches Brew,* which sold half-a-million copies in its first year. But groups such as Dreams (with Billy Cobham, Michael and Randy Brecker) or the English group Soft Machine had already been toying with the idea in 1969, and Hendrix had hinted at this fusion of idioms as early as 1967 with his revolutionary debut album, *Are You Experienced.*

Given Miles' stature in the jazz world, he was probably the only one at the time who could have solidified the movement by lending it credibility. For this reason, he may in fact be considered more of a popularizer of fusion music than its original innovator. By the time *Bitches Brew* hit, Hendrix had already been there, if only in an embryonic form.

Before Hendrix, the lines were more clearly drawn—there was rock on the one side and jazz on the other, with blues straddling the fence. After Hendrix, nothing would ever be quite so cut-and-dried. The impact of his explosive emergence in 1967 stretched the boundaries of rock, and at the time of extreme exploration (*Third Stone From The Sun* from *Are You Experienced,* or the free-form tag on *If 6 Was 9* from the follow-up LP, *Axis: Bold As Love*) touched directly into the realm of jazz whether or not he actually intended to.

There is a solid body of evidence supporting the theory that Jimi was indeed moving away from the more simplistic forms of rock and beginning to embrace jazz more closely. Right up to the time of his death on September 18, 1970, he often mentioned a dream he had for a big band setting with vocal backing that would help him work out new musical ideas he had.

In one of the last interviews of his life, appearing in *Melody Maker* magazine on September 13, 1970, Jimi revealed some startling insights about the state of his music and where he would have liked to take it: "I've turned full circle. I'm right back where I started. I've given this era of music everything but I still sound the same. My music's the same and I can't think of anything new to add to it in its present state. When the last American tour finished, I started thinking about the future, thinking that this era of music sparked by the Beatles had come to an end. Something new has to come and Jimi Hendrix will be there." He went on to speculate about this ideal orchestra to carry out these new musical ideas he was hearing: "I want a big band. I don't mean three harps and 14 violins. I mean a big band full of competent musicians that I can conduct and write for. And with the music we will paint pictures of Earth and space so that the listener can be taken somewhere."

Hendrix would come within a week of realizing his dream band. He died while on tour in England, shortly before he was to begin preliminaries on a collaboration with Gil Evans. The respected jazz arranger was fashioning an album of Jimi's tunes and wanted Hendrix himself to be playing on top of his big band arrangements, just as he had done with Miles on *Miles Ahead* in 1957, *Porgy And Bess* in 1958, and *Sketches Of Spain* in 1959. Evans eventually completed the project in 1974 using Japanese fusion guitarist Ryo Kawasaki for the guitar parts on *The Gil Evans Orchestra Plays The Music Of Jimi Hendrix*. That posthumous release contained such lyrical Hendrix classics as *Castles Made Of Sand, Little Wing,* and other selections that Evans presented in an all-Hendrix tribute concert at Carnegie Hall as part of the New York Jazz Repertory Company's 1974 season.

Jimi's body was buried at the Greenwood Cemetery in Seattle on October 1, 1970. Included at the funeral among the mourners were Jimi's father Al, his brother Leon, Buddy Miles, Mitch Mitchell, Noel Redding, bluesmen Johnny Winter and John Hammond Jr., and Miles Davis, whose presence there was as much a symbolic gesture as one of true friendship. It was in essence a statement of support for Jimi's music, and with Miles' stamp of approval, other jazz musicians could feel more comfortable about borrowing from this rock idiom as well.

Today, nearly every young fusion musician who came up with rock during the '60s and later got formal schooling in jazz conservatories will invariably list the name of Hendrix alongside the names of Coltrane, Bird, and Miles as major influences.

Mike Stern, who plays guitar in Miles' latest edition, and touted fusion guitarist Al DiMeola have both captured some of Jimi's fire in their own playing, but their appreciation of Hendrix goes well beyond the hot licks and biting sound he patented. "One of my favorite Hendrix songs," says DiMeola, "was a very pretty, very underrated tune he did on his first album called *May This Be Love*. He does this solo that sounds like his guitar is underwater, which was so totally foreign to me at the time. I mean, there I was, 13 years old in Bergenfield, New Jersey, learning everything from jazz to bossa nova to classical from my mentor [guitar teacher Robert Aslanian], and this guy comes out with underwater guitar sounds! It was so revolutionary at the time. Hendrix was such an innovator. He was just into experimenting with sounds and taking tunes out with long solos that took you on a little bit of an adventure. And this is what is gradually slipping away in the music industry today, not so much in jazz but especially in the music you hear on the radio. It's so hip to be able to be as free and experimental as Hendrix was, but today the pressure is on so much for anyone who's into the business of selling records to make pop music in the A-B-A form. And I don't think that the pressure was on as heavily back then."

Of the Hendrix technique, DiMeola adds, "His soloing was definitely in the jazz tradition, and a lot of members of the jazz community picked up on it. Not everyone, of course—there's a lot of players from the old school who couldn't stand to listen to Hendrix. But of my generation, most everyone will admit that Jimi was a leader."

Mike Stern remembers Hendrix mostly for the evocative quality of his playing on tunes like *The Wind Cries Mary* from *Experienced* and *One Rainy Wish* from *Axis*. "His playing on those tunes is so lyrical. It has that same singing quality that I dig in Jim Hall's playing or in Wes

Montgomery's playing. But the thing about Hendrix was he had that sound, he would articulate that lyrical feeling with a fatter sound on his Strat than you could get with a regular hollow-bodied jazz guitar.

"Jimi was definitely a legato player, and whether he intended to or not, he started a movement among guitar players with his long sustaining, legato lines. He sounded more like a horn player than anyone before him, and he influenced everybody that followed him. I'm after that same horn-like quality in my own playing, either when I'm with Miles or when I'm playing a straightahead bebop gig. Of course, on a bebop gig I'll go for a darker, warmer sound, more like Jim or Wes, but Miles wants me to play loud. At Avery Fisher Hall last year [where Miles unveiled his current group to New York critics at the 1981 Kool Jazz Festival], he went over and turned my amp up at one point. And he's always saying things to me like 'Play some Hendrix! Turn it up or turn it off!' Miles loves Hendrix. Jimi and Charlie Christian are his favorite cats as far as guitarists are concerned. So right now with this band he wants to hear volume. My own natural instinct is to play a little softer, which I've been able to do on tunes like *My Man Is Gone,* where my playing is a little darker. But Miles wants me to fill a certain role with this band, so I'm playing loud and my solos are usually speeded up to double-time where I have to play kind of rock-style, whatever that is. So while I'm going for Jim and Wes, there's some Jimi in there too, I guess."

Fusion pioneer Larry Coryell speaks of Hendrix as having the talent of Stravinsky. Others have likened his inventive instincts to Ornette Coleman's visionary concepts. In fact, the ultra-funky, multi-layering guitar textures that Jimi explored in the studio on cuts like *Night Bird Flying* (which was to have appeared on a double LP Hendrix was working on at the time of his death called *First Rays Of The New Rising Sun* but was later included in the posthumously released LP, *Cry Of Love*) suggest some of the sounds that Coleman would expand on years later with his electrified Prime Time band. And today, many of the harmolodic offshoots picking up on Coleman's lead—groups like Material and Curlew or solo artists like guitarist James Blood Ulmer—can trace their musical roots directly to Hendrix.

The link between Hendrix and Ulmer becomes especially eerie when you listen to Blood's vocal style on tunes like *Stand Up To Yourself* and *Pleasure Control* from his *Free Lancing* LP. His slightly strangled, semi-talking yet highly expressive singing style on those cuts is hauntingly reminiscent of Jimi's own husky-tone, sensual style.

Another fusion pioneer, guitarist John McLaughlin, calls Hendrix a revolutionary force. "Jimi single-handedly shifted the whole course of guitar playing, and he did it with such finesse and real passion."

But perhaps Jaco Pastorius put it best, in his own succinct way, when asked to comment on what influence Hendrix has made on the current state of jazz. From his base in Fort Lauderdale, Florida, where he is hard at work on his next solo album, the ex–Weather Report bassist summed it up with: "All I gotta say is . . . *Third Stone From The Sun*. And for anyone who doesn't know about that by now, they should've checked Jimi out a lot earlier."

He's referring to the extended "sound painting" that Hendrix introduced on his debut album, *Are You Experienced*. In that number, drummer Mitch Mitchell displays his fondness for jazz (his background with the Georgie Fame band gave him a foundation in jazz rhythms), and Jimi blows what amounts to free form sax lines on top of it, perhaps borrowing from the free jazz movement which was in its ascendancy at the time with John Coltrane as its leading light. Jaco invariably pays homage to Hendrix during his live performances by using *Third Stone From The Sun* or *Purple Haze* as a springboard for one of his customary fuzzed-out feedback sessions on his beat-up Fender bass. And he generally sandwiches that segment between tributes to Coltrane (*Giant Steps*) and Charlie Parker (*Donna Lee*), as if to demonstrate some kind of common thread among these three musical forces.

Of course, Jimi never presumed to be a jazz player. He was actually shy about approaching jazz musicians, probably because he could neither read nor write music. But by the summer of 1969, he was listening to more jazz, enjoying the sounds of Coltrane, Coleman, McCoy Tyner, and Rahsaan Roland Kirk—who was like an idol to him. Jimi's own musical ideas were probably closer to Kirk's than to the modal concepts of Coltrane or Miles. Since Hendrix was able to play three guitar parts simultaneously, he must have felt an immediate affinity for Kirk, who could play three wind instruments at once. And Kirk's amazing mastery of circular breathing techniques allowed him to blow unusually long, sustained lines, which matched Jimi's own legato guitar lines. From the start of their early jams in London at Ronnie Scott's club (around the early part of '67), Kirk and Jimi communicated on a mutual plane, recognizing that the blues was at the heart of their respective styles.

They also shared a common feel for rhythm, which was all-important to Jimi's playing. The rhythm of the guitar, he felt, was the key to blues, jazz, and rock. He had forged his own solid rhythmic comping style while playing backup on the chitlin' circuit during the early '60s with the likes of Sam Cooke, Ike & Tina Turner, and Little Richard before moving on to New York and taking up with the Isley Brothers and Curtis Knight. Young British counterparts like Eric Clapton or Jeff Beck didn't have anything remotely as earthy and real to draw from in their formative years as guitarists, having learned nearly all their blues licks from records and radio rather than by osmosis and experience, as Jimi had. As a result, their respective styles come across as far more precise and intellectual than Jimi's, lacking the grit and soul that was so much a part of the Hendrix style.

Listen to Jimi's extended bluesy jazz jam on *Rainy Day Dream Away* from *Electric Ladyland*. Together with organist Mike Finnigan, drummer Buddy Miles, bassist Noel Redding, and saxist Freddie Smith, Hendrix creates a swinging, intimate, smoky jazz club ambiance that is closer to Grant Green and Charles Earland than to the frenzy of a rock concert setting.

In the tradition of jazz players, Jimi loved to jam. He was wide open to a whole spectrum of musicians who were intrigued by new sounds and were not tied down to any one root. The list of names he jammed with during his brief but brilliant career is endless, including the likes of blues guitarist Johnny Winter, and jazz organist Larry Young (Khalid Yasin), who went on to play in Miles' band for the now-historic *Bitches Brew* session, recorded in Columbia Studios in New York City on August 19, 1969, the same day that the Woodstock Music Festival officially opened. At one other fabled jam, Jimi locked horns with bassist Dave Holland, drummer Tony Williams, and guitarist John McLaughlin. But McLaughlin is less than ecstatic about the result of this late-night session at Jimi's Electric Ladyland Studios in Greenwich Village. "It was just a jam, really just a party in the studio. It was four o'clock in the morning, and everybody was a bit tired. I've only heard a few minutes of it on tape, but what I heard is just not up to it. If they found something that was really good, I'd be the first one to say, 'Let's release that.' But there's maybe three minutes of material, the rest is not up to par."

Besides these celebrated jams, there are also rumors that some kind of collaboration took place between Jimi and Miles in the studio. It was around the time of Miles' *Filles De Kilimanjaro* (recorded in 1968) that he began communicating with Hendrix. By this album, with its debut of electronic instruments and heavier beats, it was clear that Miles was beginning to flirt with rock, perhaps in response to the phenomenal success he saw that Hendrix had attained. By 1969 Miles was urged by Clive Davis, then president of Columbia, to face the rock challenge head-on. The result was *In A Silent Way*, on which Miles employed electric guitarist McLaughlin.

Then in 1970 came *Bitches Brew*. As Miles has gone down in history as the Christopher Columbus of this new, uncharted land called fusion music, Hendrix might be considered its Leif Erikson. While the one consciously and meticulously established a strategy to explore this new land, the other merely sailed off course and aimlessly landed there, not really acknowledging the significance of his discovery at the time.

Producer Alan Douglas, who had worked with Eric Dolphy in his formative stages, was rumored to have tried orchestrating a summit meeting in the studio between Miles and Hendrix, but both were said to have a reluctance to work together. Douglas, who later gained control of some 600 hours of Hendrix tapes as the designated curator of the Hendrix estate, is of the opinion that Jimi was definitely heading to a closer connection with jazz at the time of his death. To further support his theory of Hendrix as the emerging jazz musician, Douglas released an album in 1980 called *Nine To The Universe,* a collection of jams with organist Larry Young and others that shows Jimi's natural affinity for the jazz idiom.

In the early stages of his career, it was easy for skeptics to dismiss Hendrix as nothing more than just another freaked-out rock star whose only contribution was his pioneering efforts in the mastery of decibels. His explosion onto the British scene in 1967, a carefully calculated campaign masterminded by impresario Chas Chandler, was met with almost unanimous ridicule by the London press, which immediately labeled Jimi as a kind of black anti-hero. One paper called him a Mau-Mau in banner headlines while another tagged him as "The Wild Man of Pop." Hendrix received similar treatment from the American press as well, at least initially. *The New York Times,* for example, referred to him as "a Black Elvis" in a laudatory review on February 25, 1968. This early scrutiny obviously focused on Hendrix' surface appeal and ignored the richness and depth of his musical ideas.

Of course, Jimi often gave the skeptics plenty of ammunition to write him off as an exhibitionist (he was thrown off a Monkees tour in 1968 for shocking the pre-pubescent teenybopper crowd with his blatant X-rated stage antics) or as a gimmicky carnival attraction (by virtue of his showy, acrobatic presence and dental daring on guitar) or as a jive-talking sexual tease (no doubt reinforced by such come-on tunes as *Foxy Lady* and *Little Miss Lover*). This was certainly a part of the Hendrix mystique in those early days of the Experience. But toward the end of his life, Jimi began expressing strong desires of shunning the whole packaged and processed world of pop and getting into more serious music.

As he put it in that final interview with *Melody Maker:* "The main thing that used to bug me was that the people wanted too many visual things from me. I never wanted it to be so much of a visual thing. When I didn't do it, people thought I was being moody, but I can only freak when I really feel like doing so. Now I just want the music to get across, so that people can just sit back and close their eyes and know exactly what is going on without caring a damn about what we are doing while we're on-stage."

But by 1970, with a collaboration with Gil Evans on the horizon, Jimi Hendrix had long grown beyond the showmanship of 1967, when he felt a certain amount of responsibility to play guitar with his teeth and smash amplifiers. He was indeed headed in more challenging musical directions, and we can only dream about how far he would've gone and where he would be today.

PART FOUR

Have You Ever Been (to University)

You've got to know much more than just the technicalities of notes, you've got to know sounds and what goes between the notes.

BEN GOERTZEL

FROM "THE ROCK GUITAR SOLO: FROM EXPRESSION TO SIMULATION"

Popular Music and Society, Spring 1991

Over the past twenty five years, the electric guitar solo has achieved a myth-ical status far beyond that of any other aspect of rock music. Consequently, the evolution of the guitar solo reveals a great deal about the history of rock. In particular, I will focus on the metamorphosis of the guitar solo from a powerful means of individual expression into a stylized, pro forma "frill." This development seems to be deeply connected with the transformation of rock music from a rebellious, experimental art into a rigidly stylized form of commercial pop music. And it fits very naturally into Baudrillard's analysis of the replacement of expression by simulation in popular culture.

Until the mid-60s a rock guitar solo rarely lasted more than ten seconds; it was little more than a simple tool for augmenting the chord pattern of a song. The transformation of the guitar solo into a powerful vehicle for sub-tle melodic and emotional expression occurred almost simultaneously with the evolution of "art rock." And as over the last ten or fifteen years "art rock" has gradually been abandoned, so has the power of the guitar solo declined. Today's rock guitar solos tend to be unoriginal and perfunctory; and the most innovative guitar soloing is taking place in jazz and heavy metal music, outside of the context of mainstream rock.

Naturally, an abbreviated history such as this cannot capture the whole "truth" about the evolution of the guitar solo. To explain even the more obvious nuances of the styles of the most famous rock guitarists would require several volumes, and the picture would still be terribly incomplete. My aim here is merely to paint in broad strokes one important aspect of the history of this beautiful and intriguing phenomenon: how, in this realm as in so many others, what was once a reality is being replaced by a system of signs.

Early rock guitar solos were short and simplistic, but they were raw and emotionally expressive nonetheless. Today Chuck Berry's solos tend to sound a bit cliché. Something new was required. And a variety of novel musical forms emerged. Only one, however, is particularly relevant to the evolution of the guitar solo: what is now called "art rock."

If a landmark is required, art rock may be assumed to have begun with the release of the Beatles' "Sergeant Pepper's Lonely Hearts Club Band" album. The song "A Day in the Life," with its creative use of dissonance and its poetic/political lyrics, made it clear that rock 'n' roll had the potential to be more than "disposable music." The Beatles were also the first to introduce a variety of instruments—violins, sitars, etc.— into rock 'n' roll. However, their innovations were soon superseded. Their compositions invariably centered around simple, catchy tunes. The next step was the emergence of electric blues and art rock as completely novel genres.

Art Rock

The Doors were an anomaly. They started out playing blues, and evolved a unique style of rock based on Ray Manzarek's intricate carnivalesque organ work and Jim Morrison's surrealistic, theatrical vocals. Robby Krieger, the Doors' guitarist, was more important as a composer than as an instrumentalist. To some extent, they were successful precisely because their sound was so different from that of the typical late-60s/early-70s rock band. Virtually every other big-name rock band of that era was dominated by a powerful lead guitar.

The Yardbirds, a 1960s band, were a paradigm case. Three of the all-time greatest rock guitar heroes—Eric Clapton, Jimmy Page and Jeff Beck—were in the band at various times. Eric Clapton went on to create extremely innovative rock music, as a part of the group Cream, on various solo albums, and in collaboration with Duane Allman under the name Derek and the Dominos. Jeff Beck went on to make interesting jazz fusion as well as rock, in the Jeff Beck Group, on his own, and with Jan Hammer. And Jimmy Page went on to form Led Zeppelin, probably the most important force in the establishment of the guitar solo as a rock 'n' roll myth. All three of these guitarists used their solos as a powerful vehicle for individual expression. Like Ritchie Blackmore of Deep Purple, Joe Walsh of the Eagles, Neil Young, and dozens of others, they were classic "guitar heroes." In concert, they often extended their songs to several times the length of the recorded version, and most of the additional duration was usually guitar solo. Their solos were almost always different, and they often presented not only harmonic subtlety and melodic complexity but the subtle interpenetration of various themes. In this they were somewhat reminiscent of the great jazz improvisers: Charlie Parker, Thelonious Monk, Miles Davis, John Coltrane . . .

But of course, remarkable as they were, it was neither Clapton, Beck nor Page who fulfilled the ultimate potential of the guitar solo. In 1965, a young black guitarist named Jimi Hendrix appeared on the London rock scene, having been discovered in New York City by Chas Chandler, formerly of the Animals. He was left-handed, but he played a right-handed guitar upside-down. He played with his teeth; he played behind his back; he played while writhing on the ground in orgiastic fury and while having mock intercourse with his guitar. And, with an astounding arsenal of physical tricks and stylistic innovations, he made the guitar spew out sounds like nothing anyone had ever heard before, from any instrument. He would bend the neck of the guitar, caress the strings, twist the strings, use the waw-waw pedal to create a unique psychedelic drone, slide from one note into another with amazing effortlessness, and somehow harness the most incredible levels of feedback toward the creation of bizarre sound effects. The most flamboyant of lead guitarists, he often described himself as a rhythm guitarist, and this was true in that he habitually played lead and rhythm *simultaneously,* thus keeping his solos in perfect counterpoint with the rhythm.

In short, Jimi Hendrix epitomized the phrase "guitar hero." He had an incomparable effect upon guitarists, not only in the specific tricks he invented but in the way he revealed that the electric guitar could be used for much more than comping chords and playing straightforward melodic solos. He sparked the birth of the age of the electric guitar as a sound-effects machine. And, at the same time, he solidified the image of the guitarist as a sex symbol, a showman, and a maverick creative force. When he played "Wild Thing" at the Monterey Pop Festival, he literally raped his guitar, pelvic-thrusting it up against the wall while he made it wail psychedelic melodies above a wall of feedback. And then he doused it with lighter fluid and set it on fire. With that, the future of the rock guitar solo was irrevocably determined.

It is worth pausing to consider the relation between sex and the electric guitar. Jimi slept with his guitar at night; he called it his Electric Lady (hence the title of his third album, "Electric Ladyland"). In concert, he once admitted that his "Manic Depression" was "a song about a cat wishing he could make love to his music, instead of the same old everyday woman." This is an extreme case, but it is certainly not out of synch with the popular image of the electric guitar. Frank Zappa once said that he played the electric guitar because, although a saxophone can sound sleazy, only an electric guitar can sound truly obscene. To many guitarists and many rock fans as well, there is something sexual about the *sound* of an electric guitar. This contributes something essential to the "guitar hero" image of the lead rock guitarist.

A large proportion of rock lyrics center around sex and love. And, of course, the steady beat of rock music is inherently sexual in nature: from the beginning, this was a large part of rock's allure. Early rock was dominated by vocalists, who usually served as sex symbols, sometimes attaining a mythical status. (Many deeply religious Elvis fans, for instance, do not hesitate to speak of Elvis and Christ in the same breath.) Given this tendency, it seems only natural that when rock became more musical and less vocally-oriented, it did so through the creation of a new class of sex symbol, the guitar virtuoso. The lead guitarist, alone under the spotlight, caressing and attacking his guitar, spinning around, not even looking at the audience—just him and his guitar, his Electric Lady, just him spinning out his individual vision, his electric, sexual dreams. As has often been observed, the guitar hero fits into the culture of machismo with perfect ease.

But sex is not the only theme of which the guitar solo is a natural expression. To some extent, art rock represented a digression from the typical themes of rock and roll—sex, partying, the travails of everyday life. The topics of contemporary rock songs are essentially the topics of early rock songs. But art rock displayed a definite tendency toward the mystical. The Beatles were perhaps the first popular manifestation of this trend, with their frequent references to Indian religion, with songs like "Tomorrow Never Knows." Jimi Hendrix's albums are about evenly divided between love songs and "cosmic songs," tales of transcendental experience. Often, as in the title song to his first album, "Are You Experienced?," mystical and sexual themes are interlinked in a complex web of imagery. The lyrics of Led Zeppelin's "Stairway to Heaven," often considered the most popular rock song of all time, are overtly religious and mystical in nature. Pink Floyd and Yes are examples of groups the majority of whose songs refer to some "cosmic" religious experience. These two bands were not so lead-guitar oriented as Cream or Led Zeppelin or Hendrix, but they both included outstanding guitarists and they both integrated tremendously inventive guitar solos into their music.

Often these mystical lyrics were extremely vague, relying on an idiosyncratic superposition of oblique metaphors, flowery language and rock clichés.

. . .

Sometimes, however, they were very concrete and visual, drawing from definite historical sources. Led Zeppelin drew a degree of inspiration from black magic, particularly the writings of Aleister Crowley. And Hendrix's second album, "Axis: Bold as Love," is named after a legendary Turkish demigod.

. . .

But the exact words, good or bad, were never all that important. What was essential was the mystical *feel,* the cosmic *impression.* To an extent, these mystical art rock songs had a more specific purpose than ordinary rock: they served to help induce in the listener a state similar to that which inspired the composition of the songs. This is particularly true when the listener is taking the same drugs as the musicians involved. The lyrics and music then appear as a sort of cipher which can only be decrypted by one who has taken the proper drug. For instance, seeing sounds as colors is a common experience among those who have taken LSD—and this certainly gives new meaning to the song "Axis: Bold as Love." Among art rock fans, one often hears comments like "You can tell he was on acid when he wrote that." The songs were often long—often from seven to twenty minutes, a far cry from the standard three-minute songs of early or contemporary rock—and this contributed to their emotional impact: they were less momentary stimuli and more comprehensive "experience."

The electric guitar solo fit into this atmosphere beautifully. Hendrix had revealed that the guitar could be used to create a vast variety of "cosmic," "unearthly" sounds, limited only by the ingenuity and technical prowess of the guitarist. Any new musical technology tends to have a futuristic, surreal sound to it at first; here this effect was amplified by conscious attempts to get as weird as possible, and to make music which would combine with mystical lyrics to form an integral whole. Other instruments also played an important role: in Pink Floyd and especially Yes, synthesizer solos came to equal guitar solos in melodic complexity and mystical power. But the electric guitar was always perceived as more *human,* more direct somehow. It packed an individualistic, sexual force to which nothing but the voice could compare.

In sum: the guitar solos of the "art rock" period were extremely adventurous and inventive, drawing inspiration from a variety of musical sources and venturing far beyond mere augmentation of the bass line and chord pattern. In this context, the guitar solo was the primary vehicle for subtle emotional expression, for elaboration on the themes of the lyrics, bass line and chord pattern. It was the primary means by which individual personality was introduced into a song. The small repertory of figures which characterized the guitar solos of early rock was replaced with an astounding variety of musical figures, bizarre sounds, and novel techniques. And this variety of tools was used creatively to transmit the details of spiritual, psychedelic experience to a receptive audience.

Post Art Rock

What's happening now? Electric blues virtuosos like Jimmy Page, Jeff Beck and Eric Clapton are still playing spectacularly, but they are well past their prime. Their recent compositions, though by no means lacking in quality, do not compare well with their compositions of ten or twenty years ago. A lack of originality and fervor is glaringly apparent. There are a number of younger electric blues virtuosos, most notably Stevie Ray Vaughan and Joe Satriani; but there is no one soloing nearly as effectively as did Page, Beck, Clapton, or Hendrix. Blues-based rock seems to have lost its originality, its vitality. In fact, Hendrix may have sensed this—toward the end of his career, he was more interested in jazz than in rock. Pink Floyd, Yes, and other mystically-oriented rock groups are still around. But their fans almost universally agree that their new music is nowhere near as creative, as mind bending, as their old. By and large they are making short songs in the standard rock 'n' roll format; they have left their symphonic tendencies behind. Since these bands were not driven by guitar soloists, their guitar solos have followed the rest of their music and become much less experimental and much less ambitious.

PAUL GILROY

FROM "SOUNDS AUTHENTIC: BLACK MUSIC, ETHNICITY, AND THE CHALLENGE OF A *CHANGING* SAME"

Black Music Research Journal, Fall 1991

From the Jubilee Singers to the Jimi Hendrix Experience

The distinctive patterns of cross-cultural circulation on which the rise of Afrocentric rap has relied precede the consolidation of coherent youth cultures and subcultures in the post-World War II world. They can be traced directly back to the beginnings of black music's entry into the public domain of late nineteenth-century mass entertainment. The worldwide travels of the Fisk Jubilee Singers provide a little-known but nonetheless important example of the difficulties that, from the earliest point, attended the passage of African-American "folk" forms into the emergent popular-culture industries of the overdeveloped countries. At that time, in the late nineteenth century, the status of the Jubilee Singers' art was further complicated by the prominence and popularity of minstrelsy (Toll 1974; Boskin 1986). One review of the earliest performances by the group was headlined "Negro Minstrelsy in Church—Novel Religious Exercise" while another made much of the fact that this band of Negro minstrels were, in fact, "genuine negroes" (Silveri 1989, 106). Doug Seroff (1990, 4) quotes another contemporary American review of a concert by the group: "Those who have only heard the burnt caricatures of negro minstrelsy have not the slightest conception of what it really is." Similar problems arose in the response of European audiences: "From the first the Jubilee music was more or less of a puzzle to the critics; and even among those who sympathized with their mission there was no little difference of opinion as to the artistic merit of their entertainments. Some could not understand the reason for enjoying so thoroughly as almost everyone did these simple *unpretending* songs" (Marsh 1875, 69; emphasis added).

The role of music and song within the abolitionist movement is an additional and equally little-known factor that must have prefigured the Jubilee Singers' eventual triumph (Dennison 1982, 157–187). The choir, sent forth into the world with economic objectives that must have partially eclipsed their pursuit of aesthetic excellence in their musical performances, initially struggled to win an audience for black music produced by blacks from a constituency that had been created by fifty years of "blackface" entertainment. Needless to say, the aesthetic and political tensions involved in establishing the credibility and appeal of their own novel brand of black cultural expression were not confined to the concert halls. Practical problems arose in the mechanics of touring when innkeepers would refuse the group lodgings having mistakenly assumed that they were a company of "nigger minstrels" (i.e., white). One landlord did not discover that "their faces were coloured by their creator and not by burnt cork" (Marsh 1875, 36) until the singers were firmly established in their bedrooms. He still turned them into the street.

The choir's progress was dogged by controversies over the relative value of their work when compared to the output of white performers. The Fisk troupe also encountered the ambivalence and embarrassment of black audiences unsure or uneasy about serious, sacred music being displayed to audiences conditioned by the hateful antics of Zip Coon, Jim Crow, and their ilk. Understandably, blacks were protective of their unique musical culture and fearful of how it might be changed by being forced to compete on the new terrain of popular culture against the absurd representations of blackness offered by minstrelsy's dramatization of white supremacy. The Fisk singers' success spawned a host of other companies that took to the road to offer similar musical fare in the years after 1871.[1] The meaning of this movement of black singers for our understanding of Reconstruction remains to be explored. It will complement and extend work already done on representations of blackness during this period (Gates 1988) and promises to go far beyond the basic argument I want to emphasize here: black people singing slave songs as mass entertainment initiated and established new public standards of authenticity for black cultural expression. The legitimacy of these new cultural forms was established precisely through their distance from the racial codes of minstrelsy. The Jubilee Singers' journey out of America was a critical stage in making this possible.[2]

Almost one hundred years after the Jubilee Singers set sail from Boston for England on the Cunard ship Batavia, another black American musician made the same transatlantic journey to London. Jimi Hendrix's importance in the history of African-American popular music has increased since his untimely death in 1970. The European triumph that

1. Seroff's (1990) research lists over twenty choirs in the period between 1871 and 1878.

2. The musical authenticity of the Jubilee Singers has been explicitly challenged by Zora Neale Hurston ([1933a] 1970a, 223–255) who refers to their work as "a trick style of delivery" and a "misconception of Negro Spirituals."

paved the way for Hendrix's American successes represents another interesting but rather different case of the political aesthetics implicated in representations of racial authenticity. A seasoned, if ill-disciplined, rhythm and blues sideman, Hendrix was reinvented as the essential image of what English audiences felt a black American should be. Charles Shaar Murray (1990, 68) quotes the following diagnosis of Hendrix's success by rival guitarist Eric Clapton. "You know English people have a very big thing towards a spade. They really love that magic thing. They all fall for that kind of thing. Everybody and his brother in England still think that spades have big dicks. And Jimi came over and exploited that to the limit . . . and everybody fell for it."

Sexuality and authenticity have been intertwined in the history of Western culture for several hundred years. The overt sexuality of Hendrix's own "minstrel" stance seems to have been received as a sign of his authentic blackness by the white rock audiences on which his pop career was solidly based. Whether or not Hendrix's early performances were parodic of the minstrel role or simply confirmation of its enduring potency, his career points to the antagonism between different local definitions of what blackness entails and to the combined and uneven character of black cultural development. The complexity of his relationship to the blues and his fluctuating commitment to overt racial politics extend and underscore this point. The creative opposition in his work between blues-rooted tradition and an assertively high tech, futuristic spirituality distills a wider conflict, not simply between the premodern or anti modern and the modern but between the contending definitions of authenticity that are appropriate to black cultural creation on its passage into international pop commodification.

Bibliography

Boskin, J. 1986. *Sambo: The rise and demise of an American jester.* Cambridge: Oxford University Press.

Dennison, S. 1982. *Scandalize my name.* New York: Garland Press.

Gates, H. L., Jr. 1988. The trope of the new Negro and the reconstruction of the image of the black. *Representations* 24:129–156.

Hurston, Z. N. [1933b] 1970b. Characteristics of Negro expression: Conversions and visions, shouting, the sermon, Mother Catherine, Uncle Monday. In *Negro,* edited by N. Cunard. New York: Ungar.

Marsh, J. B. T. 1875. *The story of the Jubilee Singers with their songs.* New York: Hodder & Staughton.

Seroff, D. 1990. The original Fisk Jubilee Singers and the spiritual tradition, pt. 1. *Keskidee* 2:4–9.

Shaar Murray, C. 1990. *Crosstown traffic.* London: Faber.

Silveri, L. D. 1989. The singing tours of the Fisk Jubilee Singers: 1871–1874. In *Feel the spirit: Studies in nineteenth century Afro-American music,* edited by G. R. Keck and S. V. Martin. New York: Greenwood Press.

Toll, R. C. 1974. *Blacking up: The minstrel show in nineteenth-century America.* Cambridge: Oxford University Press.

PAUL CLARKE
"A MAGIC SCIENCE": ROCK MUSIC AS A RECORDING ART
Popular Music, 1983

Jimi Hendrix once claimed "I'm working on music to be completely, utterly a magic science" (Henderson 1981, p. 337). It is a description that fits not just the best of Hendrix's own music, but the best of all that late twentieth-century music in which the ability to capture and control sounds (on tape or disc) has become a means of extending old musical forms and traditions and establishing new possibilities for them. Throughout his career, Hendrix drew nourishment from his musical roots in black traditions, but it was not until the summer of 1967 that he plugged himself fully into the new possibilities opened up by the technology of sound recording. Hendrix had already proved himself something of a musical "magician" in the ancient sense in that he attempted, through music, to mediate between order and disorder, using his guitar as an expressive extension of himself to flirt with the danger and power of musical disintegration (for the parallel with non-Western musical practice see Shepherd 1977, p. 72; Mellers 1973, pp. 24–6; Clarke 1982, pp. 227–9). From 1967 onwards, Hendrix was to prove himself an equally able musical "scientist" through his mastery of studio technology. The studio became

> Jimi's workshop. The endless timeless space where he was most at home. Take after take. Seemingly for days and weeks. Getting the right sound, the right pitch and intensity . . . Most could not hear the sounds he was after, yet were greatly touched by the final product. Its close perfection surrendering to the final moments when it came together. (Henderson 1981, p. 237)

On stage, Hendrix's music had always been bound by time and place but in the studio—insofar as the costing of studio time allowed (and eventually Hendrix built his own studio)—the music could be lifted out of time, captured and contained on tape, made into an aural raw material which could then be added to or manipulated. Whereas on stage Hendrix had had to judge the experiential impact of sounds each moment as he brought them into being, in the studio this instant response could be supplanted or supplemented by a more considered response; each sound, as caught on tape, became repeatable, perfectible, subject to assessment, revision, manipulation—a process not possible or concievable within the live performance tradition of music making. The *magic* of Hendrix's post-1967 music (as cut in the grooves of *Are You Experienced?* and later albums) therefore derives not just from his own innate genius as a performer, and his grounding in the spirit and techniques of black music, but also from his command of the *science* of sound recording and control—his mastery of the aural/musical opportunities provided by the multi-tracking, the adjusting of frequencies, the mixing and re-mixing, and so on, that had become possible in the recording studio.

The move made by Hendrix from stage to studio reproduces on a small scale the way in which rock music as a whole has evolved in the last twenty-five years. Rock and its related musics (soul, reggae, etc.) share roots in live performance traditions (from both Afro-American and Euro-American origins) but have emerged and developed with and through advances in the modern science of recording. To understand rock, then, we need to consider its musical origins and its technological base—and how the two connect. This is where Hendrix's term "magic science" comes in useful, in that it insists we approach rock songs with an ear not only for the "magic" of our experience of them, but also for the "science"—the technological processes—through which the music is created. As V. F. Perkins has suggested, criticism, if it intends to "contribute to a productive collaboration, rather than offer a merely rhetorical private response," should both "present a positive statement of the achievements it claims to have located," and provide a "clear definition" of what processes and combinations make these achievements possible (Perkins 1972, p. 191).

The musicology of rock

As with the emergence of jazz three-and-a-half decades earlier, the rise of rock 'n' roll can be viewed as a cultural moment in which Afro-American musical characteristics penetrated and revitalised white popular music.

And in both cases it was technological progress in sound recording and reproduction that allowed this to happen. Jazz had revolutionised popular dance music in the 1920s, bringing, through the media of gramophone and wireless, a greater concern for musical immediacy and emotional spontaneity. Rock 'n' roll saw the same process occurring within the tradition of popular song. The Afro-American concern with the expressive characteristics of the human voice, long evident in blues and gospel music, caused a shift in emphasis from words to vocal sounds, from "moon-June" lyrics to the jubilant emotional catharsis of "awopbopa-loobopalopbamboom." Colour and expression and human "feel" became valued in instrumental sounds as well, as a new rejection of (European) distinctions between "music" and "noise" made available *all* acoustic resources as potential elements of musical experience. Underlying everything else rock 'n' roll set the beat, a pounding regularity of percussion and bass instruments working directly on the physical responses of the body.

It had always been the case that, in contrast to the white tradition of notated music, in black music "the act of expression took precedence over the artefact as the final goal." Ian Hoare has observed that "it was this oral emphasis that made the music's development so compatible with the declining importance of sheet music and the rise of the record medium where the essence of the appeal came to lie in the overall sound and mode of performance rather than in the *songs* as such" (Hoare 1975, p. 124). Sound recording, by bringing musical practices which had previously been confined to live performance to a much larger and more widespread audience, thus facilitated the cross-fertilisation of musical cultures which finds expression in both rock and jazz. But although Afro-American (and Afro-Caribbean) musics penetrated and revitalised white European-based music, they did not completely overwhelm this more formal tradition. Rock is neither a black nor a white music but rather a melting pot of the two, displaying what musicologist Richard Middleton considers an ambiguous cultural stance (Middleton 1972, p. 147). It is caught up in a continuous attempt to resolve the tension between European styles of music (classical, Tin Pan Alley, music hall/vaudeville, folk ballad, etc.) and Afro-American styles (blues, rhythm and blues, gospel, soul, reggae, etc.), a tension between the view of song as an aesthetic object and song as functional happening, between the idea of passive listening and the idea of participation, between notions of composition and complex structure and notions of improvisation and subtleties of texture. Hence the breadth of stylistic possibilities that characterise rock at any given moment.

In the view of Dave Rogers the rise of rock music has been characterised by two things: "a process of cross-fertilisation and . . . an increasing eclecticism" (Rogers 1976, pp. 7–8). We have seen how the cross-fertilisation emerges out of the interpenetration of musical cultures which sound recording has facilitated. Rock's eclecticism also has its technological aspect, for radical advances in technology have transformed the recording studio—once no more than a location for the recording of performances—into what might be described as an audio workshop, with sound (performed, synthesised, natural or of any other kind) being the raw material. As George Martin—producer of the Beatles—has noted, the studio allows access to "any sound in the universe, from the sound of a whale mating to that of a Tibetan wood instrument, from the legitimate orchestra to synthesised sounds" (Martin and Hornsby 1979, p. 141). These sounds need not be produced or performed simultaneously, for with dubbing and multi-tracking techniques a song or musical piece can be constructed out of separate aural events laid down on tape at different times, and even from performances and other sound materials collected in other studios or recording locations. Paul Simon's "The Boxer," for example, "was recorded all over the place—the basic tracks in Nashville, the end voices in New York St. Paul's Church, the strings in New York Columbia Studios and voices there too" (Simon, quoted in Leigh 1973, pp. 54–6). Furthermore, each performance or sound captured on a track of tape can then be subject to a variety of treatments, so that, as Charles Keil has observed of rock records, "five instruments are sometimes made to sound like a full orchestra, or twenty instrumentalists and a choir can be given the texture of two ukelele players humming to each other in a phone booth" (Keil 1966, p. 90). Brian Eno, himself a musician much involved with the musical opportunities being opened up by new technology, has remarked that whereas "in the early days of studio recording what went on to the tape was pretty much how the record ended up," since that period "the degree of chaos in the actual making of the recording has been reduced, while the complications involved in processing have increased . . . What you have now is an incredible number of processing possibilities . . . and a very low degree of 'randomness' being generated by the recording situation itself" (Eno 1982, p. 94). Such sophistication has not been universally welcomed and many artists working in many genres, from the Dylan of *John Wesley Harding* to the Clash of their debut album, *The Clash,* still deliberately embrace the aesthetic of raw, undoctored performances, laid straight on to tape. But while technological advance has placed no *obligations* on rock musicians to juggle frequencies, assemble and mix diverse tracks and so on, it has opened up a whole range of *options,* and, from Phil Spector to Jimi Hendrix, from the Beatles to Brian Eno, it has encouraged an adventurous eclecticism of content.

Rock music as a recording art

Up until the last hundred years or so an artist or communicator wishing to address his public had two options. He could *make* something—an object, a picture, a book, a musical score—or alternatively he could *do* something, perform something—speak, mime, dance, play an instrument—embodying in that action whatever he had to say. As drama theorist Richard Southern has observed, a creation—an artefact—"you can perfect in solitude before the people see it; but an action is done before them once and is finished—the only chance of perfecting it lies in an opportunity of trying it all over again on another occasion" (Southern 1962, p. 23). So, there have always existed arts of making—creative arts—which involve "work which however exacting can be perfected whenever one chooses," and arts of doing—performance arts—which depend "on a concentrated effort on one particular occasion." The problem with rock on record, however, is that it does not fall strictly into either category. It is a *made* thing, certainly—a round, black object stored in its sleeve on the record rack; but it is also, when introduced to the appropriate equipment, a matter of *performance,* of Beatle harmonies, of Chuck Berry guitar licks, of a ranting Johnny Rotten, of Jerry Lee Lewis pummelling his piano. In fact, along with radio, cinema, television and video, rock on record is one of "those strange new products of the modern age: the recorded and transmitted arts" (ibid., p. 23).

The transmitted arts translate images and sounds (including performances) into electronic signals capable of being broadcast—literally "broadly cast"—and thus free them from having to be heard and/or seen by an audience in a particular *place.* Our concern, the technology of audio or visual *recording,* takes things further than this; it both frees images and sounds (and therefore performances) from the limitations of place, *and,* by giving transient events a solid embodiment (on cassette, disc etc.), liberates them from the limitations of *time.* The initial effect of this capability was to revolutionise the possibilities of performance art in ways that today we take for granted. Recording firstly ensured that performances (of a Charlie Chaplin, a Nureyev, a Jimi Hendrix) last beyond the moment of doing (even beyond the life-span of the doer) as lengths of eventful time removed from the time-flow to be re-inserted as and when desired. It secondly allowed the performer the opportunity to repeat and refine his musical, theatrical, choreographic action over and over in a series of "takes" until satisfied with it. But along with its marked influence on performance traditions, recording has also been instrumental in the development of what can best be described as new forms of *creative* art—forms in which the capturing of performances (on disc or tape or in digital coding) becomes not an end in itself but a gathering of raw material which can then be treated in various ways: speeded up, slowed down, chopped about, mixed, distorted and so on, as part of a process of considered composition. As early as the late fifties, in rock music, double-tracking in combination with dubbing techniques was being used to create musical experiences which had been previously inconceivable. In Neil Sedaka's "Breaking Up Is Hard To Do," for example:

> Sedaka sings in definite harmonies with himself in some sections, and in others the "front" voice sings the lyric while from behind comes the rhythmic "dum-a-dum-a-dum-dooby-do-dum-dum" phrase with which the record opens. In a sense all that happens is that one man is doing what it took three-or-four-voiced groups to do before, but the effect is entirely different. It is the aural equivalent to the splendour of a hall of mirrors— each distorting in a different way the same image, the man singing. (Laing 1970, p. 112)

Dave Laing goes on to argue that it was around this time that the disc became a truly autonomous medium, offering unique musical possibilities which finally set it apart from music on the stage or in the score. As with parallel developments in the other recording arts of film and television, these unique possibilities came about as a result of the blurring of distinctions between performance arts and creative arts, between the act of "doing" and the act of "making," and the consequent complicating of the relationship between the creator and his materials and the performer and his audience.

Thus in the recording arts our experience of an "act of doing" is no longer bound to a particular occasion; instead the action, aural or visual, can be lifted out of the time continuum and given a solid embodiment in a made "thing," to be released back into time when desired. The performer, although he loses direct contact with his public, has the chance to reach a much wider audience, and the opportunity to perfect his performance in solitude before they experience it. The "act of making," on the other hand, has aural and/or visual events as material to work with, events which may include, or entirely consist of, performances. Not surprisingly, therefore, recording arts frequently involve a variety of skills: technical, performing, organisational and so forth, and as a result tend to be collaborative rather than individual ventures. Further, the artistic process becomes entwined with a production process which requires a concentration of capital (studios, pressing plants, etc.). In each society the question of who owns and has access to (under what conditions) these technological resources will have great bearing on what it is possible for recording arts to achieve.

The recording art of *rock* is one of a number of modern musics founded on the technology of sound recording—many avant garde and electronic musics, for example, are created in the studio rather than in performance or in a score—but it is musically distinct from these other forms in that it has clear origins in certain (Afro- and Euro-American) performance traditions, aspects of which it has extended and adapted in exploring the musical possibilities of the new technology. Rock marks, then, a convergence of musical traditions and technological advances—the technology constantly extends the possibilities of what can be done with sounds, while the musical traditions provide means and motivations, forms and functions for exploiting these possibilities. Looked at in the context of the general history of song making, rock, through the development of sound recording, has added to the performance (aural) traditions characteristic of "folk" and "primitive" musics and the creative (notational) traditions typified by the "art" song of the European composer a third option: the artistic-technological capability to *create* songs directly out of *performances*. The songmaker, in the workshop of the studio with any conceivable sound as his raw material, can lift his own or other performances out of time to be repeated and revised, speeded up or slowed down, enhanced or distorted, weaved in with any number of separate recorded performances and sounds, using the tape recorder and its more sophisticated extensions as an aid to composition whereby "the inspiration of the moment may be fixed, considered, worked over at leisure" (Cole 1974, p. 153). In a sense this is the best of all worlds, combining the aural opportunities of performance with the eventual permanence of creation, combining features of both "folk" and "art." Like folk and primitive musics (in which it has its roots), rock music has as its basis the art of performance, and therefore improvises and experiments with all kinds of vocal and instrumental sound. Like notated art musics, rock song on record is ultimately a lasting creation, a made "thing."

A conception of rock music as a recording art, and of rock records as aural artefacts, can help guide us away from those blinkered critical perspectives which view rock songs solely in terms of criteria borrowed from either the performance or the creative arts. Critics preoccupied with the energy and spontaneity of *performance* will often overlook the extent to which even those recorded songs which exhibit a marked reliance on improvisation and expressive elaboration need to be evaluated ultimately as considered compositions. Thus the American rock critic, Greil Marcus, argues that Elvis Presley's Sun recordings were not "the natural (and the implicit assumption is, likely unthinking) expression of a folk culture" but on the contrary were:

> carefully and laboriously constructed out of hits and misses, riffs and bits of phrasing held through dozens of bad takes. The songs grew slowly, over hours and hours, into a music that paradoxically sounded much fresher than all the poor tries that had come before; until Presley, Bill Black and Scotty Moore had the attack in their blood and . . . didn't have to think about it. (Marcus 1977, p. 173)

Even in its comparatively primitive state in the mid-1950s, the technology of the tape-recorder allowed Presley and Sam Phillips to "delay, recheck and refine the direct musical dialectic of an aural-tradition, performance-bound art" (Wishart 1977, pp. 147–8).

The evaluation of rock music based on inappropriate criteria drawn from the *creative* arts generally takes two forms: the literary critical assessment of words, or the musicological-notational assessment of music. In both cases the aural artefact of rock song on record is valued only to the extent that it can be reduced to the form of a visual artefact—a page poem or a musical score. In the classical tradition in which music is worked out as a written blueprint, or in literature in which language is set upon the page as prose or poetry, this may be an acceptable mode of analysis. Songs made in the studio, however, should be understood as considered aural compositions in which sounds are performed, recorded, treated and combined together often with no necessity for any kind of visual mediation whatsoever. It should also be understood that these are *songs*, each a synthesis of music and language so that even when one aspect is prominent, the musico-linguistic balance tilted a particular way—towards words in a Joni Mitchell song, towards formal music in an orchestrated Beatles ballad—our evaluation must still be based (as our experience of the song is) not on any one aural strand—lyrical, musical or vocal—but on the complex of created relationships between sounds as they act on us through time.

Given these *criteria,* we can then afford a degree of critical pragmatism, borrowing or adapting musical, linguistic, literary and drama critical *terms and techniques* where necessary. This is legitimate to the extent that we borrow only terms and techniques, and do not invoke wholesale the inappropriate criteria of the foreign discipline; it is, after all, possible to follow through Joni Mitchell's use of metaphor in "A Case of You" without having to claim that the song is a poem, or the Beatles' use of strings in "Eleanor Rigby" without having to claim it as an "art" song.

Rock language

. . .

The words of a rock song work aurally, strung along a voice in real time. Whereas the "sound" of a written poem is a synaesthetic experience, its aurality derived in the imagination from visual evidence, the sound of a song is actual—words realised in a particular way by a particular voice. "The difference between the words on paper and the song," Bob Dylan once observed, is that "the song disappears into the air, the paper stays. They have little in common" (quoted in Saal 1975, p. 106). Of course, Dylan's own songs very rarely disappear completely into the air. They are caught (by studio engineers or bootleggers, depending on circumstances) on magnetic tape to be sent out again and again into the air as desired by the listener. In this sense (as part of an aural-*recorded* process) Dylan's songs have a permanence akin to that of the page poem. Nonetheless, the actual listening experience of a recorded song, each time we play it, is a matter of sounds coming at us through time, and this is the first aspect of the aural language of rock song we should consider.

When we read a poem, there is no "time" consideration in our assimilation of it. We can pause and dwell on a word or line, an image or an idea for as long as we wish before moving on. Song, however, being time-bound, has a dramatic immediacy which allows us no intermediate stage between the moment's verbal/musical statement and our reaction. Listening to a rock song we can dwell on a word, an image, an idea only for as long as the performer/creator—the songmaker—allows us to; we cannot refer back, or skip forward, or pause and ponder, our only options are to listen to the song right through, or to switch the record player off. This is part of the point Simon Frith is making when he suggests that "songs are more like plays than poems" (Frith 1980, p. 882). Like drama, in fact like all performance and recording arts, rock song "corresponds directly with the continuum of our experiencing" (Wishart 1977, p. 130).

Whenever we begin to listen to a rock song on record, then, we effectively submit ourselves to the songmaker's manipulation of the time continuum. So far as language is concerned, this allows the vocalist, like an actor, to time each word or phrase for maximum impact, to pace his words, or rush through them, or dwell on them, leave them hanging on a silence—all devices whereby the rhythm of language can be used to dramatise the content of what is being said or sung.

. . .

Another important result is that "song words are always spoken out—we always hear them in somebody's voice" (Frith 1980, p. 882). The words of a song matter not only as meaningful signs but as human noise—as sounds which convey paralinguistically something of the personality, emotion, attitude at their source. This is especially so for songs and genres in which the voice comes to matter more than the words it carries, the words being merely the means by which emotion is channelled, directed, explained. The art of Otis Redding, for example, is less a matter of words than of emotional intensity with which they are delivered, and this is true of many soul, blues, and rhythm and blues singers (and their white imitators). In Redding's "I've Been Loving You Too Long," the lyric is little more than a sequence of disjointed, fragmented utterances with key lines: "I've been loving you for too long," "I can't stop now," "you were tired," and "my love is growing stronger," repeated over and over to the point of seeming obsession. The words set the situation, they have us eavesdrop on the tragic disintegration of a relationship in which the lover/singer's "love is growing stronger" while his beloved's "love is growing cold," but the power of the song lies in the way Redding's voice charges each verbal moment with vocal passion and desperation. Simon Frith has observed that "what makes these words convincing are the sounds around them. The exaggerated oos and ees, the repetitions, the pauses and the hiccups, the slurs and interjections. What Redding suggests is the power of spontaneous feeling barely controlled by words or music" (Frith 1980, p. 882).

Most of this description is of a surface structure of paralinguistic events, events in the flow of voice—gasping and gulping, jabbering and stuttering—which convey feelings instantly and empathetically from speaker to listener. By the climactic begging exhortation of the song, in which words and phrases are crushed or dismembered into gasping, pleading sounds, we can almost feel the muscular spasms which generated each imploring "please."

Earlier in his article Simon Frith notes that such non-verbal vocal effects have their corollary "in our own daily lives where the most directly intense statements of our feeling involve not words but noises. We sigh and we gasp, we moan, we guffaw, cry, cheer, and so on" (Frith 1980, p. 882). What happens in an aural song tradition (performed or recorded) is that these sounds become part of an artist's dramatic resources. When Redding sings "Oh baby I'm down on my knees," we know that he is not, and that his traumatised voice is in response to no one at all, there is no woman on the receiving end of his dramatic pleas—but this does not mean that the voice is not *meant* for anybody. It is meant for us, the listeners, not as direct address of course, rather as an invitation for us to enter into the singer's dramatic fiction, to suspend our disbelief and infer a situation from the words and voice we hear. We do much the same whenever we read a poem and flesh out an imagined world around it on the basis of the verbal implication it provides, only in a rock or soul song it is not only words but paralinguistic sounds (intonation, rhythm, vocal texture, dynamics) involved in the delivery of words that carry implications of character and circumstance.

In evaluating rock lyrics, then, we need to keep in mind both their *aural* and their *vocal* nature: we hear a song as a continuous happening, and we hear it too in somebody's voice. The language of rock, it follows, falls somewhere between poetry and drama, another instance of the "ambiguous situation" of rock as a recording art. Like poetry, it has a lasting embodiment and involves the creative organisation of language. Like drama, it works through performance, in real time, and can draw upon the expressive resources of the human voice. There is, of course, a further point to be made. We must remember that rock words are just the linguistic dimension of a musico-linguistic synthesis—that, in Frith's words, "rock meaning cannot be detached from musical form" (Frith 1979, p. 17). As Redding cries "please . . . please . . . please" at the climax of "I've Been Loving You Too Long," he does so as part of a cacophony, his words battering hopelessly against a ruthless, rising wall of horns, just as they batter against the indifference of his lover. When, in "Sail Away," Randy Newman sings "climb aboard little wog and sail away with me," what has promised to be (in terms of musical convention) a gloriously orchestrated hymn to America is warped into a hymn to the American Original Sin of slavery, leaving us as listeners to cope with the contradictions and ironies. Even in a song as wordy as Joni Mitchell's "Furry Sings the Blues," we cannot divorce the powerful, poetic narrative from the haunting, cyclical movement of the music which frames it, or the emotional texture of its unresolved chords, or Neil Young's lonesome, vulnerable harmonica which, though wordless, perhaps best articulates the bleak world of the dying blues singer. Each song and song convention will have a different balance and interrelationship between words, voice and music, and, as Michael Parsons has observed, "to speak as if the words are the primary element and the music subsidiary to them is to reduce the impact and over-simplify the complexity of feeling of which words and music together are capable" (Parsons 1969, pp. 118–19). To conclude, then, I will consider the synthesis of music and language in a particular rock recording.

Language and music as sounds in synthesis

. . .

[Ian Dury's] "Waiting For Your Taxi" demonstrates the practical application of the criteria established earlier—criteria which are appropriate to the medium (aural-recorded), the form (musico-linguistic) and the musicology (ambiguously set between Afro-American and Euro-American) which characterise rock song. Thus the emotional potency of the song's moaning horns and the alarmingly "vocal" saxophone are clearly grounded in two essential features of Afro-American music: the use of aural order and disorder as a metaphor for ordered and disordered reality (community, environment, psyche), and the close connection of much black instrumental music with the expressive characteristics of the human voice. Similarly, a conception of rock song as a *recording art* helps us understand the way the song is made; how Dury contrives such a strange (multi-tracked) duet with his own voice, how street sounds are captured, selected and edited (on magnetic tape), how the startling saxophone playing of Davey Payne (perfected in a series of takes) comes to act as a musical reaction to those street sounds. Overall we can see how the studio is used by Ian Dury and his band, the Blockheads (as by Hendrix, the Beatles and many others before them), as a workshop within which a diversity of aural materials, including performances, can be subjected to a variety of treatments and then combined, mixed and re-mixed, pared down or augmented until judged aurally and experientially to be exactly the sound(s) desired.

So, as with Jimi Hendrix with whom we began, the "magic" of "Waiting For Your Taxi" as a musico-linguistic experience owes as much to the "science" of recording and manipulating sounds as it does to the skill and spontaneity of performances. In fact we have seen how in all rock songs, even those in which post-production mixing and editing matter little (the songs of Linton Kwesi Johnson or Otis Redding, for example), the ability to record sounds and seal them in the lasting form of an object has opened up a whole new dimension of musico-linguistic possibility. To understand and evaluate such songs (even as a prelude to placing them in a wider sociological or cultural context), we need critical theories and methods which do justice to *all* aspects of sound which count in our listening experience.

References

Books and articles

Clarke, P. 1982. "The artist in the studio: relations between language and music in the making of contemporary rock songs," unpublished MA thesis, University of Keele

Christgau, R. 1969. "Rock lyrics are poetry (maybe)," in *The Age of Rock: ...Sounds of the American Cultural Revolution*, ed. J. Eisen (New York), pp. 230–43

Cole, H. 1974. *Sounds and Signs: Aspects of Musical Notation* (London)

Eno, B. 1982. "On record," *Sunday Times Magazine,* 31 October, p. 94

Esslin, M. 1961. *The Theatre of the Absurd* (London)

———. 1973. *Pinter: A Study of his Plays* (London)

Frith, S. 1979. "Listening to lyrics," in *The Ilkley Literature Festival 1979 Programme* (Ilkley, Yorks), p. 17

———. 1980. "Try to dig what we all say," *The Listener,* 26 June, pp. 822–3

Henderson, D. 1981. *'Scuse Me While I Kiss the Sky: The Life of Jimi Hendrix* (New York)

Hoare, I. 1975. "Mighty, Mighty Spade and Whitey: black lyrics and soul's interaction with white culture," in *The Soul Book,* ed. I. Hoare (London), pp. 117–68

Johnson, L. K. 1975. *Dread, Beat and Blood* (London)

Keil, C. 1966. *Urban Blues* (Chicago)

Laing, D. 1970. *The Sound of Our Time* (Chicago)

Leigh, S. 1973. *Paul Simon: Now and Then* (Liverpool)

Marcus, G. 1977. *Mystery Train* (New York)

Mark, M. 1979. "It's too late to stop now," in *Stranded: Rock and Roll for a Desert Island,* ed. G. Marcus (New York), pp. 11–28

Martin, G. and Hornsby, J. 1979. *All You Need is Ears* (London)

Mellers, W. 1973. *Twilight of the Gods: The Beatles in Retrospect* (London)

Middleton, R. 1972. *Pop Music and the Blues* (London)

Parsons, M. 1969. "Rolling Stones," in *The Age Of Rock,* ed. J. Eisen (New York), pp. 160–79

Perkins, V. F. 1972. *Film as Film* (London)

Poirier, R. 1969. "Learning from the Beatles," in *The Age of Rock,* ed. J. Eisen (New York), pp. 160–79

Ricks, C. 1980. "Can this really be the end," in *Conclusions on The Wall: New Essays on Bob Dylan,* ed. E. M. Thompson (Manchester), pp. 47–9

Rogers, D. 1976. "Varieties of pop music," in *Pop Music in School,* ed. G. Vulliamy and E. Lee (Cambridge), pp. 5–32

Saal, H. 1975. "Dylan is back," in *Bob Dylan: A Retrospective,* ed. C. McGregor (London), pp. 105–8

Shepherd, J. 1977. "The musical coding of ideologies," in Shepherd et al., *Whose Music?: A Sociology of Musical Languages* (London), pp. 69–124

Southern, R. 1962. *The Seven Ages of the Theatre* (London)

Stevens, W. 1966. "Selections from 'Adagra,'" in *Modern Poets on Modern Poetry,* ed. J. Scully (London), pp. 153–8

Willis, E. 1975. "Bob Dylan," in *Bob Dylan: A Retrospective* ed. C. McGregor (London), pp. 89–105

Wishart, T. 1977. "Musical writing, musical speaking," in Shepherd et al., *Whose Music?: A Sociology of Musical Languages* (London), pp. 125–53

Records

Ian Dury and the Blockheads. 1979. "Waiting For Your Taxi," *Do It Yourself,* Stiff SEEZ 14A (London)

Johnson, L.K. 1978. "Five Nights of Bleeding," *Dread, Beat and Blood,* Virgin vx 100Z (London)

Redding, O. 1965. "I've Been Loving You Too Long," *Best of Otis Redding,* Atlantic K600165 (New York)

Sedaka, N. 1962. "Breaking Up Is Hard To Do," RCA 1319 (London)

Simon and Garfunkel, 1970. "The Boxer," *Bridge over Troubled Waters,* CBS 563699 (New York)

SAMUEL A. FLOYD, JR.
FROM *THE POWER OF BLACK MUSIC*
Oxford University Press, 1995

. . .

[Previously] I mentioned the indebtedness of rock 'n' roll to R&B.[1] In the transition, black and white rockers borrowed and absorbed some of the musical practices and performance traits that had been derived from the ring,[2] including characteristic riffs, boogie-woogie ostinatos, vocal lines that are internally heterogeneous, adherence to the time-line principle, timbre-distortion practices, the improvisation and *materiality* of the music making (including performance practices such as Presley's pelvic gyrations), and the general dramatic tendency of the music. The degree of timbral distortion in the rock music that emerged in the 1960s, particularly the sonic innovations of heavy metal, is one of the primary elements that mark it as different from R&B. But even this was based in the sonic values of the ring. Jimi Hendrix, known as the rock movement's "Heavy Metallurgist par excellence" (Shaw 1982, 169), had a musical conception and sound rooted in the black core culture, most particularly in the Delta blues tradition and in the music making of Chuck Berry and Little Richard. The early bluesmen, laying bottlenecks and knives to the strings of their guitars, had laid the foundation for the brass-muting jazzmen, and both set the stage for Hendrix, who used fuzz faces and other commercial devices, as well as a number of custom-made implements (Menn, 1978). Such distortions can be heard in, for example, "Are You Experienced?" and "Voodoo Chile," both available in the posthumous compilation *The Essential Jimi Hendrix* (1978–1979). Hendrix had been especially influenced by Little Richard, and their affinity can be heard as he plays with Richard on the albums *Little Richard Is Back* (1964) and *Friends from the Beginning—Little Richard and Jimi Hendrix* (1972). Another influence and teacher was Albert King, who,

> like Hendrix, was a left-handed player who used a right-handed guitar upside down. He passed on to the eager young musician his own trademark—a sound that slurred up and then dropped down, like a saxophone sound. He taught him fingerings using the thumb and frettings on the guitar to bend the strings horizontally instead of vertically. (White 1984, 128)

Hendrix's apprenticeship in R&B bands such as those of Little Richard, Curtis Knight, and the Isley Brothers, and his exposure to Ike Turner, Albert King, and other R&B stylists, contributed to the development of his own style and to his use of ring tropes. But eventually, heavy metal became his overall conceptual framework, a sound that, in spite of its current association with white-oriented rock, goes back to Howlin Wolf's recordings in the early 1950s:

> Wolf first recorded for Phillips toward the end of 1950, and in January 1951 Chess released a single, "Moaning at Midnight," with "How Many More Years" on the flip. The music was astonishing, and Phillips never did a better job of capturing a mood. "Midnight" began with Wolf alone, moaning in his unearthly moan. Willie Johnson's overamplified guitar and Willie Steel's drums came crashing in together and then Wolf switched to harp, getting a massive, brutish sound and pushing the rhythm hard. "How Many More Years" featured Willie Johnson more prominently, and his thunderous power chords were surely the most *electric* guitar sound that had been heard on records. Wolf's rasping voice sounded strong enough to shear steel; this music was heavy metal, years before the term was coined. (Palmer 1981, 234)

Aspiring rockers of the 1960s and 1970s would identify Wolf as their inspiration and model. Although the music they created was based in cultural and social values different from those of R&B, its essential sound is certainly traceable to Wolf, both directly and through Hendrix, who had also been influenced by Chuck Berry, Muddy Waters, T-Bone Walker, Louis Jordan, Bo Diddley, Little Richard, and others. In fact, the fuzz, distortions, wah-wahs, and bent notes of rock guitarists entered rock not only through Hendrix, but also by way of white imitators of Wolf, Muddy Waters, and the other Chicago bluesmen.

On *Band of Gypsies* (1970), which is thoroughly rock, Hendrix's debt to Call-Response is clear. In it, B. B. King-style guitar lines and elements of Muddy Waters's style (signature riff figures) and Wes Montgomery's mannered approach (octaves and other double stops)[3] are fused with the rock idiom. Listen especially to "Machine Gun" and "Power of Soul." Echoes of Little Richard, albeit faint, can be heard on the "Changes" vocal. One of Hendrix's most gripping performances was also one of the most Signifyin(g) events in American-music history: his 1969 performance at Woodstock of "The Star Spangled Banner." The consecutive descending thirds that open the introduction, followed by Hendrix's unaccompanied "talking" guitar passage, immediately identify this performance as ring based. As the performance progresses, Hendrix inserts "calls" at "the rocket's red glare" and "comments" appropriately at "the bombs bursting in air" and other "telling" points. Here, Hendrix is a musical teller of the narrative, using his instrument in a manner similar to that of African callers and the "tone painters" of the European classical tradition. Hendrix's sound here comes out of the tradition of Howlin' Wolf's "Moanin' at Midnight" and "How Many More Years," and his distortions from the practices and proclivities of numerous ancient and modern African and African-American music makers.

As far as rhythm is concerned, Hendrix's music is primeval. David Henderson (1983) tells of an African conga drummer's reaction to Hendrix's performance style:

> Rocki's father was a voodoo priest and the chief drummer of a village in Ghana, West Africa. Rocki's real name was Kwasi Dzidzornu. One of the first things Rocki asked Jimi was where he got that voodoo rhythm from. When Jimi demurred, Rocki went on to explain in his halting English that many of the signature rhythms that Jimi played on guitar were very often the same rhythms that his father played in voodoo ceremonies. The way Jimi danced to the rhythms of his playing reminded Rocki of the ceremonial dances to the rhythms his father played to Oxun, the god of thunder, and lightning. The ceremony is called voodoshi. (250–251)

As the basis of Hendrix's music is mythic and ritualistic, it is also related to soul music, which also relies on the primeval, mythic, ritualistic expressions of the black church, which in turn, of course, have some of their roots in the same tradition from which voodoshi derives.

Notes

1. Following the transformation of R&B into rock 'n' roll—a metamorphosis effected, mainly, by Chuck Berry, Little Richard, and Elvis Presley—the Rolling Stones ("Carol," "Come On," "Around and Around," "Johnny B. Goode") and the Beatles ("Roll Over Beethoven," "Too Much Monkey Business") borrowed heavily from Berry (Reese 1982, 58–59).

2. This sense of music completing a cycle speaks to the circle image in many traditional African religions. While the Christian symbol of the cross graphically illustrates the intersection of worldly time and eternity, the circle suggests that through experiencing the rhythmic cycles of worldly life consciously and repeatedly, we spin ourselves into a sense of the divinely eternal.

3. Listen, for example, to King's "Caldonia" and "I Got Some Outside Help" on *B. B. King "Now Appearing" at Ole Miss* (1980) and Wes Montgomery's "Polka Dots and Moonbeams" and "In Your Own Sweet Way" on *The Incredible Jazz Guitar of Wes Montgomery* (1960).

References

Henderson, David. 1983. *'Scuse me while I kiss the sky: The life of Jimi Hendrix*. New York: Bantam Books.

Menn, Donn. 1978. Liner notes. *The essential Jimi Hendrix*. Reprise 2RS 2245.

Palmer, Robert. 1981. *Deep blues*. New York: Viking Press.

Reese, Krista. 1982. *Chuck Berry: Mr. Rock 'n' Roll*. London: Proteus Books.

Shaw, Arnold. 1982. *Dictionary of American pop/rock*. New York: Schirmer Books.

Weinstein, Norman C. 1992. *A night in Tunisia: Imaginings of Africa in jazz*. Metuchen, N.J.: Scarecrow Press.

White, Charles. 1984. *The life and times of Little Richard: The quasar of rock*. New York: Harmony Books.

SHEILA WHITELEY

PROGRESSIVE ROCK AND PSYCHEDELIC CODING IN THE WORK OF JIMI HENDRIX

Popular Music, January 1990

But like, the blues is what we're supposed to dig . . . sometimes the notes might sound like it, but it's a different scene between those notes. (Hendrix quoted in Pidgeon 1967, p. 2)

Discussion of the 1960s generally identifies progressive rock as the prime organ of communication within the counter-culture. At the same time, musical analysis of the genre is an underdeveloped field of study, including only an identification of musical characteristics (Willis 1978), Mellers' analysis of the Beatles (1973) and Middleton and Muncie's analysis of five representative songs in the Open University's course, *Popular Culture* (1981). As a particularly heterogeneous genre (compared with, for example, rock 'n' roll and r&b), definitions of progressive rock equally raise problems; to what extent does the variety of styles reflect the variety of radical movements contained within the overall term counter-culture; alternatively, given the variety of styles, can progressive rock be considered a single phenomenon and, if so, to what extent does it have musical codes in common?

Although it is possible to isolate music from its social, cultural and ideological context, progressive rock was located where particular sociological factors and musical developments crossed. The question thus arises as to whether progressive rock can be interpreted as a particular expressive form of the counter-culture's social and material life experience and, if so, the extent to which it can be considered as containing cultural values and social meanings.

With progressive rock standing in a contradictory position to mainstream pop conventions, the critical imperative rests on the degree to which the music can be read as "oppositional." How does progressive rock, from within its musical structure, articulate the socially mediated subjective experience of the different groups within the counter-culture? Is it a simple contestation of existing musical frameworks and how can a musical language express an alternative "progressive" viewpoint? To what extent does this rely on personalised intuitional breaks, inflections and the breakdown of structures?

While my initial analysis of Hendrix addresses the problem of the music itself—how it is arranged, instrumentation, style etc.—the problem remains as to *how* it can provide social and cultural meanings. My starting point has been that musical facts are socially grounded: that "the socially constructed codes which are responsible for musical structures set the limits of meaning, but the music is actually created in concrete cultural situations, and these orient its received meaning in particular ways" (Willis 1978). However, while it can be argued that the sense of innovation in progressive rock challenged the more standardised structure of pop songs and as such provided a musical analogy for the counter-culture's search for alternative cognitive and social modes beneath and outside the framework of the dominant culture, the area of signification presents problems. In particular the level of denotation seems lacking or at best unclear as there is very little sense of objective reference to concepts and perceptions. On the other hand, it is possible to discuss connotation, in that music was recognised, by the counter-culture, as a symbolic act of self-liberation and self-realisation in which reality and musical experience were fused. As such the sound-shape, together with the socio-cultural element superimposed upon it, consolidate to form a distinct form of communication.

As the counter-culture was largely concerned with alternative modes of living which involved, to a large extent, the use of drugs as a means towards exploring the imagination and self-expression, Hendrix's music is analysed for psychedelic coding. Focused by a reading of Joel Fort's *The Pleasure Seekers: the Drugs Crisis, Youth and Society* (1969), this analysis explores the way in which progressive rock conveys a musical equivalent of hallucinogenic experience through the manipulation of timbres (blurred/bright/overlapping), upward movement (and its comparison with psychedelic flight and the "trip"), harmonies (oscillating/lurching), rhythms (regular/irregular), relationships (foreground/background) and collages to provide a point of comparison with the more conventionalised, "normal" treatment inherent in rock.

At the same time, it is recognised that such associations quickly become conventionalised. As Middleton and Muncie (1981, p. 87) point out,

> psychedelic elements in musical style are typically interpreted as such by reference to a sub-culture of drug usage; in other words they are defined in this way primarily because hippies said they should be. A whole group of connotations, arising from our knowledge of the drug culture, then settles on the music. But this culture has already been defined in this way partially because of the existence in it of this particular kind of music. The meaning of drug-usage is affected by the meaning of the associated music . . . The system is perfectly structured internally . . . but has no necessary connection to anything outside itself; there is no purchase on it from without.

While my analysis of Hendrix has been influenced to some extent by this awareness of intra-cultural interpretations, I have tried to establish the meaning of psychedelic elements through an examination of the musical codes involved and, more important, their relationship to each other.

This article suggests a possible approach towards correlating cultural and musical characteristics and, in particular, the correspondence in Jimi

Hendrix's music between its "progressive rock" and its "psychedelic" associations. In particular, it explores how the emphasis on self-expression, improvisation and experimentation, implicit in progressive rock,[1] related to the counter-culture's emphasis on the immediacy of the experiential here and now of psychedelic experience.

Jimi Hendrix: the relationship between structure and psychedelic coding

Prior to his move to London in 1966, Hendrix's musical career in the United States had included package tours with Solomon Burke and Wilson Pickett. His strongest influence came from the serious blues musicians who came out of the South—Muddy Waters, Willie Dixon and Little Walter— and on one occasion he backed his idol, B. B. King. Other temporary engagements included backing Little Richard, Jackie Wilson, Wilson Pickett and Curtis Knight and for a time he played with the Isley Brothers, the first band to give him a chance to play lead guitar. This broad-based experience in the clubs made him equally conversant with jazz, saxophone swing, r&b, gospel and soul.

Hendrix was brought to England by Chas Chandler who saw him playing at the Cafe Wha in Greenwich Village. Chandler took him back to London where they auditioned a rhythm section which resulted in the engagement of Noel Redding (bass) and Mitch Mitchell (drums). Calling the band the Jimi Hendrix Experience, they played their first public engagement at Paris Olympia.

"Hey Joe," with flip side "Stone Free," was the group's first single, and was released on 16 December 1966. By this time Hendrix had spent four months playing the London clubs: the Marquee, the Upper Cut, the Bag-O-Nails and the short-lived 7 1/2 Club. A review in *Melody Maker*'s "Caught in the Act" section focused on his powerful psychedelic blues style, but the press generally wrote him off as so much loud, useless noise, calling him "The Wild Man from Borneo" or "The Crazy Black Man." Rather than fight the image the group encouraged it, hoping it would increase their following in the underground. "Hey Joe" musically reinforced the image.

> Mysterious, menacing and dynamically very well paced, the record in effect picked up on the blues where the Rolling Stones had left the idiom after topping the British charts with "Little Red Rooster" in 1964, and "Hey Joe" . . . made the British top ten early in 1967. Just as Britain was beginning to feel the reverberations of the drug culture in San Francisco,

here was a young black man from the West Coast with frizzy hair, outrageously colourful clothes, and no inhibitions about using the guitar as a sexual symbol. (Brown and Pearce 1978, p. 13)

But, as Mike Clifford points out, Hendrix had everything going for him—he had a supremely cool vocal drawl, dope-and-Dylan oriented lyrics, the acid dandyism of his clothes and the stirring element of black sexual fantasy (Gillett 1970, p. 385).

"Hey Joe" is based on a simple repetitive harmonic structure. The introduction establishes the inherent menacing mood of the song with a moody, blues-like riff. The vocal is based on a heavily repetitive falling motif, coloured by inflection and muttered comments. After a shouted "I Gave Her the Gun / I Shot Her / Yes, I Did. / I took the gun and I shot her" the second verse leads into Hendrix's guitar solo. This is based on scale figures which move around the principal chord structure: three bars on G Major, two bars on E Minor. The effect of the simple repetitive harmonies is to free the melody line (the structure is easily extended to create breaks of an irregular length) while the form itself is not constrained by a set of harmonic sequence (such as the twelve bar blues). At the same time, the progressions provide harmonic motion under the strongly rhythmic figures which are themselves punctuated by Hendrix comments: "Shoot her one more time baby."

Progressive elements

Hendrix had first heard "Hey Joe" when jamming with Arthur Lee of the group Love, but whereas Lee relied on a mixture of muttered vocals and a guitar line borrowed from Jackie De Shannon's "When You Walk In The Room," Hendrix shows more the influence of two of his guitar heroes, John Lee Hooker and Albert King. The introduction, for example, with its heavily accented G, the underpinning in the vocal line with the long decay on the D over which Hendrix mutters "I said," reflects the moody and menacing style of Hooker, while the casual dexterity in the lead break is more reminiscent of Albert King. The influence of B. B. King is also present in the sensuous articulation in the break, the flurries of quick notes contrasting with the sustained G and glissando fall in bar 7. The basic falling pattern which was established in the vocal is also there, and is a typical r&b formula. However, as Hendrix himself once replied to an interviewer who was comparing his style with Clapton: "but like, the blues is what we're supposed to dig . . . Sometimes the notes might sound like it, but it's a different scene between those notes" (quoted in Pidgeon 1976, p. 62). Thus, while there are blue notes, pitch inflection, "vocalised" guitar tone, triplet beats and off-beat accenting and a call-and-response relationship in Hendrix' own commentary to his guitar solo and verse line, the way in which these elements are pulled together is typically Hendrix. The sustain tone, which originated with B. B. King, takes on an even more overt sexuality, which was particularly evident in live performances by Hendrix where he would play the guitar with his teeth or with strongly masturbatory connotations to feed both the rhythmic emphasis of the guitar line and the words themselves: "I caught her messin' with another man."

In January, 1967 Nick Jones' article in *Melody Maker* (1967) "Hendrix—On The Crest Of A Fave Rave" provided a formative account of the basic ingredients for progressive rock: "The Hendrix sound is what England hasn't yet evolved—but desperately needs. It's a weaving, kaleidoscope of tremor and vibration, discords and *progressions.*"

The album *Are You Experienced* was released in September 1967. The single "Hey Joe" appeared on side one and two other tracks also became chart hits: "And The Wind Cries Mary" and "Purple Haze." The album focused on the psychedelic, with the title pulling on drug connotations.

"Purple Haze," the name given to a particular brand of the drug LSD, is overtly concerned with hallucinogenic experience. The energy, use of distortion, fuzz,[2] wah wah and loudness coupled with precise and sinuous scalic riffs are comparable to "Hey Joe," but this time the sexual focus, the betrayal of the male by the female and the violent consequences are shifted to pull on a sense of timelessness.

"Purple Haze" begins with a bass pedal E under A# on bass and lead guitar, the two bars creating an underlying beat, a common pulse, which worked to establish a bonding between performer and audience. The pulse-like beat continues in the next two bars, but here the A# disappears as Hendrix moves into the opening riff with its characteristic bending up of notes and dipping vibratos. Whilst this is basically a pentatonic blues riff, the extremes of distortion blur the actual pitching of the notes and the discordant partials make it practically impossible to hear the pitch. However, given the blues logic of Hendrix's other songs it is probable that the underlying structure is based on the chords of E-G-A which support the earlier vocal line.

The riff has the typical feeling of muscle and crunch common to most

Hendrix numbers, and this comes through particularly in the tonal quality created by the electronic distortion, the fuzz and the resultant discordant partials. The expectations generated in the opening riff are also picked up in the main break which moves toward an overt theatricality with its hammered and pulled-off notes, the jittered bursts of broken words over the free-flowing improvisation with its wild yet controlled sense of energy. In particular, the logic of the melodic shape of the line, the downward curve from C#-B subtly supports the more overt frenzy of the delivery itself. Throughout the entire solo the impression is of doubling at the octave above, a possible effect of electronic distortion or alternatively some sort of partial harmonic. In some bars the lower octave predominates, in others the upper, with the clearest "shifts" to the higher octave occurring at bars 2 and 8.

Psychedelic coding

As an acid track, the torn sounds and muttered syllables work within the overall shape of the lead guitar line which moves from top C# to B. The movement into the *trip* is accompanied by upward moving figures. The drums gradually move from a highly active and syncopated rhythm into a fast but even pulse in quavers. In the lead break, high notes, sliding amplifications and the sheer volume of noise move against the continuous arterial throb of the rhythm to juxtapose two realities—the throb of the continuous bass heart beat against the exhilarated high of Hendrix's guitar solo, which is intensified by the doubling at the octave effect.

For the listener, the sheer volume of noise works towards the drowning of personal consciousness. The simultaneous underlying pulsating rhythm and the heightened sensation of raw power rips through the distorted amplification of the guitar sound with its sinuous *tripping* around the basic notes.

The melody line is simple and based on a recurring motif which moves towards an incantatory, mesmeric effect. Again there is an indication that the song reflects the state of mind on a hallucinogenic trip. Under the influence of acid, a particular word or phrase can take on an unreal significance to become totally absorbing and dominant within the new state of consciousness. When the passage is played at half-speed on a tape-recorder, the word "haze" in particular vibrates, dips and moves upwards to suggest a sense of fixation, and this particular effect is also present on "funny" and "sky" where the dip shapes create a strong feeling of floating around the beat.

Overall, the use of repetition in the song works toward a mood of obsessiveness and absorption. This is reflected in the motif which constitutes the total melodic structure of the vocal line, and while there are minor variations based on inflection which bend with the words, its constant use moves ultimately towards a sense of fixation and total absorption within the "purple haze." The final vocal phrase, for example, with its strong dip shapes and muttered comments is supported by an accented F chord over a pulsating beat which stops suddenly as Hendrix mutters "tell me, tell me, tell me." The effect is one of loss of time, the underlying beat has gone and all that remains is the distanced voice and a sense of other-worldliness.

The total effect of "Purple Haze" is one of drifting and while the lead break, for example, is fairly metrical with most of the bars being in eights or sixteenths plus ornaments, the deflection of accents from weak to strong beats in bars 3–5 create a feeling of being within a different time-scale. The sensation of drifting is equally fed by phrasing and articulation. In the lead break the guitar meanders in an almost raga-like noodling around the notes, again suggestive of a state of tripping where a fixed idea/concept/point takes on a new reality. In conjunction with the feedback and distortion there is a feeling of incoherence. In particular the high registers are almost pure noise and as such resonate with the imagery of the words.

Progressive elements

While "Purple Haze" makes use of many blues features, the basic falling shape of the vocal, the repetitive phrases and short motifs, the somewhat tuneless melodic line, the call-and-response between the vocal and guitar, there is overall a sensation of anti-structure which comes through in the aural experience of the delivery, the dense sound, the distorted slide notes, the muttered broken questions and the deep/throated answer, and the final rising crescendo of the high-pitched E vibrato.

Hendrix's extreme use of a fuzz effect whereby even the slightest sound of the guitar gives off a full-volumed sound also feeds the underlying sense of disorganisation. The effect was increased by his standing close to a speaker so that when a string was plucked, the guitar would pick up the sound which would then become amplified and come out of the speaker. As the sound wave would make the string vibrate at the same frequency as before, the positive interference would have the effect of making the string vibrate indefinitely, which fuzz alone could not do. Then, by using filters, Hendrix would make the feedback occur on the second harmonic, so that when the string was plucked and the guitar was held near the speaker the note would jump up an octave, maintaining itself at a much higher frequency and causing the sound to become even more piercing. This effect occurs, for example, on the second "help me, help me" which leads into the lead break. As such, while Hendrix is basically repeating the riff, the effect is one of added intensity.

Other effects used in "Purple Haze" are the wah pedal, reverb, echo, phase and tremelo, all of which are common today but relatively new at the time. Although not used as extensively as fuzz, they allowed him to extend on the expressive potential of the blues and, in conjunction with the psychedelic connotations of the words, the song moves towards a theatrical enactment of a drug-induced state.

In contrast to the raw power of "Purple Haze," "The Wind Cries Mary" is far more gentle in effect. The haunting guitar motif which opens the song has an echo effect which resonates with the evocative "and the wind whispers / cries / screams / Mary" to create an innate sense of understanding. While "Purple Haze" evokes a powerful acid experience, "Mary" (marijuana) is a much milder drug and as such the gentler pacing of the song elicits a sense of complicity between Hendrix and the audience. There is a muted understatement. Hendrix's voice is at its most evocative, the words are spoken rather than sung out with an off-the-beat inflection, against a gently moving melody which pulls on the mood of serenity and well-being that can accompany shared "smoke."

The basic chord structure is simple, moving through a repetitive C:Bb:F until the evocative: "Footprints dressed in red / And the wind whispers Mary . . ." where the move to G7–Bb has an underlying darkness which is immediately counteracted by the brighter sound of the lead break which moves upwards in fourths, with a gentle bending of slide notes to effect a musical equivalent of floating. There is an ease in tension on the penultimate note, a sudden stillness before the haunting lyrics of the last verse. "And the wind cries Mary" is then picked up by the guitar motif which gently bends the last note.

Overall, "The Wind Cries Mary" encodes the effect of marijuana through the gentleness and inner-directedness of its style. The timing is subtle, with the inflections in the melody line meandering just off-the-beat. In conjunction with the gentle drift of the key link motif: C:Bb:F the effect is one of easy well-being. The wind can blow anywhere, and the marijuana experience is universal.

"Love or Confusion" has an equally simple harmonic structure and is based on the chords of G-G6-F-F6. The effect is to free the vocal line, which follows the natural inflection of the words with accents both on and off the beat. The rising and falling phrase-shapes and the muttered asides equally support the underlying meaning of the words, rising on the word "burns" and "love," sinking on "cold," circling "round and round" and distanced on "confusion." The sense of confusion is intensified by Hendrix's guitar playing which appears to be superimposed on the vocal. It is neither in dialogue with the voice, nor does it fill in gaps as in the blues, but instead provides its own vocal line. The effect is of two simultaneous melodies, both in the G minor pentatonic blues scale. At the same time, the chromaticism in the bass line provides a certain "dizziness" in effect, which again feeds the connotations of confusion.

The overall effect of the passage is one of noise which is generated in the main by Hendrix's use of fuzz tone which sounds at times almost like snare drum accents. This functions to articulate the beginning or end of a section and here the fuzz, together with the low grinding sound of the bass guitar, moves against the rests and the drum roll. At the same time, the other instruments come briefly into focus, doubling the bass line to create a moment of coherence. The rhythm guitar, for example, actually doubles the snare drum part, but since it is so sustained and relatively free of high frequencies, the sounds are distinct. The vocal line bends heavily with the muttered "or is it confusion" acting almost as commentary on the sounds of the passage.

Psychedelic coding

The words are strongly psychedelic in their associations of colour and confusion, and in conjunction with the acute distortions of fuzz sound and the tripping around notes in the lead break, move towards a sensation of movement through time and space. The endless feedback and distortion move the listener into an equivalent state of incoherence, the montage of sound effects, reverb, echo, tremelo and fuzz, resonating with the vocal message "pounding, pounding, going 'round and 'round and 'round and 'round."

Hendrix's lead break with its bend-up notes and *glissandi* equally suggests flight. It is here that the psychedelic fuses with space rock: the electronically distorted notes encoding both the unpredictability of hallucinogenic search, the lack of certainty of a good/bad trip with the unknown element in space travel.

Hendrix's exploration of space reads like a negative reaction to the mainstream rather than a positive move towards engaging in cultural quest. The use of distortion and fuzz creates an unknown element which can connote a sense of uncertainty. This also comes through in the way in which he tuned his guitar. The top string was often tuned to D or Eb and the excessive bending and the use of the wah wah pedal served to obscure the actual notes played. At the same time, Hendrix's use of a conventional guitar, similar to that of Hank Marvin, but played upside down, can be read as a turning upside down the conventional world of such groups as The Shadows. Clearly, Hendrix could have bought a left-handed guitar (as he himself was left-handed), but his playing of the instrument upside down helped to construct his image of an inverter of norms.

At the same time, the extreme use of noise, in conjunction with the hypnotic nature of the Hendrix sound with its overwhelming sense of energy and drive, created a means through which he could tune into the "collective unconscious" of his audience. This provoked the mass sexual ecstasy often associated with his concerts which moved towards a corporeal sense of tribal unity. At this point, Hendrix's personal expansion of human consciousness would fuse with the collective experience of the hallucinogenic in the exploration of the self through mind-expanding drugs:

> Mild physical sensations particularly in the limbs, occur, but the main dimensions are perceptual . . . primarily visual, but also (including) the other individual sensory modalities and sometimes a blending or synesthesia so that one "hears" something seen or "tastes" something touched. With the eyes closed, kaleidoscopic colors and a wide array of geometric shapes and specific objects . . . are often seen . . . Illusions can occur and sometimes, depending on the interaction of the many important human variables, hallucinations. (Fort 1969, p. 182)

In conjunction with the overwhelming sense of energy and drive in his guitar playing, allied to unusual sound effects (running his hand up and down the fretboard, banging the guitar and feeding these sounds through fuzz) there is, then, the implication of a new language of sound which equates with the sense of hallucinogenic exploration implicit in his lyrics.

While "Love or Confusion" continues to draw on blues resources particularly in the single note attack with long decay and *glissando* fall, the basic melodic falling pattern, for example, "Is this love, baby, or is it confusion"—is equally typical of r&b. The forcefulness in Hendrix's guitar style can be traced back to his early experience in r&b and rock 'n' roll, but generally structures and style are growth points rather than working barriers.

In particular his use of effects works to support the sense of the unknown, the "confusion" in the lyrics. The improvisations and the often incoherent instrumental melody/sound, the apparently disordered, random and electronically dominated noise, the never-ending effect of the reverb, create a kaleidoscopic effect. Layers of sound appear to grow out of one another in a continuous flow to provide a musical metaphor for the endlessness of space itself. The emphasis on noise and the apparently chaotic sound of Hendrix's playing equally supports the idea of confusion. The overall effect is anarchic, a move against reality (with its emphasis on logic) and as such there is a fusion with the psychedelic, the unpredictability of hallucinogenic search, the juxtaposition of unknown colours with chaos and confusion.

"Hey Joe," "Purple Haze," "The Wind Cries Mary" and "Love or Confusion" were constantly performed by Hendrix in concert and appeared on seven of his LPs including the live recording *Woodstock*. As such they would appear to be representative not only of his particular style of performance, but also of his particular focus on the psychedelic, space rock and sexuality. "Foxy Lady," "Fire," "Red House," "Long Hot Summer Night," "Gypsy Eyes" and "Dolly Dagger" for example, show a comparable sensuality in vocal delivery and performing style to "Hey Joe." There are the characteristic muttered asides to evoke an erotic intimacy which is intensified by the pounding beat and sensuous guitar style. "Gypsy Eyes," for example, has the characteristic sliding *glissandos* and bent-up notes in the guitar introduction but the opening vocal has no supporting chords, and as such the focus is on Hendrix's slow sensual delivery. The overt sexuality of "Dolly Dagger" is intensified by the pounding rock beat and bass riff. In particular, the repetitive blues-like delivery of the coda in conjunction with the strongly bent-up chords moves towards an assertion of dominance and self-gratification which, in live performance, would have been intensified by the explicit masturbatory connotations of Hendrix's guitar style.

"Spanish Castle Magic" and "Are You Experienced" exhibit comparable techniques both in vocal delivery and guitar style but this time draw on psychedelic vocabulary. Initially, it is the lyrics that point to the psychedelic. "Are You Experienced" invites a hallucinogenic exploration. The "are you experienced," in particular, points to the need for guidance by a trained, trusted person for the first-time user of LSD.

> The underlying personality, mood, attitudes, expectations and setting in which the drug is taken have proven to be far more important as determinants of an LSD experience than with drugs such as alcohol, marijuana, barbiturates, or amphetamines . . . Because of the intensity and complexity of the experience, it can . . . be disorganizing and upsetting. (Fort 1969, pp. 181, 183)

With Hendrix as a "trusted" and "experienced" guide (in the sense that he was both a loved and respected performer), the experience is promised as beautiful: "Have you ever been experienced: Well, I have. Ah, let me prove it to you."

"Spanish Castle Magic" extends the "experience" itself, but in both songs the lyrics imply knowledge: "candy" = "sugar" = LSD, "stoned" = "high," pulling on the effects of LSD, the sensation of floating. Coupled with the overwhelming sense of energy in Hendrix's guitar playing and the sheer volume of noise generated by the fuzz tone there is then an implicit drowning of individual consciousness, an invitation to "experience," which is reflected in the name of the band itself.

Space rock also required experience, with the form of the music depending upon comparison and for symbolic communication. As such its form of communication is symbolic and pre-conditioned by the structures of previous symbolic transfer. Unlike Pink Floyd, however, whose space rock (e.g. "Astronomy Domine," "Set the Controls for the Heart of the Sun") is melodically and rhythmically simple, relying on electronically produced sounds to create a dramatic realisation of the vastness and potential beauty of space, Hendrix appeared more intent on *destroying* conventional reality (with its emphasis on logic), to constitute instead a sense of the anarchic through the mutation of sound. With both bands, space rock exhibits a comparability with psychedelic rock and hallucinogenic experience: both talk of light, of colours, of the *extra*-ordinariness of experience.

In "Up From the Skies," Hendrix again makes use of spoken dialogue to effect a sense of personal experience which, coupled with the use of fuzz and distortion and the upward moving figures, suggests flight and disorientation.

> Thoughts which are ordinarily suppressed or repressed from consciousness come into focus and previously unseen relationships or combinations between these are recognized . . . Ordinary boundaries and controls between the self and the environment and within the self are loosened . . . mood changes or swings can occur and sometimes intense pleasurable or esthetic experience . . . On other occasion or with other individuals, the mood changes can be highly unpleasant and labile. (quoted in Fort 1969, pp. 182–3)

The songs analysed suggest, then, knowledge and experience, not only of psychedelic drugs and their potential effects, but equally of musical style. For example, while Hendrix made use of blues resources in the repetitive structure of the riffs, the repetition of phrases and short motifs, the use of blue scales, the falling shapes of the vocal, the use of call-and-response between the vocal and the guitar, the Jimi Hendrix Experience was ultimately based on an immense vocabulary of sound. Volume affecting sustain, wah wah pedal, fuzz tone and reverb are especially important in a consideration of style and Hendrix's experience in rock 'n' roll and r&b is equally apparent in the forcefulness of his playing and the emphasis on an essentially rhythmic rather than lyrical guitar technique. Overall, harmonies, melodies and lyrics would appear to be secondary to a consideration of *effect* as what are often simple deep structures are masked by the incredible energy and forcefulness of the guitar style and the dynamics of the electronic effects themselves.

"Love or Confusion," for example, is based on the chords of G, G6, F and F6, the phrases are repetitive and memorable, but overall the effect is one of anti-structure which is due to the aural experience of the delivery, the dense sound, the feedback and distortion which move toward pure noise. "Purple Haze" is also based on a repetitive riff over a simple harmonic structure: E, G, A, but again the underlying logic of the chord progressions is transformed by Hendrix to produce a feeling of intuitive incoherence and lack of rationality through the use of fuzz tone which distorts the hammered and pulled-off notes.

The blues, then, is a growth focal point rather than a working barrier, and Hendrix's guitar style, while reflecting the influence of B. B. King, John Lee Hooker and Albert King, demonstrates his own physical feeling for sound, not only in the virtuosity of technique but also in the use of electronic effects which enhance the feeling of raw energy which characterises all his songs.

The muttered vocals which are common to all Hendrix songs also demonstrate a physical feeling for sound rather than melody and as such make their impact musically rather than semantically. In "Love or Confusion" for example, the musical effect of "or is it, or is it confusion" is to focus the confusion in the sound itself, the fuzz tone, the low grinding sound of the bass guitar against the roll on the cymbal. In "Long Hot Summer Night" the muttered "I'm so glad that my baby's coming to rescue me" again works as a sound source to effect a strongly sexual rhythmic focus before the lines are repeated twice to an upward melodic line to suggest, in context, an orgasmic high. "Foxy Lady" again focuses on a repetitive rhythmic motif: preceded by the highly charged "give us some," the repeated "foxy" symbolically moves to an expression of the rhythm of the sexual act itself. The falling shape on "Ah" in "Are You Experienced" followed by the muttered "but you are experienced" is also rhythmic in effect, the lack of melody moving towards an underlying intimacy and sense of personal hallucinogenic knowledge which is finally focused by the spaced out utterance: "Not necessarily stoned, but beautiful."

The muttered vocals show, then, a comparability with Hendrix's essentially rhythmic guitar style. To quote Greil Marcus, the "words are sounds we can feel before they are statements to understand" (quoted in Frith 1978, p. 176). While it is difficult to describe verbally the aural quality of the rhythmic delivery and the sensuality in the vocal style, the overall effect is to give an underlying rhythmic weight to the content of the words and as such there is a parallel with the blues where repetitive lines are coloured by inflection to impart an underlying expressive tension.

Like their close contemporaries, Cream, the Jimi Hendrix Experience show a development of blues resources, and while both Clapton's and Hendrix's guitar styles show the influence of B. B. King there is nevertheless a difference in delivery—"where Clapton played with attack and tension, Hendrix tended to take his time and stay relaxed" (Gillett 1983, p. 385)—relying more on electronic effects to create the effect of raw energy. At the same time, contemporary reviews of the two guitarists were curiously similar. "Hendrix: Progressive and beautiful in his ideas": "Clapton: Progressing with ideas and techniques" (*Melody Maker,* June 1967). As such it would appear that the concept of progressiveness was strongly determined by the way in which the two musicians could take on the basic resources of the blues and produce new and unexpected developments. As Zappa said at the time: "If you want to come up with a singular, most important trend in this new music, I think it has to be something like: it is original, composed by the people who perform it, created by them."

Acknowledgments

Grateful acknowledgement is made to Peter Winkler, State University of New York, Stony Brook, for his help in transcribing "Purple Haze" and "Love or Confusion."

Notes

1. My own research, of which the analysis of Hendrix constitutes only a small part, indicates that progressive rock was characterised by a sense of creative development from a base style and involved an underlying sense of uncertainty and surprise through extensive improvisation; that performance (live and recorded on LPs) would demonstrate both originality and self-expression.

2. The "fuzz" effect, so important in Hendrix's music, is effectively a severe distortion. The first deliberate distortion of this type was produced in the mid-1960s by damaging the speaker cones of an amplifier system. This meant they could no longer give a true response and thus introduced some distortion. The first properly controlled fuzz was produced in much the same way as it is today, except that valves were used rather than amplifier transistors. The input signal from the guitar is greatly amplified to exceed the signal level above the supply voltage. As this is not possible, the signal becomes saturated at the supply voltage level. This has the effect of clipping the top of the wave form to produce the distortion (see Figure 1). This effect was used by rock musicians to produce the "aggressive" quality through the introduction of many high-frequency harmonies. Naturally produced sound waves have only a few harmonies, but these "clipped" waves have many, especially at a high level, and this is what gives off the piercingly painful effect. Natural guitar sounds at loud volume are not nearly so painful to listen to, and hence far less aggressive.

Figure 1

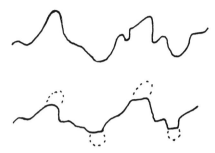

Hendrix took this use of fuzz much further by using amplifiers with a much higher gain. This meant that most of the signal was clipped, leaving only the bass part (see Figure 2). This greatly increased the effect by making the signal much harsher. At times he also used extremely high-gain fuzz, which left practically none of the original signal and the output was similar to a square wave (Figure 3). It is probable that Hendrix later used transistors in his fuzz box. These have much higher gain than valves, as they saturate faster, giving very square cut-offs as opposed to values which tend to saturate more slowly, thus giving a more rounded and softer fuzz.

Figure 2

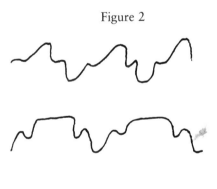

Figure 3

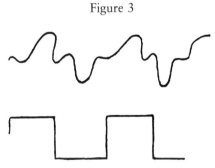

Brown, H. and Pearce, D. 1978. *Jimi Hendrix* (London)

Fort, J. 1969. *The Pleasure Seekers: the Drug Crisis, Youth and Society* (New York)

Frith, S. 1978. *The Sociology of Rock* (London)

Gillett, C. 1970. *The Sound of the City* (London)

Mellers, W. 1973. *Twilight of the Gods* (London)

Melody Maker, June 1967

Middleton, R. and Muncie, J. 1981. "Pop culture, pop music and post-war youth: countercultures," in *Politics, Ideology and Popular Culture (1) (Popular Culture, Unit 20)* (Milton Keynes)

Pidgeon, J. 1976. *Eric Clapton* (London)

Willis, P. 1978. "The Creative Age," *Profane Culture* (London)

PART FIVE

1 9 8 3 . . .
(a n d
B e y o n d)

*Everybody seems
to be busy showing
what polished per-
formers they are
and that means
nothing these
days—it's how you
feel about what
you are doing that
matters.*

JOHN ROCKWELL

HOW THE ELECTRIC GUITAR BECAME A WAY OF MUSIC

The New York Times, 15 July 1974

The enormous adulation—even adoration—accorded such a diffident instrumentalist as Eric Clapton on his current American tour is but the most recent proof of the place the electric guitar has gained in our musical life.

The electric guitar is *the* instrument most characteristic of popular music today. But it is more than that, and more than a mere amplified extension of the normal, acoustic guitar. It has become the inspirer of its own style of music, a classic instance of the medium affecting the message.

Guitars in general are the common man's piano: relatively inexpensive and easy to play at a functional level, convenient to carry around and associated—especially since Bill Haley shook up the parental world with "Rock Around the Clock" in 1955—with the machismo of the self-contained teen-age subculture.

General Similarities

Both acoustic and electric instruments look roughly the same (apart from some of the more fantastical shapes that some custom-designed electric guitars have assumed); both use strings that one stops on a fret-board with the left hand and strums or picks with the right. The chord patterns and fingering techniques on both kinds of guitars are transferable, at least in a general sense.

But the differences are pronounced, too—so pronounced that they suggest two different instruments altogether. The acoustic guitar (even with such enthusiastic variants as flamenco) is best suited to intimate expression. It is the perfect instrument for love music, for the soulful confidences of the folk singer. Even when it is translated into a large hall, by classical guitarists such as Andres Segovia, what sticks in the mind afterward is the image of tiny, delicate pins of sound reaching out into the vast hall.

With the electric guitar, the pins become giant hammers crashing on the eardrums. The nature of amplification has reached such a level that everything affects the sound of the instrument, from the slightest pluck to a sleeve brushing against the strings to the performer's body bumping against the body of the guitar. That volume has enabled guitarists to take the leading role in bands: No longer, nor ever again, need they worry about being drowned out.

Filters to Fuzz Boxes

If volume is the most immediately remarkable aspect of the instrument, its other characteristics are just as distinctive. A true electric guitar—unlike an amplified acoustic guitar—is a piece of electronic equipment. In the older instrument, the plucked string set up resonances in a sound box. In an electric, the action of plucking the string disturbs a magnetic field within the instrument, and that disturbance is transferred through coils wrapped around the magnet to an amplifier, and then to loudspeakers. The signal can be modified by any number of bits of electronic gimmickry, from frequency filters to fuzz boxes to wah-wah pedals.

Perhaps the most striking ability of these modern electric guitars, when compared with their acoustic predecessors, is the way they can spin out long legato lines. After the initial contact with the string, the resultant sound has to decay into eventual inaudibility (unlike the organ, which sustains a note as long as a key is depressed). With the electric guitar, however, the amplification can prolong the decay, so that guitarists like George Harrison, Roy Buchanan and Mr. Clapton can make the instrument seem to sing, linking the notes songfully together—or it "gently weeps," as Mr. Harrison puts it in a song.

The Art of Feedback

Wah-wah and echo effects increase the rhythmic complexity of a guitar line, not to speak of their strange sound colors. Feedback—letting the noise emerging from a loudspeaker generate new noise from the guitar—has been refined into an art by guitarists like Pete Townshend of the Who, who controls his effects by teasing the face of his guitar closer and farther from the banks of loudspeakers.

All of these new instrumental sounds have resulted in a music totally different from guitar music in the preelectrical era. Electric-guitar music can be massive and overwhelming, a gargantuan cacophony of chordal color. Or it can be simple and pure, the sound stretching out lazily between the notes. Above all, its range of possibilities has multiplied immeasurably: In terms of variety, the electric guitar stands to the acoustic guitar as the mighty Wurlitzer stands to a virginal.

The 1948 Breakthrough

The first really popular electric guitars came out in the nineteen-thirties, but it was not until 1948 that the first widely distributed solid-body guitar (one that dispensed with the resonating hollow body needed for an acoustic instrument) reached the market. By the early fifties most jazz bands used amplified or electric guitars, but only after the rise of rock in the mid-fifties did the rock guitar begin its ascendancy.

Since then, there have been numerous notable jazz electric guitarists, and even an occasional "serious," classical piece that makes use of the instrument. But the true exploiters of the electric guitar's sound potential were electrified black bluesmen like B. B. King and white and black blues-rockers. It was they more than any others who revealed the variety hidden within these unassuming bits of wood or plastic. Aside from Mr. Clapton, Mr. Harrison, Mr. Townshend and Mr. Buchanan, other well-known, inventive rock guitarists today include Jerry Garcia and Keith Richard.

All of them, however, owe a large debt to the late Jimi Hendrix, the black bluesman turned rocker. Anyone who saw the film of the Woodstock Festival will remember Mr. Hendrix's astonishing version of "The Star-Spangled Banner," complete with screams and wails and machine-gun bursts and diving, exploding bombs—all produced by one man, alone onstage, with nothing but his electric guitar. Mr. Hendrix gave us the best vision not only of what an electric guitar can do, but of the almost mystical way in which electric guitarists relate to their instruments.

HOMAGE TO JIMI: A NEW MUSIC COMPOSITION
Guitar Player, March 1981

Over the last few years there has been an increasing number of exciting, innovative works written for the electric guitar, including duets, concerti, and compositions for solo guitar, guitar and electronic tape, guitar in chamber ensemble, and guitar with orchestra. In the past the electric guitar was neglected in "serious" composition because of the ignorance of composers as to its potential and a prejudice toward something associated solely with "popular" music. Prior to the violin's acceptance as being worthy of serious consideration in the Baroque era, it, too, was considered by some to be a vile instrument, suitable only for taverns and dance halls! A similar attitude existed in some minds as to the place of the electric guitar.

The advantages of the electric in serious music are essentially twofold: sustain and volume. Composers in the past were limited in writing for the classical guitar in an ensemble texture because of the quick decay of the instrument's sound, making sustained melodic lines impossible. Unless special care was taken in scoring and balancing in an ensemble, the classical guitar would be buried. Although amplification has, in many cases, eliminated this problem, difficulties in tone reproduction remain. By contrast, the electric guitar's sustain and volume characteristics make it the practical choice for the serious composer wishing to write for guitar with chamber ensemble or orchestra. But the electric is not merely a substitute for the classical model, having its own beautiful sound and wide range of tone, articulation, nuance, and expression capabilities.

In writing for the electric guitar, the composer can reach a wider audience, such as those who listen to jazz and rock and those whose ears and minds are open and interested in anything played on the instrument. This will allow a greater interaction between the popular and classical worlds. It was in this spirit that *Homage To Jimi* was written. This piece was composed for electric guitar and percussion in response to a 1979 commission from professional percussionist John Gardner. The guitar part was written on piano, which resulted in unusual sonorities, some with unorthodox fingerings that are difficult yet playable. Although I am a classically trained composer, my musical education began in rock. Like most guitarists of my generation, I was profoundly influenced by Jimi Hendrix. *Homage To Jimi* is not intended primarily as a vehicle for the duplication of actual Hendrix techniques and sounds. Instead, it is a more subtle and abstract attempt to capture some of the demonic fire and lyric beauty that was, to me, the essence of Hendrix' music. To achieve this, I combined a pantonal—not 12-tone—musical language with references to Jimi's music. I wished to give the impression of a work that at first sounds like my own, but gradually gives way to Hendrix' influence, hopefully fusing the two.

The percussionist plays a total of 23 instruments. This multiple percussion setup consists of small brass wind chimes, four almglockens (large cowbells), three automobile brake drums (each producing a high pitch), one hi-hat, one Pang cymbal (this instrument has an upturned rim), one sizzle cymbal, one suspended cymbal, one tam-tam (a non-pitched gong), three small gongs (pitched low to high), one snare drum, four Remo Roto-Toms, one bass drum, and one African log drum. These instruments are played with a variety of mallets. In the score each instrument is assigned a line or space on one of two staves. Each one also has a corresponding symbol listed in the legend accompanying the text.

In addition to the exotic nature of the instruments themselves, there are several special percussion effects. For example, using a Super Ball mallet (a stick with a Super Ball on it), the percussionist rubs the top of the log drum, producing an effect similar to a lion's roar. At times, the percussionist also *bows* his cymbal. By rubbing a cello or bass bow on the edge of a cymbal or gong, a high-sustained pitch is produced, with each cymbal sounding a different note.

In contrast, I chose to limit the electric guitar effects to a few special devices, leaving most of the interest in the music itself (Hendrix references, unusual chords, atonal melodic lines). I use only an Electro-Harmonix Big Muff fuzz and an old Vox wah-wah pedal. I use the wah-wah backwards: That is, I plug my guitar (a 1978 Gibson Les Paul Custom) into the output, and the input into a pre-CBS Fender reverb amp. This produces feedback. By switching pickups I can change the pitch. By operating the volume control on my guitar I can execute an effective ascending or descending glissando. By operating the pedal I can produce an effect that sounds like a sea gull's cry, especially if reverb is added. As you might imagine, I discovered this by mistake and decided to try to use it creatively and dramatically in this piece.

The remaining special effect is a tape that is played toward the end of the work, containing the bridge of Hendrix' "If Six Was Nine." I made a tape loop out of it so it would play over and over, and recorded it on another tape for about 30 seconds. In performance the tape starts unobtrusively, as if someone had a radio on in the theater, and then grows louder until it matches the volume of the percussionist and guitarist. Then it dies away, leaving the duo to finish the piece alone.

The work also uses many contemporary techniques, such as changing meters (often every bar), difficult rhythms, and proportional notation that doesn't specify when or how long to produce a certain sound. All of the special effects and techniques are not used as gimmicks, but as expressive devices to help capture the spontaneous spirit and huge emotional range of Jimi's music. The work is basically programmatic; that is, each section depicts a certain phase or style of Jimi's music. The first half deals primarily with the demonic fire, while the second half concerns itself with the lyric beauty.

. . .

The mercurial nature of the electric guitar allows one to write a work that would appeal to both musical worlds, and *Homage To Jimi* has received very positive reaction from both classical and rock fans. The electric guitar can be further used as a link, introducing the classical world to aspects of jazz and rock, and exposing the rock world to classical music through transcriptions, arrangements, and new music. There are many more innovative works for electric guitar written by composers with jazz and rock backgrounds, and the potential for further works is enormous. Perhaps through these compositions we can combine the best of different musical worlds.

MICHAEL ROSENSTEIN
IF SIX WAS NINE: LA MUSICA DI JIMI HENDRIX PER JAZZ ENSEMBLE
Cadence, April 1993

Splasc(h) 376: If Six Was Nine / Little Wing (Ballad N. 26, Little Wing) / Castles Made of Sand—Indians / Angel (Power to Love—Night Bird Flying, Angel, Figurati, Manic Depression, Stone Free—Fire) / Driftin' / Third Stone from the Sun (Third Stone from the Sun, Room Full of Mirrors, Spanish Castle Magic, Burning of the Midnight Lamp—Bold as Love, La Luna e la Torre) / A Purple Lady in Voodoo (Voodoo Chile, Foxy Lady, Bag Man, Purple Haze). 59:24.

Lucia Cappelli, vcl; Diego Carraresi, ss, ts; Dario Cecchini, bars, b cl; Alessandro Fabbri, d, perc, electronics; Sergio Gistri, tpt, flgh; Stefano Scalzi, tbn, tba, t flgh. Firenze, Italy, 3/9–19/92.

An Italian Hendrix cover band with no guitarist, no bass player, no amplification or feedback, and a female vocalist with an Italian accent? This seems an unlikely project, but from the first funky attack of "If Six Was Nine" to Carraresi's R&B inflected tenor tear through "Purple Haze," this sextet delivers a set of riveting interpretations of Hendrix hits and obscurities. Gil Evans attempted to imagine what Hendrix might have sounded like with a jazz band, and most homages and tributes get caught up in his guitar psychedelics. Arrangers Carraresi and Fabbri take a different approach by exploring Hendrix' themes, recasting these familiar melodies, lyrics, and rhythmically propelled song structures for two brass, two reeds, vocals, and drums, resulting in unexpected resonances.

The arrangements group the horns for a full ensemble sound, shifting leads and ensemble roles evenly. Cappelli's vocals don't even try for Hendrix' raw blues inflections, but rather are imbued with a soaring emotionalism, investing even the raps from "If Six Was Nine" and "Bold as Love" with heartfelt exhilaration. Scalzi's tuba and Cecchini's baritone share the bottom, stripping the grunge from Noel Redding's bass lines while still capturing the rhythmic urgency. Pieces are woven together in suites delivering some songs whole and using themes from others as bridges. Check out "Anthem," which mixes themes from two tunes for an intro into the lyrical balladry of "Angel," only to head off into the chamber counterpoint of an original interlude by Carraresi intertwining lines of atonality. The blues riff from "Manic Depression" then leads into "Stone Free" with a searing tenor solo and dancing tuba line. The piece concludes with a quick, punchy allusion to "Fire." The ensemble jams through these striking arrangements with an invigorating originality. You may never listen to Hendrix in quite the same way again.

GARY VARGAS

THE HENDRIX PROJECT: A MOVING EXPERIENCE

Straight Ahead, January/February 1993

The immense talent of Jimi Hendrix combined with the sweep of his artistic vision to produce the most influential style in the history of the electric guitar. Twenty-odd years after his death his mastery of the plectrum remains unequaled, so just imagine the difficulty a dancer would have in translating the full range of Hendrix's fretwork into footwork. That is what Bebe Miller attempts in her artful and ambitious Hendrix Project, which she brought to the University of California at Santa Barbara on October 13, 1992.

A dancer and choreographer of great renown, Miller is interested in "finding a physical language for the human condition." In a preconcert interview she voiced her unhappiness about the current state of society: "It's time for change, radical change." The Hendrix Project, she explained, responds to problems such as homelessness and the destruction of the environment by invoking the revolutionary spirit of the Sixties. The five compositions Miller chose to interpret indicate an awareness of Hendrix's work that, with the combined talents of her six dancers, allowed her to explore the depth of his music.

The program began boldly with Miller spinning, reaching, and clutching at the whining-missile and machine-gun riffs of Hendrix's tortured version of "The Star-Spangled Banner" from Woodstock. One by one the other dancers joined her as the piece swelled into a ballistic ballet driven by the violent energy of the music. In contrast, the finale explored every nuance of Jimi's Albert Hall performance of "Little Wing" with a superb black-and-white male duet that had the erotic grace and muscle of a Mapplethorpe set in motion. In between, the dancers stomped and boogied to the "freak flag" spirit of "If Six Was Nine," freewheeled through Jimi's Monterey performance of "Like a Rolling Stone," and explored the dark, sexy heat of "Red House," Hendrix's classic blues as performed in San Diego.

Overall, Miller's hyperkinetics were a fine match for the music's motifs, and her dancers exuded enthusiasm and a marvelous sense of unity. Hendrix once said that he looked more for a feeling of closeness between musicians than for originality. Miller's dancers had that closeness, and, inspired by Jimi's artistry, they performed with the exhilarating freedom inherent in his music. However, for sheer excitement, Miller's extended solo on "Like a Rolling Stone" was the highlight of the show. She first matched Jimi's languid introduction with studied, powerful moves that resembled a martial art. Then, as the tempo rose, she exploded into arm-pumping, hip-slapping moves of her own—captivating enough to momentarily make you forget who was playing guitar.

We will never see the like of Jimi Hendrix again, and the chance to see his oeuvre interpreted by a world-class dancer-choreographer is an opportunity not to be missed. Miller is planning a broadcast performance of the Hendrix Project, but if you are fortunate enough to live in a city where they will be appearing, check out the Bebe Miller Company for a truly unique "Experience."

DOUGLAS J. NOBLE
HENRY ROLLINS ON JIMI

UniVibes, 17 February 1995

Noble: When did you first hear Jimi Hendrix?

Rollins: *I first heard Hendrix when I was a little boy. My mother as well as my step-brother were into him and I heard the records.*

Noble: What sort of impact did it have on you?

Rollins: *Being young and not knowing anything, I didn't really get the full impact of Hendrix until I saw him on television. I can't remember when that was, probably a rerun of Monterey or something. I was only ten years old or so when he died, so I wasn't aware of the musical impact he had on the world until I was older.*

Noble: Which is your favourite Hendrix album and why?

Rollins: *I prefer the boots to the "real" records at this point just because I have played them all so many times. But as far as the records you can find in normal shops, it would have to be* Electric Ladyland. *I've never heard such a cohesive amount of music that goes so far and wide yet works as an entirety like that record. I think he should have put the alternate mix of "1983 . . ." on there. My favourite Hendrix song would have to be "Voodoo Child (Slight Return)," especially the version from Woodstock—the San Diego version is great, too. It's the ferocity of the song that's so overwhelming to me. A real tour de force. Coming in second would have to be "Machine Gun"—the unedited Isle of Wight version on the* Island Man *boot.*

Noble: Do you think of Hendrix as being closer to Black Sabbath or John Coltrane?

Rollins: *Interesting question, putting Coltrane and Hendrix in the same sentence, because I see them being on the same path totally. Both were uninterested in convention and were dedicated to a spiritual exploration of themselves through music. Even their musical progression I find similar as far as the sometimes critically slammed music they were going for at the time of their passing. I find a lot of parallels in classic jazz and the finer moments in rock music—Hendrix, Zep—in that they were really going for something and not just working through the idiom. Considering Hendrix died when he was twenty-seven and had accomplished all that he did, I get the feeling he was the only real genius rock music ever had.*

Noble: Do you think there's a Hendrix influence in any of your work, either musically, lyrically or spiritually?

Rollins: Sure, Hendrix is an influence and an inspiration. Not being a guitar player, I don't know the exact extent of the influence—perhaps just to stick to my plan and go for it. Like when you said that you like "most" of my work. It's the Hendrix spirit that makes me not give a fuck what you think of me or my work. And there you go!

ELECTRIC LADY STUDIOS ALUMNI LIST

52 West 8th Street
New York, NY 10011

ARTIST	ALBUM/SINGLE (TITLE)
AC/DC	Back in Black
Bryan Adams	Heaven
Aerosmith	Dude Looks Like a Lady
	Love in an Elevator
Anthrax	State of Euphoria
B-52's	Cosmic Thing
Beastie Boys	Too Much Posse
Jeff Beck	It Gets Us All in the End
Bon Jovi	Wanted Dead or Alive
David Bowie	Young Americans
The Cars	Door to Door
	Greatest Hits
	Heartbeat City
Cheap Trick	Tonight It's You
The Clash	Combat Rock
The Cult	Electric

ARTIST	ALBUM/SINGLE (TITLE)
Culture Club	Move Away
Brian Ferry	Slave to Love
Foreigner	4
	Head Games
Peter Frampton	I'm in You
Aretha Franklin	Jumpin' Jack Flash
Free	Alright Now
Daryl Hall	Three Hearts . . .
Hall & Oates	Big Bam Boom
	H2O
	Private Eyes
	Voices
Debbie Harry	Rockbird
Heart	Barracuda Live
Jimi Hendrix	Electric Mojo Man
Billy Idol	Rebel Yell
Iron Maiden	Somewhere in Time
	Powerslave
Joe Jackson	Blaze of Glory
Mick Jones	Mick Jones
Kashif	Say You Love Me
B. B. King	The Thrill Is Gone
Kingdom Come	Kingdom Come
Kiss	Animalize
	Asylum
	Creatures of the Night
	Kiss Alive
Led Zeppelin	Houses of the Holy
	II
Huey Lewis & The News	Sports
	Small World
Little Steven	Sun City
Joni Mitchell	Mingus
Ric Ocasek	This Side of Paradise
Yoko Ono	Hell in Paradise
Robert Palmer	Riptide
Rolling Stones	Emotional Rescue
	Some Girls
Run-DMC	You Be Illin'

ARTIST	ALBUM/SINGLE (TITLE)
David Sanborn	Close Up
Scandal	Warrior
Patti Smith	Horses
Soundtrack	Hail! Hail! Rock 'n' Roll
	Ishtar
	Rocky IV
	The Last Emperor
Steps Ahead	Magnetic
Thompson Twins	Here's to Future Days
Traffic	Live at Stony Brook—1970
Van Halen	Finish What You Started
Various Artists	Live at the Fillmore East—1970
John Waite	Missing You
Jody Watley	Love Injection
Stevie Wonder	Talking Book

JON PARELES

THE JAZZ GENERATION PAYS TRIBUTE TO JIMI HENDRIX

The New York Times, 4 December 1989

Jimi Hendrix receives a tribute, acknowledged or not, in virtually every hard-rock guitar solo. A different kind of tribute took place on Friday night at Town Hall, where members of the jazz generation that grew up in the rock era played their own arrangements—usually radical reworkings—of Hendrix songs. "The Hendrix Project," conceived and directed by Craig Dennis Street, used small and large ensembles to honor Hendrix, the composer.

The concert didn't prove that Hendrix's melodies, harmonies and words, in themselves, established his greatness. Much of his legacy is straightforward 12-bar blues songs, transformed by performances in which he carried the primal cry of the blues through an electronic whirlwind. But Friday's concert showed that his experimental spirit—his determination to smash though limits of timbre, harmony and structure—has continued to inspire all kinds of musicians since his death in 1970.

The trombonist Craig Harris wrote the most ambitious arrangements, using a 14-piece band of brass, saxophones, drums and guitars. For an atmospheric "Hear My Train A-Coming," he evoked an old-time whistle stop, using rustling percussion, Brandon Ross's slide guitar and the rhythmic, frenetic honking of Mr. Harris's didjeridoo (Australian log horn), with blues riffs glimmering from muted cornet (Graham Haynes) and clarinet (Don Byron). "And the Wind Cries Mary" coalesced from Cyro Baptista's whistling percussion sounds to a richly reharmonized horn arrangement that carried Mr. Harris's rambunctious trombone solo. And for the closing "Freedom," Mr. Harris turned the ensemble into a funk band, bouncing riffs back and forth with ever-increasing power.

The brothers Mark and Scott Batson, both pianists, made a spectacular, virtuosic entrance into New York jazz with a duet on "Castles Made of Sand"—an arrangement by Geri Allen that set impressionistic delicacy against percussive impact, then brought the two together for a gospel-tinged finale. Mark Batson returned with Ms. Allen's arrangement of "Manic Depression," which moved from abstraction to jagged two-part counterpoint to splashing, crashing modal chords—all played with the dynamic control and unpredictable timing of a jazz master. Mark Batson is a senior at Howard University, from which Scott Batson recently graduated; they're young, but they won't be unknown for long.

Naturally, there were guitar showcases. Jean-Paul Bourelly arranged "Voodoo Chile" for two acoustic guitars (Mr. Bourelly and Brandon Ross) and David Torn's electric guitar, separating out Hendrix's blues, rhythm and noise. Mr. Bourelly deployed a big band for "Are You Experienced," with jabbing horn punctuations behind his own singing and his wriggling, wailing guitar solos. His arrangement of "Electric Ladyland" featured Mark Ledford, a singer who can croon tenderly or swoop through astonishing melismas, amid gauzy, muted horn chords.

Mr. Torn performed a solo version of "Cherokee Mist/And the Gods Made Love" that bogged down as he toyed with echo effects. And the guitarists, eventually joined by the drums, also collaborated on "The Star-Spangled Banner," a spacy, staggered version of Hendrix's full-scale assault on the anthem.

* * *

"Villanova Junction," an unreleased Hendrix song, turned out to be another blues piece, arranged by Graham Haynes for a brass quartet oompahing behind Vincent Henry on harmonica and Vincent Chancey on French horn. Oliver Lake played an alto saxophone solo, part aching melody and part sprinting lines and squeals, that had considerable dramatic tension but little audible connection with its avowed source, "Little

Wing." Mr. Ross's arrangement of "Drifting" created molten, oozing chords, for guitars and Melvin Gibbs on bass, behind Mr. Ledford's suave singing and Mr. Lake's saxophone obligatos. And "Voodoo Child: Slight Return" was played and arranged by Mr. Baptista, Rodney Holmes and Kevin (K-Dog) Johnson, on percussion and trap drums, pounding out the song's basic riff and volleying solos.

Funk, rhythm, blues, jazz, rural twang and futuristic noise—Hendrix swirled them together, leaving the arrangers to extrapolate from what was already in the songs. And while "The Hendrix Project" owed as much to the arrangers' ingenuity as to their original source, the concert showed that first-rate jazz repertory doesn't have to be jazz.

CHUCK PHILIPS

EXPERIENCING JIMI HENDRIX

Los Angeles Times, 26 November 1989

Some sounds speak directly to the subconscious—the blast of a cherry bomb, the howl of a siren . . . the scream of Jimi Hendrix's feedback at the start of "Foxy Lady."

If Jimi Hendrix were alive, he would be 47 on Monday. To mark the occasion, the Black Rock Coalition—a nonprofit organization formed to fight racism and combat negative stereotypes in the music industry—will present the first "Jimi Hendrix Birthday Celebration" at the Music Machine in West Los Angeles at 8 p.m. on Monday.

In a field almost exclusively populated by white musicians, Hendrix has served as a role model for a cadre of young black rockers. His achievement was to reclaim title to a musical form pioneered by black innovators like Little Richard and Chuck Berry in the 1950s.

For years, critics and musicians in pop circles have hailed Hendrix—who died on Sept. 18, 1970, as a result of inhalation of vomit due to barbiturate intoxication—as one of the most creative and influential rock guitarists ever. But his impact on today's budding crop of black rock musicians runs even deeper.

"I think of Hendrix in the same context as Martin Luther King Jr. and Malcolm X," said Vernon Reid, guitarist for Living Colour and a founder of the Black Rock Coalition.

"To me, he was one of the seminal black figures. Unfortunately, people get so wrapped up in his guitar playing that they tend to overlook what he did with sound and composition. Like Coltrane, Miles [Davis] and Ornette [Coleman], Jimi's presence fundamentally changed the equation."

Lenny Kravitz, whose '60s-influenced solo debut album, "Let Love Rule," has received kudos from critics and in college and alternative radio circles, cites Hendrix as a crucial link in the development of black music.

"For Jimi radio airplay wasn't the premise," Kravitz said. "He didn't just write hit songs or hooks. Back then rock music was about free expression and Jimi was an innovative artist at the top of his form. People tend to forget that rock 'n' roll *is* black music—not just white people either. Black people forget too. Hendrix opened the doors for guys like me. He is the perfect example of a black artist doing what he wanted to do."

Billy Nelson, who plays bass for the BRC (Black Rock Coalition) All Stars, the band that will open the Music Machine bill (local rockers Total Eclipse and East Coast rappers Culture Shock are also scheduled), says it would be impossible to overestimate Hendrix's importance in the local black rock community.

"Hendrix did for rock what Charlie Parker did for jazz," Nelson said. "He was like a modern-day Bach or Beethoven, a musical mastermind who came in and completely changed the entire scene."

Proceeds from the Hendrix tribute will be used by the BRC to underwrite the coalition's ongoing campaign to secure a star for Hendrix on the Hollywood Boulevard Walk of Fame. Local BRC co-director Ray Jarvis says the coalition chose to single out Hendrix's contribution because his music represents the "essence of what the BRC is all about."

The BRC was established in 1985 by Vernon Reid, writer Gregg Tate and film producer Konda Mason. Local directors MaryAlice Bailey, Norwood Fisher, Mason and Jarvis opened the Los Angeles chapter in May.

"It's funny, this idea of treating black rock like it's a separate sub-genre of rock," Reid said. "When a white band like AC/DC plays rock, they're actually playing black music. Rock 'n' roll was created by black musicians."

Reid believes that Hendrix's race is central to his relevance. "Who could listen to 'Machine Gun' without thinking about black soldiers in Vietnam?" Reid asked. "It's because he was black that his version of 'The Star-Spangled Banner' is so powerful. It's too bad that Jimi was taken from us before he could really explore the jazz direction."

* * *

BRC member Dr. Frank Gilliam, a professor in UCLA's political science department, says one reason Hendrix is so revered is because his music helped many middle-class black rock fans overcome a social identity crisis they experienced during the late 1960s.

"Some of us in the BRC were raised in the suburbs, the first wave of black working-class children," Gilliam said. "When we were growing up, rock was not cool music for black kids to enjoy. Either you listened to 'soul' music or else you were considered 'whitewashed.'"

According to Gilliam, Hendrix's music and his anti-war, pro-civil rights political stance offered black teen-agers who loved rock 'n' roll a new ethnic role model—a black man internationally respected for modernizing black roots music who was unafraid to experiment with Anglo cultural influences.

"Jimi personified the 'transculturation' of America for middle-class blacks," Gilliam said. "He validated our position in society, the fact that we were proud to be black, but also not enslaved by the black experience."

Hendrix's penchant for loud, dissonant feedback altered the course of funk music too. Many R&B musicians who cut their teeth on James Brown and Sly & the Family Stone were stunned by the power of his eclecticism.

George Clinton, whose work has influenced black stars from Prince to De La Soul, says Hendrix's psychedelic approach to the pentatonic scale not only taught him to respect blues music, but also encouraged him to experiment in new directions.

"Jimi was definitely the one we held up when we wanted to reach for something," Clinton said. "The way he could control feedback and make it sound so symphonic truly transcended logic. There were no boundaries to his playing. One minute he would sound like Curtis Mayfield, next thing he'd be doing Ravi Shankar. His music gave me the freedom to go out and be anything I felt like being musically."

Coalition members also consider Hendrix to be the first rock musician to seriously explore atonal improvisation with amplified feedback and electronic distortion. During the late 1960s, his efforts in this regard drew praise from respected figures in the jazz community like Miles Davis and Gil Evans. In Davis' 1989 autobiography, the trumpeter credits Hendrix with influencing his shift toward a more rock-edged sound.

* * *

James Marshall Hendrix was born in Seattle on Nov. 27, 1942. Before bursting on the pop scene as a headliner in 1967, he worked the chitlin circuit as a sideman. Between 1963 and 1965, he toured with and/or performed session work for many R&B stars, including King Curtis, Ike & Tina Turner, the Isley Brothers, Jackie Wilson, James Brown, Solomon Burke and Little Richard.

Little Richard remembers Hendrix as a consummate showman who strongly resented the racism he encountered in the music industry: "Jimi helped open up rock 'n' roll to black music. He broke down the doors and burned up all the wood. He was one big package."

Hendrix moved to England when he was 23 and began pioneering new musical genres like metal and fusion before they even had names. Within a year of linking up with drummer Mitch Mitchell and bassist Noel Redding to form the Jimi Hendrix Experience, Hendrix was cutting gold albums and selling out international tours.

After that integrated power trio folded in 1969, Hendrix created the Band of Gypsies with black musicians Buddy Miles (drums) and Billy Cox (bass) and began to publicly support the political struggles of blacks, American Indians and Vietnam veterans.

During his life, Hendrix's playing not only dazzled his fans and peers, but it also impressed many of the artists whose styles he emulated. During the course of his career, he jammed with pioneers like Roland Kirk, B. B. King and Muddy Waters.

Curtis Mayfield, whose influence on Hendrix is evident in compositions like "Little Wing" and "Electric Ladyland," says that even though he had the opportunity to play with Hendrix, he still stands in awe of the late guitarist's abilities.

"Jimi's approach to music transcends racial barriers. His imagination spoke to people on a deeper level than that," Mayfield said. "With the psychedelics and what have you, he was almost like a scientist, studying the effects."

Although Hendrix released only five albums during his brief career, his legacy lives on. In the 19 years since his death, six official compilations and more than 400 bootleg records have appeared on the market.

Bob Merlis, head of publicity at Warner Bros. Records, says Hendrix is still the label's most consistent seller. His original five albums have all reached the 3 million sales mark. Nine albums have been digitally remastered and reissued as CDs on Warner Bros./Reprise. "Smash Hits," a best-of collection first released in 1969 and containing such classic Hendrix numbers as "Foxy Lady" and "Purple Haze," was re-released early this month in CD, and comes complete with a new high-tech graphics track that allows fans who own JVC's new CD-plus-graphics unit to view synchronized psychedelic imagery while listening.

For serious fans, a musical transcription series called the Jimi Hendrix Reference Library is also available in album-and-book packages from Hal Leonard Publishing. The latest addition to the catalogue is called "Variations on a Theme: 'Red House'—Evolution of the Blues," featuring narration and singing by blues legend and Hendrix fanatic John Lee Hooker.

Unlike other prominent music figures of the 1960s' anti- Establishment drug culture, Hendrix seems to have little difficulty competing in today's techno-synth market. Producer Alan Douglas, who runs Are You Experienced, the Hollywood company that merchandises all official Hendrix estate music and memorabilia, estimates that 75% of Hendrix's current audience is between 12 and 20 years of age.

"Jimi is no nostalgia figure," Douglas said. "He is still a relevant force in rock. Kids today relate to his music as if he was still alive."

FRANK OWEN and SIMON REYNOLDS
WHY HENDRIX STILL MATTERS
Spin, April 1991

Historical revisionism and the endless stream of tired imitators that followed in his wake sometimes makes it difficult to appreciate what a radical listening experience the music of Jimi Hendrix was and still is. Yet for those with the ears to hear, his influence is everywhere in contemporary rock.

In the Stone Roses and their guitarist John Squire's polychromatic action-painting style of playing. In My Bloody Valentine, a group which has worked with Roger Mayer, the guy who invented effects boxes and distortion pedals for Hendrix. In Loop's noise symphonies. In Sonic Youth, whose unusual tunings would not have been possible without Hendrix's reinvention of the guitar. (Drummer Buddy Miles, who played with Hendrix, recorded an album called *Expressway to Your Skull* in 1968. Nineteen years later Sonic Youth recorded a song with the same name.)

In the wah-wah heaven of Dinosaur Jr. In the raga free-form folkadelic blitz of Hüsker Dü's "Recurring Dreams" on *Zen Arcade*. In the wigged out, apocalyptic, nouveau acid rock of the Butthole Surfers. (Think of their "Jimi" as a fin de siècle version of Hendrix's "Third Stone from the Sun.") In the oceanic rock of A. R. Kane. In the black rock of

Living Colour and 24-7 Spyz. In the thrashing metal-funk of the Red Hot Chili Peppers (who covered Hendrix's "Fire" and inherited his febrile hypersexuality and imitated his bad-ass virility). Not to mention obvious examples like Prince and George Clinton.

And then there's heavy metal as a genre. If Hendrix paved the way for this music, it was because he showed that the blues could be blown up from a porch-side lament into a mountain range. Hendrix invented the "air guitar," not in the sense of an imaginary instrument played by hair farmers in front of their bedroom mirrors, but rather in the sense of a guitar that refused to be bound solely by earthly roots, a sound that grew wings and took flight. An aerial guitar, if you will.

The Hendrix influence on rap is also profound, and not just in the way that boho homeboys like De La Soul and A Tribe Called Quest dress. Hendrix samples on rap records include Digital Underground's "Who Knows?" the Beastie Boys' "B-Boy Bouillabaisse," A Tribe Called Quest's "Go Ahead in the Rain," and Monie Love's "Just Don't Give a Damn." Moreover, every rap use of rock comes via Hendrix, from Run-DMC to Schoolly D. Rap's dissonance is Hendrix's guitar still reverberating and feeding back.

As SPIN colleague Nathaniel Wice puts it: "He dominates both *Yo! MTV Raps* and *Headbanger's Ball*. He fathered both, dominating everything that music has become. Not only won't he die, but it's impossible to imagine how to kill him off."

There's even a case to be made that Hendrix is responsible for that hideous mutant, jazz-rock. But we'll pass discretely over that, except to mention Hendrix's profound influence on Miles Davis's brilliant late-'60s and early-'70s work.

Jim Morrison may be the subject of Hollywood mythmaking, but Hendrix is not a corpse to be resurrected. Hendrix is the living, breathing soul of today's rock'n'roll.

. . .

In 1975 rock's biggest egghead, Brian Eno, referred to Hendrix as "probably still the greatest guitar player of all time." Eno wasn't talking about Hendrix's guitar-god virtuosity: "He was the first guitar player to realize that guitar was more than a piece of wood that hung around his neck, and he really understood that there was a relationship between the room acoustics and the amplifier he was using, the whole situation."

Beyond the instrumental showmanship (setting fire to the guitar with lighter fluid, playing it with his teeth, smashing it into smithereens), Hendrix was the first environmental guitarist, the inventor of rock's first truly 3-D music. Before Hendrix, rock was a matter of tunnel space. The guitar distinctly positioned coming at you from one particular direction. Hendrix replaced rock as riff with rock as radiation. His guitar comes at you from all sides: behind you, from inside you, through you. It's Sensurround sound that permeated the listener's flesh.

* * *

Why should SPIN, a magazine supposedly devoted to all that is new and cutting-edge in popular culture, feature Jimi Hendrix on its cover? Surely, in remembering a figure such as Hendrix, we are colluding with the CD consciousness/retroculture to be found in magazines such as *Rolling Stone*. Are we not impeding the flowering of the new and the now? Should we not be killing our idols?

The '60s is the latest wing added to our museum culture (the '70s wing is already under construction, as it has been for some years now). Museum culture makes it possible to reexperience the '60s, at the same time making it impossible for people to put into practice the ideals of the '60s (breaching the gap between art and life, perpetual play, et cetera) in their lives now. In order to relive the '60s, what is important about that overmythologized decade has been killed in a process that is part neutering, part necrophilia.

The failure of the '60s, implied in it becoming mummified in a museum, lets everyone off the hook; it's easier to live with that period if you take for granted the idea that its unrealistic dreams were always doomed. (As the situationists used to say, "Be reasonable, demand the impossible.") So you can defer your responsibility to remake your life as an adventure.

But Hendrix has somehow survived this deadly process, his music still potent and still a reproach to our prematurely forgone possibilities. After all these years he still challenges us to break the bounds/bonds of our "measly little world." He's the perfect hero for the multicultural '90s, our postmodern replay of the '60s.

That's why he's on the cover of SPIN. Jimi Hendrix, R.R.I.P.—refuses to rest in peace.

PART SIX

Criticism (Slight Return)

Everybody has soul. I really don't like that word in connection with the Experience. I like the words "feeling" and "vibration."

TOM NORDLIE
JIMI HENDRIX
Spin, April 1992

A true story: It was a slow Thursday night at the triplex movie theater where I am paid obscene amounts of money as a union projectionist. I spoke with concessionist Donna F., the most hard-core mainstream-rock fan imaginable. Cheap Trick is her favorite, but Stevie Nicks, Aerosmith, former Led Zep personnel, and Peter Frampton will draw Donna literally hundreds of miles.

In the middle of bimonthly detailing of the stolen riffs of *Led Zeppelin,* Donna demanded, "Why was Jimi Hendrix so good?"

Like any would-be metal deity, I answered for ten solid minutes: "Jimi Hendrix expanded the popular vocabulary of electric-guitar sounds so thoroughly that his contribution was comparable to the development of color photography after decades of black-and-white.

"Granted, some of Jimi's fundamentals were already familiar when he broke big in the summer of 1967, following the Monterey Pop Festival— Bo Diddley liked extreme volume and distortion, Pete Townshend smashed his gear, Jeff Beck conjured monsters-from-Mars feedback and hit eerily beautiful 'outside' notes.

"But before Hendrix, most assaultive or abstract rock instrumentation was used as embellishment, even gimmickry, with carefully defined boundaries. Jimi Hendrix integrated all the possibilities. He played loud and strong but so tenderly—look at his face in the films. He was both self-discovered genius and brazen thief of ideas. Traditional blues cadences gave way to square-wave speaker damage in the bend of a string. His rhythm playing was so intricate that it was almost lead, while his solos relied on repeated multistring figures. Even body language was impossible to separate from his technique.

"No doubt, Hendrix's belief that all guitar noises were equally legit was enhanced by his use of LSD, a drug notorious for decalibrating one's normal sense of priorities. That Jimi's hands were so large he could wrap his thumb over the entire fretboard while playing normally with the other four fingers didn't hurt.

"Most importantly, Hendrix wrote from the whole cloth of his imagination. The postnuclear undersea retreat "1983 . . . (A Merman I Should Turn to Be)" is no mere *song* brushing through the listener's day, it's a trip to Atlantis. "Little Wing" is but a delicate mosaic of small chords, trickling arpeggios, harmonics, and pick noise, yet altogether it soothes as much as any church hymn.

"He left so many kettles on the fire, among them jazz fusion (*Nine to the Universe*), large-ensemble work (the uncompleted double album *First Rays of the New Rising Sun*), and an unrealized interest in conventional music theory. Who knows where he would have gone? But since he's dead, he can't make beer commercials and will instead remain as an inviolate symbol of the overwhelming spiritual and physical potential of music." I think I gasped for breath then.

"He could have *given* that guitar to somebody instead of burning it," Donna admonished. Sterling Morrison of the Velvet Underground once told me the exact same thing. Yin flowed into yang again.

KEN RICHARDSON
JIMI HENDRIX EXPERIENCE: *RADIO ONE*
High Fidelity, March 1989

Readers of this magazine know that we usually love CDs from Rykodisc, but I'll be damned if I'm going to embrace the Jimi Hendrix product that Alan Douglas has been exhuming for the company. You'll remember that *Live at Winterland,* a dispiriting performance with often foggy sound, was released in 1987 to the unknowing cries of "the definitive Hendrix concert disc" and (here's a laugh) "by far the best-sounding CD I have ever heard." Now we have *Radio One,* collecting 17 BBC radio recordings from 1967, and the problems multiply. First, the sound quality for most of the tracks, no matter what Rykodisc has been able to do, still borders on the bootleg, with Tin Man guitar all over. Second, that sound is some-times much closer to fake stereo (bass on left, treble on right) than the true mono claimed for the original recordings. Third, the repetition factor is getting ridiculous. ("Killing Floor," "Fire," "Purple Haze," "Hey Joe," and "Foxy Lady," all on *Winterland,* are here, too—as if we needed those last three in the first place. "Spanish Castle Magic" is here as well, even though *Winterland* boasted its appearance there as "the only live version known to have been recorded." Hmmm.) Fourth, *Radio One* is marred by filler ("Radio One Theme") and bad covers ("Day Tripper," "Hound Dog"). And fifth, Leland Stein's even-worse-than-*Winterland* liner notes are quite possibly the worst of 1988. (Samples: "A treat!" "Simply wild!" "Nuff said!" "When your battery needs recharging, plug this in for a daz-zling jolt of rhythmic energy. Guaranteed to get you a speeding ticket!" For "Hey Joe": "In concert he often improvised an extended intro and played the solo with his teeth." *You don't say.* For "Burning of the Midnight Lamp": "Change in chord progression at end a novel touch." Hey, Billy, when you're done with the Bangles elsewhere in this issue, I've got another one who thinks a mere *key* change is "novel.") Fortunately, Hendrix's first session for the *Top Gear* radio program (excepting "Hound Dog") is excellent, with well-balanced original sound that finally gives a warm, realistic tone to the guitar during three good tracks: "Drivin' South" (fiercest Hendrix soloing heard in years), "Catfish Blues," and the de-psychedelicized "Midnight Lamp." Those three tracks total 14 minutes and would have made a smashing CD-3. The rest of this hour-long CD proves that Rykodisc and Douglas should go back to superior original material—like, I'll say it again, *Hendrix in the West*—or simply stop this game. Just as I should stop this entirely too long "mini" review. But really, folks, buy any other Rykodisc CD you want—just don't be fooled by such an out-of-character money-grabber as *Radio One.*

GREG BAKER
SCARY JIMI ESSENTIAL
December 1995

Scariness made and makes Jimi Hendrix transcendent, potentially immor-tal. That and the stone-cold fact his music was so revolutionary and so substantial that ancient Hendrix tracks still outburn anything pretending along the same lines.

Hendrix had presence: a big man with big hair and big fingers and, well, big everything. His lyrics, while reflecting the free sex and chemical mindblowing of young America, somehow went beyond the moral pale without the detraction of contrivance; they seemed naughty, at least, even if you couldn't figure out the metaphors. (A line such as "Making love is strange in my bed" could busy a convention of Freudians for hours.)

Beyond the suggestive lust lay some hard lessons for the Establishment—the taking of one's wine and herb remains a valid political concern today. Without hammering home maxims, Hendrix was able to smirk the status quo into jeopardy. To the straights, these above-it-all lyrics were hails from hell itself, musical advocacy for the open overthrow of everything safe and simple. As one Jimi song suggested, white-collar conservatives freaked.

As for singing, Hendrix could sing in the sense that Springsteen, Petty, and, well, Dylan could sing. Rock and roll forgives the communicators their technical difficulties.

With all that, it was his guitar that spoke loudest. Groundbreaking guitar. Scary guitar. Essential guitar. Upside down, wacky-tuned, supernatural. And the body of work he conjured up with pick and axe melded so many genres (jazz, blues, rock . . .) that it came to represent a genre unto itself. To ignore Hendrix's musical influence and historical importance is akin to ignoring the existence of Joplin and Morrison. Or Beck and Clapton. Or every metal band that ever existed. Punk too. Garage and grunge and anything employing feedback. From the new noise-rock of To Live and Shave in L.A. to ol' Neil Young and the plaid shirts, the electric church owes its heritage to Jimi.

And though his is a relatively small body of (legitimate for public distribution) work, Hendrix's magnificent musical presence has barely diminished over the decades. The diluvial distribution of record after tape after CD box-set of postmortem material might revolt anyone who ever put forth any effort to understand and appreciate Hendrix as a human being, which, believe it or not, he actually was. Here's *Jimi Plays Woodstock*, *Jimi Plays Monterey, Jimi Plays the Isle of Wight, Jimi Plays the Blues, Jimi Plays Acoustic, Jimi Plays with Himself.* . . . Dehumanizing, sure, but nothing new. In 1978 there came *The Essential Jimi Hendrix*, followed a year later by *The Essential Jimi Hendrix, Volume Two.* Isn't it all essential? Yes it is, to the point that even at his worst Hendrix was never boring, at least not in context. But the deluge takes away, makes Jimi seem like a product.

Jimi was a musician, an enduring one. No matter how you shuffle the deck of Hendrix songs, every hand, even his most busted flushes, sparkles with new lights, little beams of recognition and delight and some awe. Songs you've heard so many times shift their complexity around to reveal new nuances, like when you look at the stars each night, and even though they're the same stars, they make the sky appear always different, slightly but amazingly different.

More than anything, Hendrix achieved with his art the ability to alter states. "Purple Haze" really was a drug, a dose of screaming glories lingoized as riff, melody, distortion, back to the riff . . . but really something more, as the failure of a decent Jimi disciple to emerge in all this time indicates.

There exist countless guitarists of extraordinary prowess, maestros and inventors and entertainers. Though he possessed it in abundance, because he possessed it in abundance, guitar prowess was about as important to the Hendrix mystique as any given bandana. It was his deviations, an utter disregard for convention tossed off deadpan, that made his particular guitar talk in tongues, burn and explode and shine down from heaven above. You can lose yourself in the twisted cries of "You Got Me Floatin'" or "Drifting," rethink reality, drift, float, stone trip.

The fuck-upping power of Hendrix's gift is as obvious as Woodstock. After some introductory patter, he hears a fan loudly ask him if he wants to get high. In his most inscrutable whisper, Jimi says, "I have mine, thank you. I have mine." When he slams into those already-got-the-zipper-down spirals of "Fire," you wonder what his is.

Unlike certain counterparts, Hendrix sought psychochemistry toward the fostering of love and peace and grooviness more than in protest or to chase demons or to simply demonize himself. You need only hear his music to know that. (If you've never tripped on music, you've never heard rock and roll, or at least you haven't felt it.) A casual disregard for sanity and an ability to take guitar to new places in order to take listeners to new places was a turning point in rock. Even the noblest projects of the day— Sgt. Pepper, Tommy—and the endless jams of countless forgotten longhairs stopped short of transcendence, being what they were: experiments based on the traditional tools of manipulation. Hendrix allowed his music to be manipulated by those hearing it, a bold and giving approach borne of confidence and freakiness.

The notion of guitar god as benevolent guru was a new step over the musical rail, and comes across treacly, silly really, post-Nam and post-Watergate and post-Reagan. Yet tunes such as "Angel" still fly down on wings of silver, sweet and warm like a baby on a cold night, saved from sappiness by an alien quality. Hendrix worships, respects, loves his characters without painting them as one-dimensional icons. A bit of scaled repetition on his guitar, fuzzy little chord changes that would be mistakes if they didn't sound so damn cool, and the overheated primary rhythms of the Experience—you're lost in space, which isn't supposed to happen in silly love songs.

This is the big secret, the essence of Jimi's transcendence. But it's not what makes his music so essential to an understanding of rock and roll's inherent value. For all his grace, Hendrix had that other thing, a frightening acumen for chaos.

Apart from a natural feel for peaks and valleys, Hendrix boasted a knack for evocation that was never too obvious. The wicked riffs and head-on jams of "Crosstown Traffic" don't really sound like crosstown traffic so much as they make you feel like you're sitting at a red light dying to move on, break through, achieve the linear accomplishment that Hendrix sets up as the track's thematic bond.

The way instrumentation interlocks, how phrases drop off when you expect them to be reprised, all that complexity made Hendrix a star. The way he could mesmerize thousands of people by milking new and amazing sounds from a venerable and traditional instrument made Hendrix essential. Without him, no one would ever have played air guitar. Well, whatever. But there's no denying that the whole notion of cock rock, the overwhelmingly masculine fantasy of dazzling the masses while holding a six-string, ascended at the hands of Jimi Hendrix.

Anyone can dig up a reference—"Spanish Castle Magic" from *Axis: Bold as Love* predicated some of the shuffle guitar on Bruce Springsteen's second album, . . . Truth is, nobody was or is like Hendrix. From Frank Marino and Robin Trower to Steve Vai and Eddie Van Halen, many have pretended to the guitar-stud throne. For all their pyrotechnics, none fits the crown as comfortably or nobly as Hendrix did. His histrionics didn't emphasize the music, the music moved him to histrionics. That's no pose, son, that's the real shit.

That no one has been able to pin down Hendrix's persona proves there's still much to learn by listening to him. "Musically, we don't have any actual direction"—Jimi tossed that off without explaining that it's possible to go in many directions at once. His excursions into the blues might seem redundant to someone with a decent stock of Muddy, B. B., and the Alberts, but there in "Born Under a Bad Sign" you hear hubble-bubble lead lines leap off bass snaps and know no one but Hendrix would go there; or you listen to "Catfish Blues" and hear those snakey rattles and remember it's Jimi. There remain shifting galaxies to explore, reanalyze, enjoy.

And that one guy (a dark-skinned one at that!) could cloak himself in hippie clothes, dose up a bunch of chemicals, speak in billowy non sequiturs, and find a new universe for the electric guitar without ever giving the Establishment a reasonable target frightens those who need frightening the most. Jimi said flat out that his music was meant to change people's souls. What could be scarier?

Revolution begins in the mind. Change the world by changing the way people think, even if it's only how they think about music. Jimi knew this, he just didn't spout off about it. He played it out.

As cultural icon, social provocateur, historical figure, fashion plate, and of course musician, Hendrix was one scary motherfuckin monster. Still is, thanks to the music. The zeitgeist now is a new one, the social order unrecognizable to the sixties. The history books are written. Bell-bottoms will never come back no matter how hard designers try. The flowers are dead, the mystique and magic have been co-opted. Which leaves Jimi Hendrix remaining essential for a single reason: the music.

MARK HALE

FROM *HEADBANGERS: THE WORLDWIDE MEGABOOK OF HEAVY METAL BANDS*
1993

JIMI HENDRIX EXPERIENCE: bn. UK, 10/66. Jimi Hendrix, gtr., vcls. (dec. of drug overdose, Notting Hill Gate, London, UK, 9/18/70; Noel Redding, bs. (out 1968); Mitch Mitchell, dms. *Others:* bs.—Billy Cox (rep. N. Redding ca. summer 1969); dms.—Buddy Miles (rep. M. Mitchell for LPs #5 and #7 only). *Personnel notes:* see *Career notes.*

RECORDINGS: LPs: #1–*Are You Experienced* (Reprise RS 6261), summer 1967. #2–*Axis Bold As Love* (Reprise RS 6281), 1967. #3–*Electric Ladyland* (Reprise 2RS 6307), fall 1968. #4–*Smash Hits* (Reprise MS 2025), summer 1969. #5–*Band of Gypsies* (Capitol STA 0472), spring 1970. #6–*The Cry Of Love* (Reprise RS 2034), early 1971. #7–*In The West* (Reprise MS 2049), late 1971. Recording notes: Billboard Top 40--LP #1–(77 wks., top=5). #2–(13 wks., top=3). #3–(17 wks., top=1 for 2 wks.). #4–(17 wks., top=6). #5–(23 wks., top=5). #6–(17 wks., top=3). #7–(9 wks., top=12). Platinum LPs: #1 through #4. Gold

LPs: #5, #6, #7. A live split LP w/Otis Redding, *Live At The Monterey Pop Festival* (Reprise MS 2029), 1970, also went gold as did another split LP, *Rainbow Bridge* (Reprise RS 2040), 1971, and a comp LP, *Crash Landing* (Reprise RS 2204), 1975. LPs #1 through #4 are considered the absolute classics. A huge number of live, comp and bootleg HENDRIX LPs exist, including early recordings w/Little Richard and Curtis Knight.

LIVE: The JIMI HENDRIX EXPERIENCE debuted with several UK gigs in 1966, making their TV debut on the UK program "Ready Steady Go" in 12/66. Played Monterey Pop Festival (6/67), toured w/Monkees (1967), played Woodstock Festival (8/69), played Isle of Wight Festival (1970). They were major stars of the underground ballroom circuit. The JIMI HENDRIX EXPERIENCE were known as a very exciting live act, although, like many 60s bands, they were not very tight. Hendrix was one of the most sexual performers and personalities in 60s rock; onstage he would stick out his tongue a la Gene Simmons and play his guitar from between his legs to emphasize this. He is also well-remembered for "tooth-picking" his guitar and setting it on fire at Monterey; an enduring image of 60s rock is Hendrix with his left arm raised high in the air, producing overpowering waves of guitar noise with his right hand alone. *Career notes:* Few musicians in any style have been as revolutionary and influential as Jimi Hendrix. He got sounds from the electric guitar that no one else had even dreamed of, and brought the concept of *pure noise* (as opposed to musical tonality) to rock. Hendrix was the first guitarist to use the vibrato bar, feedback, distortion and Marshall amplification to their full potential, and was also an early heavy riffer, powerchorder, and pre–VAN HALEN "hammer-on" virtuoso. Along with Jim Morrison and Mick Jagger, he was one of rock's pioneer superstud sex symbols, aside from Phil Lynott, the only black performer truly revered by white HM fans. Hendrix could have been the first metal superstar had he restricted himself to material like "Purple Haze," "Foxy Lady," and "Manic Depression," but his experimentations went far beyond metal to a style of music unique to himself; at the time of his death it seemed that he might be moving in an avant-garde jazz direction, though no one can be sure what his music would have become had he lived past 1971. It would have been interesting to hear him work with later musicians (such as John Bonham or Stanley Clarke), who could have pushed him to even greater heights than he achieved in his lifetime.

Hendrix was almost instantly popular after forming the EXPERIENCE in London, a major star until he died, and well-remembered ca. 1990. It would be hard to find a modern metal guitarist who has not been influenced by his music. See: RANDY CALIFORNIA, THREE MAN ARMY.

MARK PRENDERGAST
RACIAL REHABILITATION
New Statesman & Society, 28 April 1995

This year it'll be a quarter century since Jimi Hendrix died. Hendrix is possibly rock's greatest loss, a potent mixture of genius, talent and latent fury who sky-rocketed across the globe in a blaze of glory that today is impossible to imagine. During four action-packed years, Hendrix re-invented the notion of rock music and its appendant stardom like no one before him or since. Yet his death left much unresolved, a central issue being Hendrix's notion of blackness.

A new album titled *Voodoo Soup* attempts to place Hendrix firmly within the black milieu of American culture of the late 1960s. Its back cover shows him performing to a mixed audience in Harlem in September 1969. Most of the tracks feature Hendrix with the Band of Gypsies, an all-black group with bassist Billy Cox and drummer Buddy Miles. But is such pigeon-holing justified, or is the album simply a well-meaning anachronism? A reading of the history reveals that Hendrix was interested in developing a music where soul, funk, jazz and rock would be unified, yet his white management constantly pressurised him to return to the Experience days where he fronted a white English group and appealed to a massive white audience.

Today, in a so-called PC western world, we are used to issues of race being worked out in full. Is not the OJ Simpson trial in America so rivet-ing because it focuses a glaring light on barely-under-the-skin racial ten-sions that have infected the United States since colonial times? Yet in the 1960s there was a full-scale racial civil war raging in America. When Hendrix came to England it was a relief after the years spent scuffling in R&B and Soul bands on the segregated black American scene. For English musicians like Eric Clapton who worshipped the blues, he was a god. His transit to the UK, the contradictions of a black American in an English group, his psychedelic dandyism and love of pop form, sealed his integrity in the UK forever. According to Kathy Etchingham, his most important girlfriend, "Jimi saw no racial differences. The music was something he did. Here, in those days, a lot of people couldn't see colour. It wasn't a point of contention at that time. He once said to me that 'racism cuts both ways.' You've got to remember that Jimi was very aware; he chose to be very proud of being black, yet at the same time chose to be above it."

Harry Shapiro, author of the definitive Hendrix biography, *Electric Gypsy*, agrees. "At a time when young black audiences were into soul and funk, he was moving back towards older forms like black blues—and blues was associated with times best forgotten. Hendrix was his own man. He rejected alignment with black power politics and rejected the notion of the hippies. And though he made statements about Vietnam, you must remember that, as a former paratrooper, he supported the war there as late as 1968. I never got the impression that Hendrix was colour conscious. I believe wholeheartedly that Hendrix was colour blind."

Shapiro believes that attempts this anniversary year to make Jimi PC are "bullshit." Yet to myself, a black Irishman, Hendrix was a great hero. Someone who was loud and proud, flash and brilliant, who was feted for doing his own thing his own way. And his music really took off when he returned to the US and recorded the very black *Electric Ladyland,* an album still regarded by many as rock's highest peak. Today, to the likes of Terrence Trent D'Arby, Vernon Reid and Lenny Kravitz—all black rockers—Hendrix is the very reason they pick up a guitar.

Although stories of his part Cherokee Indian/Irish blood may be apocryphal, the historical evidence does point to Hendrix being very aware of his difference. After a row with Pete Townshend at Monterey Pop in 1967, the Who's guitarist asked Hendrix a favour on the way to the airport. Hendrix simply said: "Do you want me to autograph it, honkie?" From 1969 to 1970 (the period covered by *Voodoo Soup*), Hendrix went through a variety of groups, Gypsy Sons & Rainbows, Sky Church, the Ghetto Fighters and the Band of Gypsies in an attempt to come to terms with black pressures to form an all-black group. Etchingham sees it differently. Bypassing issues of race, she says: "At the time he'd had terrible problems on the road with the Experience musicians. People like the Band of Gypsies were old friends whom he could feel comfortable with."

There are many instances during their long tours of America of the Jimi Hendrix Experience witnessing or being subject to ego-crushing racism. During the 1960s, de-segregation was still an issue—it wasn't that long since Billie Holiday had had to darken her face to play black venues and make alternative dining arrangements when she played white halls. Yet it's fundamentally true that once Hendrix had broken up the Experience and was living and working in the US, all sorts of new possibilities, many with black artists, were beginning to take shape. He was meeting the likes of Sly Stone and Stevie Wonder and affiliations were being drawn with Miles Davis. Music rehearsals with orchestral jazz arranger Gil Evans, which fused Gospel and other black idioms, were due to take place at the time of his death. Harry Shapiro concurs: "It's probably true that had he lived he would have directed more at black audiences."

Today, the likes of white American producer Bill Laswell can quite unself-consciously make records where hardcore American black musicians like Bootsy Collins, Eddie Hazel and Sonny Sharrock openly play in the spirit of Hendrix, but within an idiom that is more completely black. Who could ask for more?

"DREAMER," FROM THE TALK OF THE TOWN
The New Yorker, 31 December 1990

Pepe Karmel is an art historian who is preparing a comprehensive catalogue of Picasso's Cubist drawings. In Paris this summer, he came upon a stockbook of the art dealer D.- H. Kahnweiler detailing the order in which Picasso and Braque delivered various pictures to Kahnweiler's gallery—a development that is in the process of yielding new dates for several key works in early modern art. Pepe is also working right now on a long article about a forgotten collector named Frank Haviland, who may have been the subject of a long-lost portrait by Picasso, a version of which Pepe believes may be present in a 1912 photograph of Picasso in his studio. One afternoon earlier this month, however, Pepe put aside all these labors long enough to visit Sotheby's exhibition galleries, on York Avenue, and, walking past some Japanese lacquerwork that was to be auctioned later that week, headed for a gallery devoted to the pre-sale exhibition of artifacts and memorabilia related to the other consuming passion of his life—the American electric guitarist Jimi Hendrix.

"I was listening to the 'Live at Winterland' CD last night," Pepe said to a friend whom he had invited to join him in inspecting Hendrixiana. "It's a posthumous release. I heard it for the first time on the radio one afternoon while I was working on Picasso, and it has become my favorite Hendrix album. You know, the point of Hendrix's genius was to take blues and break open its rhythmic structure—open it up to space and silence and freeform noise. In this sense, he's very much a swimmer against the tide of the rock trends of his time, where the whole point was either to reimpose a classical sense of time and order, as the Beatles did, or to pare down and amplify blues rhythm until it became a brutal, overwhelming force. Clapton did that, and so, in another way, did Jimmy Page. Hendrix was a dreamer at extremely high volume. What flutes, harpsichords, and violins had been to an earlier time, fuzzboxes, wah-wah pedals and tremolo bars were to him."

With that, Pepe plunged downstairs into Sotheby's exhibition space, where framed sheets of hotel stationery with Hendrix's drafts of song lyrics hung on the walls, and items of memorabilia (old clothes, old totems, old love belts) were inside vitrines. Pepe walked up to the nearest wall and began to scrutinize Hendrix's lyric sheets.

"They're written in such a careful, studied hand," he said. "So few erasures or crossouts. What's more—" He broke off to look at a sheet titled "Purple Haze," whose first few lines read, "Purple Haze . . . Beyond insane Is it pleasure or is it pain—Down on the ceiling looking up at the Bed See my Body painted Blue and red." "Ha!" he said. "Look at that, a *totally different* original lyrical conception of 'Purple Haze'! The final draft, as you know, is much more erotic—'That girl put a spell on me,' and so on. This is much more self-directed, more self-regarding. I always sense in everything Hendrix wrote a powerful note of insecurity. Now, *this*"—Pepe moved to the next item on the wall—"is *related* to the lyrics for 'Crosstown Traffic' but not *identical* with them. I think we're beginning to develop a whole new picture of Hendrix's technique here. The number of lyrical pentimenti is astounding!" He continued to glide along the wall, and was soon looking at a contract signed by Hendrix. "Well, it's hard to understand what this is about, but one feels for a certainty that he was getting screwed. And now this." He stopped and pored over one more sheet of Hendrix's handwriting, and then said softly, "Now, this is a *fundamental* discovery." The paper bore a simple lyric and elementary chord patterns (E, B, F-sharp, and D, A, E) and the words "Repeat twice—then break with guitar and Bells—Guitar 1st E string ring open as B and G strings playing slight oriental pattern together. B string notes start on 7th fret with G string on 6th. (Like so: 7 [1,2,3] 10 [1,2,3] 12 . . . then 5 [1,2,3] 7 [1,2,3] 10) Repeat with low click of bass and slide guitar coming from down notes to up—Then vocal, and at the same time guitar hitting G chord and bass string and bass guitar hitting A . . . then syncopate chords of B min, C# min, D, up to G . . . then to B."

"Isn't that amazing!" Pepe said. "He knew in advance *exactly* what he wanted to do in each solo, and could articulate it quite precisely. All the fog and fuzz of slides and wails and feedback were precisely calibrated in advance, and articulated to the band. *That's* fundamental. I don't think he could read music, and so when he wanted to transcribe his musical ideas he had to do it in this way—as a *narrative*, a little memo to himself."

Pepe concluded his tour of the Hendrix memorabilia (which was scheduled for auction on December 17th), and afterward, over a hamburger, he mused for a few moments about his feeling for the musician. "I used to think that noise played the role for Hendrix that chance played for Pollock," he said. "How much can you incorporate and still have art at all? In that sense, the discovery of his extreme premeditation might be surprising. But lately I've come round in any case to the feeling that that's a very superficial analysis. Hendrix's music is really a question of timbre: the howl of feedback, the roar of distortion—all those elements that a musicologist would call 'coloration.' He got rid of chordal complexity so he could concentrate on tonal complexity. So that sheet is really an attempt to put his search into words. In the hands of his imitators, of course, Hendrix's example, like Picasso's, was to offer a catalogue of effects. For Hendrix, though, the noise was never noise, and the effects were never effects. It was all simply music."

TOM GOGOLA
JIMI HENDRIX 1942–1995
New York Press, 27 September–3 October 1995

As the last searing notes of "Hear My Train A Comin'" dissipated into the Cleveland evening, Jimi Hendrix stood bathed in light and looked out at the fans and celebrities who'd gathered for the opening ceremonies of the Rock and Roll Hall of Fame.

He was weeping.

Jimi's first performance outside the Seattle club scene in five years had been a difficult one. Al Hendrix, his father and manager, had urged him to play the opening, even though the Hall of Fame mandarins had insisted Jimi play only old Experience numbers and absolutely forbade him from playing *any jazz at all*. It had taken a lot out of Jimi to play "Purple Haze" without the benefit of a bank of Theremins and a chamber orchestra, but he'd managed to crank it out in a spirited, if perfunctory, manner.

The crowd grew silent as Jimi looked out, crying. "You know, a lot of my friends, old and new, are here in memory only. Kurt, Janis, John— I'm here to commemorate them today." At the mention of the three fallen idols, the crowd respectfully applauded, then grew silent again. All eyes were on Jimi, including those of Mitch Mitchell and Billy Cox, his core band over the past twenty-five years. The promoters had demanded that Jimi close his set with "Voodoo Chile (Slight Return)," and they were waiting for the opening wah-wah riff when Jimi cracked a joke: "When are the Plaster Casters gonna get an exhibit here?" It broke the maudlin spell; turning to Mitch and Billy, Jimi shouted, "Let's take them all the way back—it's time for a sacrifice!" He bashed out the opening chords to "Smells Like Teen Spirit," and broke into "Wild Thing."

The promoters were delirious. This was even better than "Voodoo." Jimi was the Wild Man From Borneo all over again! Summer of Love redux! Jann Wenner later claimed to have ejaculated "the moment Jimi hit those chords."

Ten minutes into it, Jimi had taken "Wild Thing" to the furthest reaches its I-IV-V progression would allow. Then, as he'd done at Monterey nearly thirty years before, he produced a can of lighter fluid and splurted the accelerant on his Stratocaster.

Those closest to him onstage would later remark that Jimi entered into a transcendent state of pure ecstasy and cosmic redemption at this point: "It was as though the whole terrible business with Kurt Cobain had finally been purged," said Mitchell, "and he was starting over."

Jimi squatted down, lit a match, and dropped it on the Strat. But he'd used *too much* fluid, and friends, fans and family who'd just watched his rebirth now recoiled in horror as the flames engulfed him. When the smoke finally cleared, Jimi Hendrix, the greatest musician of the twentieth century, was dead at fifty-two.

* * *

Hendrix's death came almost exactly twenty-five years after his near-fatal overdose on sleeping pills in London. This strange and terrible twist of fate is all the more ironic because when Jimi came out of his drug coma in late September 1970, he was a reborn man. He would never take another pill, drink another jug of wine, smoke another joint or take another hit of acid. Remarkably, his output over the next twenty-five years would stretch as far and deep as the universe that was forever unfolding before him. And he was straight for all of it.

When Jimi came out of the coma, his dad, Al Hendrix, and fiancée, Monika Dannemann, were in the room; they'd kept a vigil, and both were determined to protect him from himself and the worst temptations of the rock lifestyle. John Lennon was there, too; he and Jimi would be close friends until Lennon's assassination in 1980.

While Jimi recovered, Al stripped the Hendrix operation to its bare bones. Longtime roadie Gerry Stickells was fired. Jazz producer and manager Alan Douglas was gone. Engineer Eddie Kramer would last only until friction between he and Bill Laswell led to Kramer's exodus. Manager

Mike Jeffery was kept on for a few months, until Al had full control of the books; then he was out, too.

A shaken Hendrix put his faith in his father to straighten out his finances and personal life. When his friend Janis Joplin died within days of his emergence from the coma, Al's nearly desperate protectiveness made all the more sense to Jimi.

"Death is the ultimate mystery, the ultimate god; it's the mystery train hooting its horn through the mist," Jimi told *Rolling Stone* that October, recovering at his Woodstock retreat. "Dig, I saw it—the white light, everything. Coming out of that, you think it's time to get serious, really start feeling the blues, the power of soul, the mud in your toes and all that. Coltrane came around eventually too, but it was too late for him. This is a family affair now, and we're gonna work it all out."

Jimi had a commitment to Reprise to finish work on *First Rays of the New Rising Sun,* but first he wanted to memorialize Joplin, and went into Electric Lady in December of 1970 to record *Pearl Diver.*

Pearl Diver was initially lambasted for exploiting Janis' death, and for its cover art, a Robert Williams painting of Hendrix swimming toward a giant gaping and *hairy* clam at the bottom of the ocean. Jimi's sizable endowment flutters in the current as a bright white glow comes from the bisexual bivalve's center. "Big Muff Diver is more like it," sneered writer Richard Meltzer. But its apparent misogyny was a misinterpretation; the cover symbolized Hendrix's exploration of the spiritual side of sexuality, its fluidity in act and identity alike.

"We just thought, what would Janis want it to be," Hendrix told *Billboard,* after his elegiac cover of "Piece of My Heart" shot to number one in April of 1971. "Janis was raunchy, yeah, so we thought she woulda dug this imagery. I was snorkeling in Jamaica after we finished the record, and this idea just came to me, of finding Janis down at the bottom of the ocean, holding court over all the freaky fishes and such."

Most fans dug the cover; the tribute itself, featuring soul rave-ups and freak-outs of Janis' best material, absolutely *smoked.* When Jimi himself came out as a bisexual later that year, admitting to Ellen Willis in a seminal *Village Voice* piece, "Breaking the Plaster Cast," that he'd had a fling with gay, black sci-fi writer Samuel Delany in 1969, the emergent gay and feminist movements pilloried the straight-white-boy rock-crit establishment and praised Jimi for his campy, self-referential cover art. "Jimi has come a long way from grinding his crotch with the yellow-underwear girl in the third row and drooling over his own tit-splashed cover art for *Electric Ladyland,*" Willis wrote. "He'd always been the spokesman of the radical hippie male; now his feminism is fuzzy, in all the warm ways."

* * *

By January 1971, Electric Lady Studios was thrumming with the sounds of the finishing touches of *First Rays of the New Rising Sun.*

When *First Rays,* the first—and last—quadruple rock album ever recorded, was released that spring, critics mused that Jimi had taken the excesses of his former life and channeled them into his music.

"Yeah, you could say that," Jimi told writer Robert Christgau. "I had all these writings, these crazy drug scribblings and doo-dads of songs I wanted to get out; that I had to get out. Like when America went to the moon—I had to get there, get it done."

Although Reprise balked at the idea, the label knew this would be Jimi's last studio record with them, and they ultimately decided to go out with a bang—but only after Al and Jimi appeased the money men by knocking two points off Jimi's take. Mike Jeffery had warned Jimi about the unmarketability of a double album; with a four-album opus in the works, he left the Hendrix operation fully convinced that Al was slipping Jimi some new drug.

First Rays was a smash, debuting at number one and staying there for twenty-four weeks. It produced five hit singles ("Ezy Ryder," "Freedom," "Angel," "Room Full of Mirrors" and "Dolly Dagger"), a record which wouldn't be eclipsed until Michael Jackson's *Thriller* (and Jimi played guitar on that, too!).

Jimi was content to stay in the studio for a while, which pleased Al; record-high revenues from album sales eased the labels' pressure on him to tour, as did revenues from a series of live concerts from 1967 to 1970, which Reprise released that May.

But Jimi had to play out sometimes, so Al arranged dozens of impromptu appearances throughout 1971 and early 1972 at Greenwich Village clubs; all of these were recorded and released in Jimi's lifetime, on Third Stone, the family label.

(Through 1995, the label's catalogue boasted an astonishing 479 releases—all by Jimi. The vast majority were inexpensive cassette releases of the "Jimi Jams" series; the rest were the dozens of live double LPs, and nine "official" studio albums.)

* * *

The first Third Stone release was Jimi's autobiographical *Black Gold,* which he'd been working on since 1970. Consisting of loose, bluesy jams recorded off the cuff at Electric Lady beginning in the summer of 1970, it was, in effect, a sort of aural *Prozac Nation,* describing in graphic, self-deprecating ways Jimi's recently concluded drug years, his dabble with death, his relationship with Monika, and the whole mess that had been his life in the late sixties. It was pretty lightweight on the musical end; the high point was the acoustic "Seattle Sunset," a bitter ode to his home city that would find its way onto his repertoire when he moved back there in the eighties.

Released while *First Rays* was still churning out hit singles, *Black Gold* was lauded for its lyrical honesty. ("Acid burned a hole in my soul / I thought I saw God / in a lightnin' rod / but it was just my soul / achin' for black gold / mesmerized by nothing / nothing at all . . .")

But hard-core Hendrix fans were worried: "Has Jimi gone soft in the simpering seventies?" wrote Michael Lydon in *Ramparts.* "Has he copped to singer/songwriter-itus and abandoned his magic wand, the Fender Strat he waves like a maestro? What's goin' on?"

Jimi Hendrix was, quite simply, entering adulthood, confronting his past and looking forward to the future. His experimentation would forevermore be confined and focused to his music. Jimi was settling in: He and Monika were married in Woodstock on Thanksgiving Day, 1971. By the end of 1972, they'd had a set of twins, Atlantis and Masala.

If *Black Gold* was a reflective contraction, then the second Third Stone record was an attempt at expansion. In early 1972, *Wah-Out,* Jimi's much-anticipated collaboration with Miles Davis, hit the streets. Then it quickly hit the cut-out bins.

Jimi and Miles' only musical project is everything the title implies and more: a triple-album freakout of tuneless, funked-out wah-wah pedal excess. Jimi plays through a Crybaby *and* a Morley pedal at the same time for most of the album, while Miles nearly blows his brains out trying to keep up. Jimi had Juma Sultan on congas; Larry Lee on rhythm guitars; cameos by Herbie Hancock and Pharoah Sanders; and Mitch Mitchell, Tony Williams and Elvin Jones on drums throughout. Roland Kirk and Eric Dolphy contribute horns, and Billy Cox, Jaco Pastorius and Ron Carter contribute a bowel-blowout bass suite for much of the second side. Despite the attendant hoopla in jazz circles upon its release, *Wah-Out* was critically and commercially rejected as an all-star noise festival, despite some stellar jazz phrasings and wonderfully out solos by Hendrix, Sonny Sharrock and John McLaughlin on side three.

Wah-Out was recorded in a series of sessions through the summer of 1971. The tensions between Miles and Jimi blare through clearly, expressed either as rag-tag meanderings or a screeching battle of the wills. In 1970 they'd feuded over women and Jimi's inability to read musical score, but had set their differences aside—after Jimi sandbagged a planned project with Gil Evans at Al's insistence—for what should have been a stellar pairing of geniuses.

But once they got into the studio, serious spiritual fault lines quickly became apparent: Davis openly mocked Hendrix's hero status among white fans and critics—along with his newfound personal asceticism—while Davis' heroin and cocaine habits didn't sit well with Al Hendrix. Nor did Davis' criticism of Al for bagging Alan Douglas—who'd worked with much of the personnel on *Wah-Out* and knew how, as Davis bluntly told *Downbeat,* "to mix a motherfucking jazz album."

Defending his managerial and production skills, Al told the jazz mag, "We were tryin' to hook the two maestros onto a solid vibe that would pulse through and pulverize the land. Unfortunately, Miles was such a motherfucker to work with—the cat even stole my girlfriend!" Jimi and Miles would never play together again—one of the great tragedies of musical history.

* * *

Miles was right that *Wah-Out* needed Alan Douglas. But his critique of Hendrix for Uncle Tom-ing to white audiences was flat wrong. By 1971, Jimi's popularity had expanded well beyond the white hippies. The title track to *Black Gold* explicitly deals with the tensions Hendrix felt as a crossover musician: "Been from the chitlin circuit to a white man's circus / There's Jim Crow jamming / at a counter that won't serve us / But I'll play for black, for white, yellow and for brown / You can call me Uncle Tom, but it's just my heart's sound." Earnest, yes. But Jimi was sincere about his multicultural roots and the imperative of jazz to bridge the gaps, not contribute to the divide.

After *Wah-Out,* only the most liberatory-minded of the white hippies would stay with Hendrix as he moved further out of psychedelia into experimental soul, free jazz, "acid funk" and what he dubbed "free blues." It wasn't that Jimi abandoned his white audiences: Anyone could come along for the ride, but Jimi was gonna drive that bus! Jimi wouldn't cater to white audiences screaming for the "Wild Thing" bump-and-grind, playing-with-his-teeth shtick, but he wouldn't turn his back on them either.

Among black fans, his relationship with multi-saxophonist Roland Kirk is telling: Kirk appears briefly on *Wah-Out,* and became a lifelong friend of Jimi's despite the album's flop—and despite the fact that Hendrix, unlike Kirk, rejected Islam for its misogyny and militant sectarianism among Black Muslims. But he'd still play with anybody.

"People just want to hear the jammin'," Jimi told Christgau that fall. "It's up to me and whoever's pounding and pulsing along, to bring it all to a higher plane. It's gonna be a long ride, sometimes bumpy, but that's what experimenting is all about."

No one would have ever guessed what a ride it would be when, on the heels of *Wah-Out,* in early 1972, the seminal *Free Blues* LP was released. *Free Blues* shattered all conceptions of what was marketable in the countercultural music bins. The double album was hailed as simultaneously the best rock, blues, jazz and R&B record of all time. It is the Iron Man of albums, charting on *Billboard*'s Top 200 Albums to the day he died, leaving the second-longest charting album, *Dark Side of the Moon,* in the dust by years.

The sidelong remake of "My Favorite Things" and the astonishing complexity and yet breezy spontaneity of the title track mesmerized the nation. That thirteen-minute-long track swings, it shivers, it swan dives, it swoons. It is apocalyptic and redemptive, Coltrane's *Meditations* with a backbeat.

But more important than its commercial success, or its remarkable feat of bringing jazz to arena-jazz status, *Free Blues* reenergized the militant agitators from the New Left. For the increasingly diasporic activists who'd originally coalesced around the Civil Rights and Vietnam War movements, *Free Blues* became a new clarion call, the unofficial soundtrack for Democrat George McGovern's run for president that year. In June, the hardcore activist remnants of the New Left embarked on a voter registration drive beginning in the rural south, while Jimi and Al planned to take the Electric Church through the same territory. The synergy was amazing. Kicking the tour off in Atlanta, Jimi opened his show with "Drivin' South," the masterful boogie instrumental that he'd written during the Curtis Knight era. It was the first single off of *Free Blues.* By mid-June, as rebel activists cranked it up on I-95, tooling toward the Delta, "Drivin' South" was the number one single in America.

While Jimi played in rural cotton fields, fairgrounds and large roadhouses throughout the South, the activists registered record numbers of sharecroppers, factory workers and disfranchised blacks. And, as McGovern rose in the polls that summer, media attention to the two trains runnin' side by side through the South was keen and sustained.

By September, Jimi and the activists were hitting the northern industrial cities, and by election night, the whole parade was back in New York for a final show at Madison Square Garden. Critics would compare that concert to two other seminal Hendrix shows: his remarkable second set on New Year's Eve at the Fillmore East ushering in 1970, and his devastatingly bluesy improv set in riot-torn Newark following the assassination of Martin Luther King in 1968.

After blistering through the opening vamp of "Killin' Floor" (his opener during the Experience years), Jimi jumped on the tune, changing the lyrics to fit the moment: "I shoulda quit you Nixon, a long time ago." The Garden rocked in a hopeful, celebratory mood as Jimi pulled "Lover Man" out of the bag, then tantalized the crowd with the first few notes of "The Star-Spangled Banner" before kicking into "Drivin' South," the "new national anthem."

By now, the electoral tally was being projected on a giant screen behind Jimi. It was going to be close. Jimi kicked into "Machine Gun" and stayed on it as the vote was tallied and updated. When New York went for McGovern, his amps wheezed and swooned in delight. When Maine went for Nixon, they shivered and howled in disgust.

Three hours later, the staccato mantra of "Machine Gun" fired its last bullet when Nixon took California. Hendrix met the angry, unsettled roar of the crowd with a final electronic cataclysm. Then there was silence. "This one's goin' out to Tricky Dick," he hooted, obscenely lurching into the "Banner."

Richard Nixon had beaten George McGovern by the narrowest margin in the history of American Presidential elections. Nat Hentoff and Robert Christgau were seen hugging and sobbing backstage.

* * *

Nixon quickly struck back at Hendrix. He called on the Congress to draft a Constitutional amendment outlawing any attempt to "desecrate through obscene renditions the spirit and sanctity of the National Anthem." By mid-1973, Nixon had pressured the IRS to audit Hendrix, and ultimately brought to bear a $6 million back taxes charge against Jimi. The FBI harassed him over charges brought to light first in the *Wall Street Journal*—later learned to be planted by Pat Buchanan—that $300,000 of undeclared income had been funneled by Jimi to the Weather Underground, helping finance their jailbreak of Timothy Leary, a number of bombings, and the purchase of the 11th Street Townhouse. In truth, as

Al told *Rolling Stone,* the missing income was all from the pre-1971 era, and most of it had likely been spent on drugs by Jimi's out-of-control entourage.

Jimi's legal troubles ended with Nixon's resignation in 1974, and he left America for a two-year world tour. He wouldn't record another studio album until 1981; every release in the decade-long interim were "Jimi Jams."

During the world tour, Jimi became an Alan Lomax of World Music, collecting sounds and jamming with musicians from a staggering diversity of backgrounds and approaches. He traveled to Egypt, India, China, New Zealand, all across the African and Asian continents, Argentina, Brazil, Venezuela and Thailand. Monika joined him from New York with Masala and Atlantis for vacations, and he'd send her back with hundreds of hours of tapes, which would eventually be released as "Jimi Jams." Back in the States, Al catalogued the tapes, and put out a number of live releases from the 1972 tour, working out of the family compound near Woodstock.

America was a different place when Jimi returned in 1976. He encountered two distinctly different musical trends: punk and disco. The former sounded doomed and nihilistic; the latter, glibly celebratory. Both sounded to Jimi like the very soul of music had been ground out, viciously and deliberately.

Jimi and Al sorted through the catalogue of world music he'd amassed, and planned the release of the first batch of new "Jimi Jams." In Al's view, although everything his son played was quality commodity, most of the material didn't warrant the expense of a full studio treatment. Instead, the "Jams" were marketed and manufactured cheaply, on cassette, and provided a consistent source of income for the family.

A lot of the "Jams" are noodling shit, or half-baked alternate takes of stuff, studio chatter, Jimi recording sounds at the zoo. A third of the "Jams" have a version of "Red House" on them. Some feature Jimi playing solo, while others are fully orchestrated but commercially suicidal projects.

Explaining the "Jams," Jimi told *Guitar World*: "It got to a point where people just wanted to hear everything I ever played, like when we'd be gettin' the horns together, waiting for the various players to show up in the studio, other folks would always stop by and we'd do a few oldies but goodies. Or, I'd be traveling, and maybe do a little pickup band thing in Zaire that we'd record on the portable. We're not going to put that on vinyl, but people still want to hear it all. Now they can."

The best of the "Jams" are Jimi plowing through R&B standards during studio warm-ups; a few soundcheck gems also pop up here and there. "Purple Haze" is covered no fewer than forty times, ranging from a fully orchestrated version to one with steel drums to a bizarre take with Robert Plant on recorder, Ravi Shankar on sitar, Allen Ginsberg on concertina and Jimi on drums.

With the "Jams" series coming together, Jimi wanted to do a short tour at the end of the summer of '76. Despite his misgivings about dance music, "Disco Jimi," as the rock press derisively called him, got into a heavy, synthed-out groove for much of the tour. The stakes were nowhere as high as they'd been in '72, as Carter rode high in the polls and America swapped partners and did the hustle. Old Band of Gypsies numbers ("Message of Love," "Changes") were funked out even further, speeded up and given fat electronic beats to make them more danceable. Jimi double-billed with gay disco superstar Sylvester at the Hollywood Bowl in mid-August, and jammed again with Sly, Bootsy and George Clinton. It was a happy, laid back time for Jimi and his family.

But the year ended in tragedy when his son, Masala, was hit by a car and killed in New York City during a holiday shopping trip. Jimi would spend most of 1977 at the family compound with Monika recovering from the terrible shock. They decided to have another child, and in September of 1978 Monika gave birth to their second son, Leo.

Punk rock had no sympathy for Jimi's troubles. When a batch of fifteen "Jams" were released in early 1978, Lester Bangs, writing in the *Village Voice,* fired the opening salvo. "It's time to jam these 'Jams' into an incinerator. This latest orgiastic free-for-all features Jimmy Smith, Johnny Winter, Rod Stewart, the entire population of Peoria, the editorial board of the *New York Times,* and my mother performing an overindulgent, hour-long 'Voodoo Chile' blowout. I say it's a doo-doo pile. I want my money back. Bring me the clenched, minimalist sphincter of the Ramones, immediately!"

The "Jams" *were* excessive—witness the hour-and-a-half cover of Jimi's pre-fame garage tune "Hornet's Nest." Jimi does one pass through as the song was originally played, a rawboned, trebly guitar part with a Hammond organ riffing a greasy, surfed-out hornet's buzz. But on each successive pass he replaces the organ with humming Tibetan Monks, ululating African warriors and an embarrassing orgasmic tremolo-howl by Patti Smith. By the record's end, they're all ululating and orgasming in tandem.

Taken as a whole, however, the "Jams" are a testament to Jimi's ability to play with *anyone*. A random sample: Nusrat Fateh Ali Khan, David

Bowie, Archie Shepp, McCoy Tyner, Borbetomagus, Nina Simone, Curtis Mayfield, Jim Croce, Rudolph Grey, Jandek, Charles Gayle, Howlin' Wolf, Pat Benatar, Lou Rawls, Frank Tovey, Alex Chilton and Morrissey.

In 1981, a year after his close friend John Lennon was assassinated, an angry Jimi released *Pistol*. His first bona fide studio recording since *Free Blues*, it was a bitter testament to his slain friend, but also a reaction to the thrashing he had endured from punk rockers. Shuffling between Woodstock and New York through the late seventies and early eighties, Hendrix had explored no-wave and the "industrial" scene (though disgusted by Throbbing Gristle's self-mutilating stage antics, according to Monika he did go in for a Prince Albert piercing "the size of a dumbbell" after marveling at Genesis P. Orridge's) and it had obviously rubbed off.

Pistol was Jimi's equivalent to Neil Young's unfortunate *Trans*. It was a reactionary, gimmicky, callow effort characterized by senseless feedback loops and atonal guitar frenzies. Some critics insisted it was Jimi's way of forcing a positive review out of Bangs, who'd written a rave of Lou Reed's *Metal Machine Music* in 1976 and now was faced with an even more remarkably jangled and pointless recording to mull over. But Bangs ignored it. If there's a telling moment, it's the remake of "Manic Depression" in which the song is slowed to a bizarre, codeined slur.

After *Pistol*, an exhausted and spiritually drained Jimi left his family behind in Woodstock and embarked on a year-long pilgrimage along the southwest coast of Africa, where the Namib Desert meets the Atlantic Ocean. Returning to the States in late 1982, he got to work on his next studio LP, *Super Nova Surfboard*. His jaunt along the unforgiving desert coast had had the desired effect: *Super Nova* was the first album to successfully mix experimental jazz with surf rock, Indian raga and tribal drumming, the high point being the entire second side, a remake of "Third Stone from the Sun," featuring the surf-riff maestro himself, Dick Dale.

Dale and Hendrix had been friends since the late sixties, and Dale's appearance on "Third Stone" was more than just another ace musician joining Hendrix in the studio. When he first recorded "Third Stone," in 1967, Jimi said, "And you'll never hear . . . surf music again." The line was a tribute to Dale, who'd been diagnosed with colon cancer that year and wasn't expected to live. He did, of course, and became a hardcore vegetarian health nut.

On the remake, Dale and Hendrix are laughing when they get to that line, and change it to, "And you'll never eat . . . surf 'n' turf again." The album was well-received critically; the combination of blistering surf licks with seagull-squawk saxophones, careening sitars, and relentless West

Indian drumming, all played at the speed of comets, was a welcome relief from Jimi's various debacles of the past half-decade.

* * *

Jimi's fascination with science fiction and time travel was always a constant source of inspiration and material. In 1984 he recorded a concept album based on Ray Bradbury's 1952 sci-fi story "A Sound of Thunder." In it, a time-travel company takes customers back to shoot dinosaurs from a platform they've set up in a prehistoric jungle. The company has already gone back and found a dinosaur that was about to be killed by a falling limb, and the hunter shoots it right before its natural death would have occurred, eliminating any chance that the shooting might alter the course of evolution or history.

In his first *Rolling Stone* interview in over a decade, Jimi explained the idea behind the album: "This guy, see, he goes back in time to shoot this big T-Rex, but he chickens out and falls off the path they've set up. He falls into the mud, and without realizing it, he carries this butterfly through time, on the bottom of his boot, this butterfly he's killed when he fell. The death of this delicate, silent creature changes everything, man.

"When they get back to the future, instead of the cool President Keith there's like this President who's just like Nixon, this mad fascist. And it's this whole scenario where there's just too many damn dead butterflies crushed under the boot, the Nazi jackboot. . . .

"I'm fascinated with the idea that one slight change, like this dead butterfly, can ripple through history and, like, change everything, ever-so-slightly but nonetheless changed."

A Sound of Thunder didn't sell very well—despite indie-rock guitar god Thurston Moore's whacked-out dinosaur sounds—as the yuppie imperatives of the mid-eighties outpaced Hendrix's militant, if playful, agitating. During one section, the only discernible "song" on the album, Jimi takes the Orwell year and re-flips it, covering "If Six Was Nine" as "If Four Was Eight" ("I'll be late, to the fascist state").

Jimi was very excited about the project, which musically had strains of death metal, pure noise, acid jazz, and balladeering arranged masterfully. But there wasn't a salable single from the Bradbury tribute, and his twenty-eight-minute-long concept video never made it onto MTV, which had evidently decided by then that Michael Jackson would be its black freak of choice. Jimi had provided the guitar solo for "Beat It"; it wound up being the only Hendrix anyone would ever hear on MTV, until his Kurt Cobain tribute in 1994.

The late eighties found Jimi playing assorted jazz and rock festivals, but mostly devoting his time to raising his family and traveling. The Hendrixes moved to France for two years, and Jimi traveled to Moscow, then to India, Turkey and Vietnam, collecting sounds and jamming.

By 1987, Al Hendrix was determined to move the family back to Seattle. Monika liked the idea, but Jimi was skeptical until Al told him about Seattle's burgeoning music scene. Jimi took an exploratory trip and found that many of the new bands were playing derivations of his early efforts (albeit more tattered versions). The family made the move, and soon enough, Jimi was sighted at various small clubs in Seattle, sitting with a club soda and a grin as he took in the new sounds.

"Wither Hendrix?" wondered *Rolling Stone* in late 1988. By then, Jimi was a regular city father/scenester. Michael Azerrad reported seeing "cheap, white, grubby imitations of Hendrix in the form of bands with names like Mudhoney, Nirvana and the Sky Cries Mary."

Hendrix's career had come full circle. Before long, he was playing blues and old R&B numbers with pickup bands around town; this had always been his most comfortable forum for expression. Heavy on his repertoire was "Hear My Train A Comin'"—as its lyric dealt with "leavin' this town" only to come back and buy it—and a folky "Spanish Castle Magic."

It was Greenwich Village circa 1971 all over again. The buzz about Hendrix's appearances fed the blossoming music scene and led to a media fixation with the city. Al, working with Sub Pop records, released a number of "Jams" chronicling the rise of the Seattle music scene.

In 1991, Jimi released his autobiography. That fall, *James Marshall Hendrix* rose up the bestseller lists in tandem with Nirvana's ascent on the music charts. Hendrix watched with pride as his prodigal bands basked in the spotlight. Punk rock had forgiven Hendrix's excesses and, in Seattle at least, had taken the best of them and rolled them into a grinding mash called grunge.

Rolling Stone revisited Seattle in mid-1992 and declared that Nirvana's Kurt Cobain was the "John Lennon of his Generation," marveling at the irony of Hendrix and Nirvana's planned collaboration. But the Nirvana project was cut off violently when Eddie Vedder, the jealous and unstable lead singer of the previously unknown band Pearl Jam, shot and killed Cobain while he and Hendrix were checking out the Spinanes at the Crocodile Club in 1994.

At his trial, Vedder's lawyers tried to prove that he'd been victimized by bullies in high school and never got over the humiliation. Under cross-examination, Hendrix admitted that Vedder had blurted out something incomprehensible about some kid named "Jeremy" before shooting Cobain. But the jury didn't buy it and gave him life.

Hendrix channeled his despair into music. Earlier this year Third Stone/Sub Pop released his tribute album to Cobain, which featured former members of Nirvana and other Seattle musicians. His bluesy solo cover of the slow-churning "Been a Son" charted at number one; an acoustic "All Apologies," recorded live in Seattle, made MTV's heavy rotation.

* * *

Jimi had wanted to play the tribute material at the Rock and Roll Hall of Fame, but instead was compelled to rummage through the old Experience catalog. When he abruptly ended "Foxy Lady" right before the solo break, he told the audience:

"You know I did this album a few years ago, maybe y'all heard of it, called *A Sound of Thunder*. And dig, there was the sound of thunder from the dinosaur roaring, and the sound of thunder when the guy got shot, the guy who'd ruined everything by killing that butterfly. He'd fallen off the path 'cause he was scared. Man, things didn't have to work out that way."

When he then broke into a staggeringly sad "Hear My Train A Comin'," everyone knew he was playing it for Kurt.

Moments later, the train would thunder down the track for Jimi, and he'd join all the other dead dinosaurs and butterflies who'd been crushed out before their time.

ANDY ELLIS
STILL REIGNING, STILL DREAMING
Guitar Player, September 1995

The story of electric guitar will forever be told in two parts: Before Jimi and After Jimi. Before Jimi, visionary players used the instrument as a powerful voice *within* an accepted musical setting. Great pioneers such as Charlie Christian, T-Bone Walker, Les Paul, B. B. King, Chuck Berry, Jimmy Bryant, Jimmy Nolen, Wes Montgomery, Dick Dale, Jeff Beck, and Pete Townshend pushed the instrument's boundaries in the context of their chosen genre. These players gave us marvelous and diverse sounds, expanded our horizons, and bequeathed us lifetimes of work to study, emulate, and build upon.

But when Jimi exploded on the scene with "Purple Haze," "Manic Depression," and "Third Stone From The Sun," in a flash we understood: Here was a *music* beyond anything ever heard before, conceived and born of electric guitar. The instrument was inseparable from the song. A sonic universe, full of strange and compelling textures and timbres, issued from Jimi's wailing Stratocaster. Hendrix liberated the electric guitar from playing mere notes and rhythm. In his hands, it became a three-dimensional sound machine—a second voice, capable of utterances beyond our comprehension.

What was he thinking? Why hadn't anyone else ever even *hinted* at this tidal wave of incandescent sound? Jimi's music made perfect sense, once you got over the shock. But imagine how Hendrix must have felt as he nurtured his vision, alone and unknown.

Here's the mystery: What the hell happened to Jimi in the summer of 1966? Listen to him as a sideman on Curtis Knight recordings cut at that time, and you'll hear a merely competent R&B player: Ike Turner and others would have *smoked* him. Then came Jimmy James And The Blue Flames, the short-lived petri dish in which Jimi cultured his newfangled ideas (this was the band Chas Chandler heard at New York's Café Wha?). Within a year, Hendrix gave us "Purple Haze" and blew our minds.

It's amazing, when you think about it: Jimi's electrifying music emerged fully formed. There's nothing tentative about *Are You Experienced*. Jimi didn't need a few albums to discover his voice and hit his stride. With his mates, he cut that first record fast and cheap on a lumbering 5-track reel-to-reel machine. Bang, bang—Hendrix knocked out such gems as "The Wind Cries Mary," "Fire," "Hey Joe," "May This Be Love," "Foxy Lady," "Third Stone From The Sun," and "Are You Experienced?" No one does that today.

Jimi's genie was out of the bottle.

Not necessarily stoned, but beautiful

Many postulate that Hendrix' purported acid experiences instigated this incredible burst of creativity and was the inspiration for his entire *oeuvre*. Anyone who has listened to Hendrix while tripping knows that Jimi *played* the sound of LSD. However, if it came down to a mere magic pill, we'd all be voodoo chiles. How many players, in an attempt to achieve Jimi's luminescence, instead went up like a Roman candle. Flame on, game over.

Ultimately, it doesn't really matter whether, as Hendrix himself alluded to in his interviews and lyrics, he was visiting from another planet or he simply managed to wrest open the doors of creativity most of us keep welded shut. Onstage and in the studio, Jimi's message was *let go and play*. His music reminds us that scales, modes, and chord inversions are but TinkerToys in the grand scheme of music creation. Put away the childish things, his guitar still whispers, reach higher and deeper, and follow your heart.

Some music soothes and heals. To these ears, that's *not* what Jimi was about. A thunderbolt from the sky, destined to shake us to our core, Jimi was on a mission to wrench us from complacency. He was a disruptive force. In today's eclectic world, it's tough to appreciate how radical he appeared in 1967. He dressed and played and talked and lived differently from the rest. Jimi stretched our concept of sound, songwriting, and social behavior. He reminded us that guitar's roots lie deep in Gypsy soil. Its heartbeat is heard around campfires, not in a classroom.

Jimi was a pathfinder: To those who like warping a guitar signal beyond all recognition, he is the father of electronic guitar. Others who love '50s blues and R&B see Jimi as the keeper of the flame. By holographically encoding the sound of this era in his music, he preserved the message so today's teens can rediscover it. Hendrix was the prototypical black rocker—a model for Prince, Vernon Reid, and Lenny Kravitz, among others—yet he also transcended race, class, and nationality. To devotees of the psychedelic state, he was a cosmic cartographer, exploring uncharted territory and recounting his journeys in song.

Will I live tomorrow?

Players love to speculate about what Hendrix would be playing today, were he still alive. Though you may disagree, it's hard for me to imagine that Jimi's slight frame could house such an intense, magical, freaked-out, guitar-fevered force for this long. While most of us drone along at our allocated psychic voltage, Hendrix was clearly operating at a higher amperage. Ever have one of those nights onstage where everything just flows? Jimi *lived* there, as a host of concert CDs and videos will attest. But there's a limit to how brightly anyone can glow before blowing a fuse. I believe that eventually Jimi would have tripped a circuit breaker had he not gone off line.

Though Hendrix is gone—it'll be 25 years this September—his music is more alive and vital today than most anything we hear on the radio. No matter how often you spin "Voodoo Child (A Slight Return)," "Axis: Bold As Love," "Stone Free," "Little Wing," or "Castles Made Of Sand"— name your fave Jimi song—each hearing reveals something new.

Tomorrow, like tonight and yesterday and countless nights before, when I need a dose of psychic Liquid Wrench to loosen my mind from whatever it's reflexively gripping, I'll reach for my Hendrix stash, pop in a disc, and turn down the lights. You too?

See y'all in Electric Ladyland . . . and don't be late.

PART SEVEN

Dig

*I'd like to get
something together,
like with Handel,
and Bach, and
Muddy Waters, fla-
menco type of
thing [laughs]. If I
can get that* sound.
If I could get that
sound, *I'd be
happy.*

BOB HICKS
JIMI HENDRIX: A MEMORIAL
Northwest Passage, 29 September 1970

Jimi Hendrix died the other day. They say it was an overdose of drugs, and I believe them, though of course I've heard it whispered that it wasn't that at all, that he was murdered because he was becoming a threat to THEM. Maybe so, but I doubt it. They said that about Lenny Bruce, too. Both were tortured men.

Hendrix was horrified by self-destruction, and at the same time fascinated by it. It—and its exposure—were ultimately to be his life's work. Ironically, in the process of staving off self-destruction—of keeping from giving up by living a large, intense life—he became to many a pop political-worship figure which encouraged them to destroy their own human potentialities by living a vicarious life through the accomplishments of others. And in the end, of course, he lost his own battle for life.

Jimi Hendrix was a complicated man and, I think, within the limited sphere of the music world, an important one. He was a genius (I would have said "unquestionably a genius," but many fine musicians who unfortunately live entirely in the past have either never heard of him or, because they do not understand the present in which he worked, dismiss him as a dangerous musical charlatan or an inconsequential quack).

Though current critics tend to think of him as the consummate craftsman of a somewhat limited form of entertainment, I sense that history will define his role as a more important one than that. Hendrix' music seems to be creating the same sort of Caliban-to-Prospero metamorphosis in rock that the music of Charlie Parker created in jazz 25 years ago. As Parker had done a generation earlier, Hendrix added an ever-present, intensely controlled and controlling intellect to a guts-and-blood emotional form of communication. With a handful of other rebel electromusicians, Hendrix began to change rock from a sexual substitute for frustrated abstainers and can't-get-enoughers into a powerful, articulate and wide-ranging *art* form.

I saw Jimi Hendrix perform live only once, about two years ago in Vancouver. He was playing with the Experience then, and still perfecting his style, but even at that time there was no question that he was the most musically mature and technically proficient personality on the hard rock scene. He played complete electric guitar, like Charlie Byrd, before he sold out to Columbia Records, used to play complete acoustical guitar. Then, Hendrix' most obvious merit was strength, an awesome primeval power of the psyche more than capable of knowing, understanding, manipulating not only the electrodal torrent of infuriated fire careening through his equipment, but also the thousands of screaming, self-lost idolaters come to worship at the feet.

I was a somewhat unwilling member of that Vancouver audience, having witnessed mass hysteria in the past and not wishing to repeat the experience. Even so, there was a kind of deadly fascination at the sight of 500 people, with single mindlessness, trampling forward, animal cries wrenching from their throats, at god-worship, and Hendrix, accustomed to it as he was, responding with a sad contempt, ordering the mob back to its seats before he would play, treating it with the same authority but with none of the love or respect he gave the wild electric forces within his equipment. The electrodes, mindless explosive non-creatures of nature, he treated with firm control. Powerful as they were, he gave them life and purpose, created a sensible unity out of what had been no sense and no unity. To the mindless he gave mind, but in the process, without wanting to, he sucked away the individual intellects of the swept-over in the audience, involuntarily making them want to cease functioning, to live their lives through him, to throw on him the burdens and responsibilities of their own lives, to make him think for them, act for them, play for them, sweat for them, screw for them, BE for them, while they sat in orgasm of self-annihilation.

This, I think, was one of the things that tore up Jimi Hendrix the man. Like every man who has ever been worshipped by other men, he knew he was not fit to be worshipped, and felt a revulsion and horror toward that mass which so willingly denigrated itself before his ultimately frail personal strength and power. By so articulately expressing his own vulnerable humanity he encouraged others to throw their humanity, their human potential, away; to give up the work of life, let others live for them.

Yet this was not a problem of his making. If many chose to make him a god, it was not because he asked to be one. It was because those people felt they needed a god, one they could see and hear and touch, to make their decisions for them; and because modern mass communications provided the means of god-making. Though the god-experience might have had a souring effect, though it might have added a motif of bitterness to his music—bitterness is almost omnipresent in the harsh thunderings of Hendrix' sounds—it is not as a reluctant fold-political phenomenon that he is most important. He was, and through his music is, an artist of high rank.

I do not mean to imply that Hendrix' music does not carry many political overtones. On the contrary, I believe his work was very political (not, of course, in the same sense that his personality became a political force), just as were the works of Picasso, Dostoevski, Beethoven, Chaucer and many others. To very roughly paraphrase Spinoza, whenever a man's work is plugged in to his times, it cannot help being political. But an artist creates an image which has a beauty and a truth of itself. The work of art is an image both complete and full—that is, it mirrors not only external, political reality, but the internal, psychological reality of the artist as well. In this Hendrix excelled.

For me, Hendrix reached his highest level of artistic maturity at the counter-culture's great white Bacchanalia—Woodstock. Not surprisingly, his work there was also his most politically deep and significant.

When a popular group comes up with a good performance, we usually say it "got it together." At Woodstock Hendrix did much more than get it together—he sculpted an electronic musical monument as carefully composed and finely rehearsed as any orchestral concert piece. It was a chillingly contemporary work, a vision of cultural crisis, of structural breakdown and chaos, screeching to an almost unbearable tension which must, somehow, burst.

The first movement—Hendrix' interpretation of "The Star Spangled Banner"—is a slimy, rotting ooze seeping obliviously on through a madman's maze of snarling unleashed demonia. It is the vast underbelly of a culture sinking, in Hendrix' mind, smugly into its death pit. Self destruction: the mouth tears great chunks of flesh from the bowel.

The bombs burst, the rockets flash. The mother weeps over her dead child; the child wanders wailing from the brutalized body that had been its mother; the bayonet gorges; the cities flame; the armies crust; hollowed men stumble from starvation; children betray their parents, betray their brothers; crowds crush each other, gasp for breath; and always, always the song drones on, through the laaaand of the freeee, and the hooooome of the braaave!—and then crash the song is over the power failure has come America it was falling down all around you and you didn't even look and chaos/struggle and suddenly a new raw driving orderly force and listen there's a melody, a vibrant honest melody.

Now a new order is begun and only the strong can live the cancer the rot the weeds must go. Every individual must be an energy unit capable of sustenance, capable of contribution, capable of self determination. A strong life, harsh but sweet in its fullness; a tonal glimpse of one future. A future of emotion, yes. But also a future guided by firm honest intellect.

Then the new song ends, and slowly slowly the voice of the crowd 400,000 strong deepens and rises and rises and splits the sky with a roar that lasts and lasts an age. Do they understand? Do they hear the message LIVE A LIFE, or do they merely sink a little lower toward self-destruction; grasp a little more firmly at one who lives his life, thinking he will live theirs too?

So. I was not surprised to hear that Jimi Hendrix was dead. He looked too deep too soon, and burned out. But he showed us part of what he saw. I admire him. I stand in awe of his work.

Discography

Hendrix recorded three studio albums with the Experience and one live album with his Band of Gypsys (see lists of songs below); *Smash Hits* is the only other Experience title he sanctioned during his lifetime, and that merely packaged previously released material. I'd recommend acquiring the titles below, on vinyl or cassette, in that order. Buy a bootleg and risk crappy sound reproduction and out-of-context jams. *Don't* buy reworked/reissued/repackaged/rereleased product at all; you'll risk bad karma.

Jimi Hendrix
Are You Experienced?

Purple Haze
Manic Depression
Hey Joe
Love or Confusion
May This Be Love
I Don't Live Today

The Wind Cries Mary
Fire
Third Stone from the Sun
Foxey Lady
Are You Experienced?

The Jimi Hendrix Experience
Axis: Bold as Love

EXP
Up from the Skies
Spanish Castle Magic
Little Wing
If Six Was Nine
One Rainy Wish

You've Got Me Floating
Castles Made of Sand
She's So Fine
Little Miss Lover
Bold as Love
Wait Until Tomorrow
Ain't No Telling

The Jimi Hendrix Experience
Electric Ladyland

. . . And the Gods Made Love
Have You Ever Been (to Electric Ladyland)
Crosstown Traffic
Voodoo Chile

Little Miss Strange
Long Hot Summer Night
Come On (Part 1)
Gypsy Eyes
Burning of the Midnight Lamp

Rainy Day, Dream Away
1983 . . . (A Merman I Should Turn to Be)
Moon, Turn the Tides . . . gently gently away

Still Raining, Still Dreaming
House Burning Down

All Along the Watchtower
Voodoo Child (Slight Return)

Hendrix
Band of Gypsys

Who Knows
Machine Gun

Changes
Power to Love
Message of Love
We Gotta Live Together

In addition to listening to the music, be sure to watch, if you can, *Jimi Hendrix* (1973) by Warner Home Video; it includes the Woodstock "Star-Spangled Banner," the Monterey "Wild Thing," and "Machine Gun" with the Gypsys. Great interviews, too, with Lou Reed, Mick Jagger, Al Hendrix, and the way cool Allen brothers.

Bibliography

Alexie, Sherman. "Because My Father Always Said He Was the Only Indian Who Saw Jimi Hendrix Play 'The Star-Spangled Banner' at Woodstock," *The Lone Ranger and Tonto Fistfight in Heaven,* pp. 24–36. New York: The Atlantic Monthly Press, 1993.

Alterman, Loraine. "Hendrix's All-New Band of Gypsys," *Rolling Stone,* 7 February 1970, p. 10.

Altham, Keith. "Hendrix IS Out of This World," *New Musical Express,* 15 April 1967, p. 4.

Aronowitz, Alfred G. "Brash Buccaneer with a Wa-Wa," *Life,* 15 March 1968, p. 8.

———. "The Final Tribute to Jimi Hendrix," *Circus,* November 1970, pp. 44–47.

Atlas, Jacoba, and Tony Glover, "A Jimi Hendrix Doubleheader," *Hullabaloo,* February 1969.

Bach, Frank. "Victims of the Plague," *Sun/Dance,* February 1971, pp. 2ff.

Bangs, Lester. "Death May Be Your Santa Claus: An Exclusive Up to Date Interview with Jimi Hendrix," *Creem,* April 1976, pp. 25ff.

Baraka, Amiri. "The 'Blues Aesthetic' and the 'Black Aesthetic': Aesthetics as the Continuing Political History of a Culture," *Black Music Research Journal,* Fall 1991, pp. 101–109.

Barnes, Bertrum, and Glen Wheeler. "A Lonely Fork in the Road," *Red Hot and Blue,* July 1990; reprinted in *Living Blues,* November/December 1990, pp. 26–28.

Baxter, Bob. "JH: Should He Have Played Right-handed?" *Guitar World,* September 1975, p. 72.

Bayles, Martha. *Hole in Our Soul*. New York: The Free Press, 1994.

"Blind Date: Jimi Hendrix," *Melody Maker*, 10 June 1967, p. 8.

Brackman, Jacob. "Overdosing on Life," *The New York Times*, 27 October 1970, Section L, p. 45.

Breskin, David. "Voodoo Child: The Rolling Stone Interview with Vernon Reid," *Rolling Stone*, 8–22 July 1993, pp. 87ff.

Brode, Douglas. "Jimi Hendrix," *Sepia*, September 1975, pp. 70–76.

Brown, Charles T. *The Art of Rock and Roll*. New York: Simon & Schuster, 1992.

Burks, John. "An Appreciation," *Rolling Stone*, 15 October 1970, pp. 8–9.

———. "The End of a Beginning Maybe," *Rolling Stone*, 19 March 1970, pp. 40–42.

Canby, Vincent. "'Jimi Plays Berkeley' at Garrick," *The New York Times*, 14 September 1971, p. 46.

Caruso, Paul. Letter to the editor, *Rolling Stone*, 22 June 1968.

Chenoweth, Lawrence. "The Rhetoric of Hope and Despair: A Study of the Jimi Hendrix Experience and the Jefferson Airplane," *American Quarterly*, Spring 1971, pp. 25–45.

Clarke, Paul. "'A Magic Science': Rock Music as a Recording Art," *Popular Music*, 1983, pp. 195–213.

Cromelin, Richard. "Tribute at Roxy Holds True to Hendrix Spirit," *Los Angeles Times Calendar*, 28 May 1986, p. 1ff.

Crouch, Stanley. "Bringing Atlantis Up to the Top," *The Village Voice*, 16 April 1979, pp. 65–67.

"Dreamer," from The Talk of the Town, *The New Yorker*, 31 December 1990, pp. 27–28.

Drummond, Norrie. "Bad Shows Bring Jimi Down," *New Musical Express*, 10 June 1967, p. 8.

Duff, S. L. "Jimi and the Monkees," *Guitar World*, March 1988, pp. 35ff.

Ellis, Andy. "Still Reigning, Still Dreaming: Why Is Hendrix Still So Damned Exciting?" *Guitar Player*, September 1995, pp. 57–61.

"Festival Pop Star Dies After Party," *The London Times*, 19 September 1970, p. 1.

Fisher, Annie. "Stadium Stomp," *The Village Voice*, 29 August 1968, pp. 36ff.

Fleming, Charles, and Jeff Giles. "Jimi, Rest in Peace," *Newsweek,* 16 January 1995, pp. 64–65.

Flooke, David. "Whitenoise?" *Crawdaddy,* September-October 1967, pp. 17–18.

Floyd, Samuel A., Jr. *The Power of Black Music: Interpreting Its History from Africa to the United States.* New York: Oxford University Press, 1995, pp. 201–203.

Fricke, David. "Jimi: The Man and the Music," *Rolling Stone,* 6 February 1992, pp. 40ff.

Gent, George. "Stars' Drug Deaths Stir Rock Scene," *The New York Times,* 3 November 1970, p. 26.

Gilroy, Paul. "Sounds Authentic: Black Music, Ethnicity, and the Challenge of a *Changing* Same," *Black Music Research Journal,* Fall 1991, pp. 111–136.

Goertzel, Ben. "The Rock Guitar Solo: From Expression to Simulation," *Popular Music and Society,* Spring 1991, pp. 91–101.

Gogola, Tom. "Jimi Hendrix 1942–1995," adapted from "Jimi Hendrix: A Life," *New York Press,* 27 September–3 October 1995, pp. 1ff; reprinted in *Guitar World,* January 1996, pp. 47ff.

Goldman, Albert. "SuperSpade Raises Atlantis," *Freakshow.* New York: Atheneum, 1971, pp. 85–91.

Goldstein, Richard. "Pop Eye," *The Village Voice,* 29 June 1967, pp. 17ff.

Gonzalez, David L. "Is There Life After Jimi?" *Newsweek,* 30 April 1990, pp. 68–69.

Goodman, George. "Black & White Fusion in the Now Music," *Look,* 7 January 1969, pp. 36–38.

Guitar Player, Jimi Hendrix edition, September 1975; September 1995.

Gwiazda, Henry. "Homage to Jimi: A New Music Composition," *Guitar Player,* March 1981, pp. 66–67.

Halasa, Malu. "Be Black and Rock," *News Statesman & Society,* 24 November 1989, pp. 52–54.

Hale, Mark. *HeadBangers: The Worldwide Megabook of Heavy Metal Bands.* Ann Arbor: Popular Culture Ink., 1993, p. 152.

Harris, James F. "The Experience Machine," *Philosophy at 33 1/3 rpm: Themes of Classic Rock Music,* pp. 134–136. Chicago: Open Court Publishing, 1993.

Hatay, Nona. *Jimi Hendrix: The Spirit Lives On . . .* San Francisco: Last Gasp, 1983.

Henderson, David. *The Life of Jimi Hendrix: 'Scuse Me While I Kiss the Sky.* New York: Doubleday, 1978.

"Hendrix Experience Hits New Noise Peak at N.Y. Concert with SRO 18 1/2G," *Variety,* 6 March 1968, p. 68.

"Hendrix' One-Year Retirement Plan," *Rolling Stone,* 17 May 1969, p. 10.

Henshaw, Laurie. "'Jimi Has Enough Talent to Hold an Audience Himself,'" *Melody Maker,* 16 November 1968, p. 7.

Hicks, Bob. "Jimi Hendrix: A Memorial," *Northwest Passage,* 29 September–13 October 1970, p. 19.

Hollingworth, Roy. "Hendrix Today," *Melody Maker,* 5 September 1970, p. 7.

Howard, Lucy, and Carla Koehl. "From Handel to Hendrix," *Newsweek,* 17 April 1995, p. 8.

Isler, Scott. "Jimi Hendrix in His Own Words," *Musician,* November 1991, pp. 32ff.

James, Dawn. "Wild, Man!" *Rave,* August 1967.

"Jimi," *Kudzu,* September 1970, p. 7.

"Jimi a Hit in Sweden—Refused Hotel Room," *Melody Maker,* 3 June 1967, p. 2.

"Jimi Hendrix and the Band of Gypsys: The Fillmore East," *Rolling Stone,* 4 June 1987, pp. 71ff.

Jimi Hendrix: A Selected Press Anthology 1967–70. Reid A. Paige Associates, 1995.

"Jimi Hendrix Blasts the Old Year Out with 'Space Rock,'" *The New York Times,* 1 January 1970.

"The Jimi Hendrix Experience," *Ebony,* May 1968, pp. 103–105.

"Jimi Hendrix in Concert: Paul Sauve Arena (Montreal)," *Logos,* May 1968, p. 20.

Jimi Hendrix obituary, *The London Times,* 19 September 1970, p. 14.

"Jimi Hendrix Paved the Way," *Soul,* 11 April 1970.

"Jimi in 3–D!" *Melody Maker,* 1 March 1969, p. 14.

Jones, Nick. "Hendrix—On the Crest of a Fave Rave," *Melody Maker,* 21 January 1967, p. 8.

Josephson, Mary. "Joplin and Hendrix: A Note on the Rhetoric of Death," *Art in America*, September 1971, pp. 96–97.

Keil, Charles. "'Ethnic' Music Traditions in the USA (Black Music; Country Music; Others; All)," *Popular Music*, May 1994, pp. 175–178.

Kennely, Patricia. "Season of the Witch," *Jazz & Pop*, January 1971, pp. 42–43.

Knight, Curtis. Interview with Nona Hatay. "His Guitar Was His Amulet," *Jimi Hendrix: The Spirit Lives On . . .*, San Francisco: Last Gasp, 1982, p. 43.

Kofsky, Frank. "The Scene," *Jazz & Pop*, December 1968, pp. 44–47.

Landau, Jon. "A Whiter Shade of Black," *The Age of Rock: Sounds of the American Cultural Revolution*, ed. Jonathan Eisen, pp. 298ff. New York: Vintage, 1969.

Lawrence, Sharon. "Castles Made of Sand," *San Francisco Chronicle, Image*, 25 November 1990, pp. 13ff.

Leo, John. "Rock Music's Din and Decline," *U.S. News & World Report*, 30 May 1994, p. 19.

Lipton, Michael. "Jimi Hendrix: *Blues*," *Musician*, July 1994, pp. 89–90.

Lydon, Michael. "Jimi Hendrix 1942–1970," *The New York Times*, 27 September 1970, Section II, p. 26.

———, and Ellen Mandel. "The Electric Guitar," *Boogie Lightnin'*, pp. 145–158. New York: The Dial Press, 1974.

McClendon, William H. "Black Music: Sound and Feeling for Black Liberation," *The Black Scholar*, January–February 1976, pp. 20–25.

Mandel, Howard. "The Hendrix Project," *Down Beat*, February 1990, p. 49.

Mangelsdorff, Rich. "Jimi Hendrix 1945–1970," *Nola Express*, 2 October 1970, p. 3.

Marcus, Greil. *Ranters and Crowd Pleasers: Punk in Pop Music 1977–92*. New York: Doubleday, 1993.

Marsh, Dave. "Hendrix LP Not Essential," *Rolling Stone*, 16 November 1978, p. 49.

———. "Jimi Hendrix: The Voodoo Lives On," *Musician Player & Listener*, October 1980, pp. 46ff.

———. *The First Rock & Roll Confidential Report*. New York: Pantheon, 1985.

"Massive U.S. Campaign to Push Hendrix," *New Musical Express*, 18 March 1967, p. 9.

Menn, Don. "Jimi's Favorite Guitar Techniques," *Guitar Player,* September 1975, pp. 12–13.

Milkowski, Bill. "Jimi Hendrix: The Jazz Connection," *Down Beat,* October 1982, pp. 17ff.

———. "Hendrix' Youngbloods," *Guitar World,* March 1988.

Miller, Jim. "Jimi Hendrix: *Axis: Bold as Love,*" *Rolling Stone,* 6 April 1968, p. 21.

Morthland, John. "Hendrix Is Buried in Home Town," *Rolling Stone,* 29 October 1970, pp. 18–20.

Mortifoglio, Richard. "Vindicating Jimi Hendrix," *The Village Voice,* 11 September 1978, p. 93.

Murray, Charles Shaar. *Crosstown Traffic: Jimi Hendrix and the Post-War Rock 'n' Roll Revolution.* New York: St. Martin's Press, 1989.

"Necessarily Stoned, but Beautiful," *The Economist,* 24 November 1990, pp. 102–103.

Noble, Douglas J. "Henry Rollins on Jimi," *UniVibes,* 17 February 1995, p. 5.

Nordlie, Tom. "Jimi Hendrix," *Spin,* April 1992, p. 52.

O'Rourke, P. J. "I Don't Live Today," *Harry,* 3 October 1970, p. 14.

"Oval Jimi?" *The London Times,* 1 September 1970, p. 6.

Owen, Frank, and Simon Reynolds. "Why Hendrix Still Matters," *Spin,* April 1991, pp. 28ff.

Palin, Chuck. "The Sexual Jimi Chicks Wanted to Ball," *Daily Planet* (Florida), 18 October 1970, pp. 18–19.

Palmer, Tony. "Eric Clapton: Why Did Hendrix and Joplin Die?" *The New York Times,* 8 October 1970, p. 28.

Pareles, Jon. "The Jazz Generation Pays Tribute to Jimi Hendrix," *The New York Times,* 4 December 1989, Section C, p. 16.

Pattison, Robert. *The Triumph of Vulgarity: Rock Music in the Mirror of Romanticism.* New York: Oxford University Press, 1987.

Pekar, Harvey. "From Rock to ???" *Down Beat,* 2 May 1968, pp. 20ff.

Philips, Chuck. "Experiencing Jimi Hendrix," *Los Angeles Times/Calendar,* 26 November 1989, pp. 62ff.

Phillips, Tom. "Integrated Rock," *Jazz & Pop,* 5 July 1968, pp. 24–25.

Piccarella, John. Hendrix entry, *The New Grove Dictionary of American Music,* pp. 370–372. New York: Macmillan, 1986.

Prendergast, Mark. "Racial Rehabilitation," *New Statesman & Society,* 28 April 1995, pp. 40–41.

Pringle, Douglas. "Jimi Hendrix at Maple Leaf Gardens," *Arts Canada,* August 1969, p. 45.

Redd, Lawrence N. "Rock! It's Still Rhythm and Blues," *The Black Perspective in Music,* Spring 1985, pp. 31–46.

Redding, Noel, and Carol Appleby. "Bad Trips: The End of the Jimi Hendrix Experience," *Musician,* September 1986, pp. 88–96.

———. "Standing Next to a Mountain," *Musician,* August 1986, pp. 62–78.

Reynolds, Simon. *Blissed Out: The Raptures of Rock.* Serpent's Tail: London, 1990.

Richardson, Ken. "The Jimi Hendrix Experience: *Radio One,*" *High Fidelity,* March 1989, p. 79.

Richman, Robin. "An Infinity of Jimis," *Life,* 3 October 1969, pp. 72–75.

Rick. "Hendrix," *Berkeley Tribe,* 2 October 1970, p. 25.

Rockwell, John. "How the Electric Guitar Became a Way of Music," *The New York Times,* 15 July 1974, p. 33.

Rosenbaum, Michael. "Jimi Hendrix and Live Things," *Crawdaddy,* May 1968, pp. 24–29.

Rosenstein, Michael. "*If Six Was Nine:* La Musica di Jimi Hendrix per Jazz Ensemble," *Cadence,* April 1993, p. 100.

Rubin, Mike, "Reel to Reel: *Jimi Hendrix at the Isle of Wight,*" *The Village Voice,* 16 July 1991, pp. 64–65.

Ruby, Jack. Jimi Hendrix interview, *Jazz & Pop,* 17 July 1968, pp. 15–17.

Santoro, Gene. "Heart Full of Hendrix," *Down Beat,* July 1990, pp. 36–37.

———. "The House That Jimi Built," *Guitar World,* September 1985, pp. 24ff.

Schwartz, Jeff. "Writing Jimi: Rock Guitar Pedagogy as Postmodern Folkloric Practice," *Popular Music,* 1993, pp. 281–288.

Senoff, Pete. "Jimi Hendrix: *Band of Gypsys,*" *Jazz & Pop,* September 1970, pp. 57–58.

Sexton, Paul. "Jimi at 50: Gone but Still a Star," *Billboard,* 28 November 1992, pp. 1ff.

Shaw, Arnold. *Black Popular Music in America: From the Spirituals, Minstrels and Ragtime to Soul, Disco and Hip-Hop.* New York: Schirmer Books, 1986.

————. "Jimi Hendrix: Reactive Noise and the Big Nasty," *The World of Soul: Black America's Contribution to the Pop Music Scene,* pp. 261–267. New York: Cowles Book Company, 1970.

Shurman, Dick. "Guitar Shorty: Blues on the Flip Side," *Living Blues,* January/February 1991, pp. 23–27.

Simpson, Frank. "The Black Elvis," *Melody Maker,* 16 March 1968, p. 5.

Smith, Steven G. "Blues and our Mind-Body Problem," *Popular Music,* January 1992, pp. 41–52.

Souster, Tim. "Rock, Beat, Pop—Avantgarde," *The World of Music* (Berlin), XII/2 (1970), pp. 33–43.

Stern, Chip. "Jimi Hendrix: A Slight Return," *The Village Voice,* 28 April 1980, p. 59.

Straight Ahead (Box 965, Novato, CA 94948–0965), 1995.

Swenson, John. "The Last Days of Jimi Hendrix," *Crawdaddy,* January 1975, pp. 39–45.

Szatmary, David P. *Rockin' in Time: A Social History of Rock and Roll,* 3rd ed. Englewood Cliffs, NJ: Prentice-Hall, 1996.

Szyfmanovicz, Roland. "Jimi Hendrix," *Jazz Hot,* May 1972, p. 46.

Tucker, Bruce. "Living Metaphors: Recent Black Music Biography," *Black Music Research Journal,* 1983, pp. 58–68.

UniVibes (Coppeen, Enniskeane, County Cork, Republic of Ireland), August 1995.

Vargas, Gary. "The Hendrix Project: A Moving Experience," *Straight Ahead,* January/February 1993, pp. 21–22.

————. "Jimi's Back Pages: Bob Dylan," *UniVibes,* November 1993, pp. 42–47.

"The Voice of Experience," *Newsweek,* 9 October 1967, pp. 90–92.

Von Tersch, Gary. "Jimi Hendrix: *Band of Gypsys,*" *Rolling Stone,* 28 May 1970, p. 48.

Voodoo Child (Jimi Hendrix Management Institute [JIMI], Indianapolis, IN 46220), Spring, Fall, and Winter 1994.

Wale, Michael. "An American Experience," *Melody Maker,* 22 July 1967, p. 7.

Walsh, Alan, "'I Felt We Were in Danger of Becoming the U.S. Dave Dee," *Melody Maker* (20 July 1968) p. 5.

Weinstein, Deena. *Heavy Metal: A Cultural Sociology.* New York: Lexington Books, 1991.

Weisberg, Jack. "A Sociological View of the Mind, Soul and Body of the Hendrix Experience," *Circus,* September 1969, p. 29ff.

Welch, Chris. Caught in the Act: *Melody Maker,* "Jimi Hendrix, a fantastic American guitarist . . ." 31 December 1966, p. 12; "The Other (Wrestling) Side of Jimi Hendrix," 14 October 1967, p. 4.

———. "Who Says Jimi Hendrix Can't Sing? (He Does!)" *Melody Maker,* 15 April 1967, p. 3.

Weller, Sheila. "Jimi Hendrix: 'I Don't Want to Be a Clown Any More . . . ,'" *Rolling Stone,* 15 November 1969, pp. 28–29.

Whiteley, Sheila. "Progressive Rock and Psychedelic Coding in the Work of Jimi Hendrix," *Popular Music,* January 1990, pp. 37–59.

Wilmer, Valerie. "An Experience," *Down Beat,* 4 April 1968; reprinted in *Down Beat,* February 1994, pp. 38–42.

Yorke, Annette. "Heroine to the Rescue: Jimi Hendrix Is Innocent," *Rolling Stone,* 21 January 1970, pp. 1ff.

Yorke, Ritchie. "Redding on Jimi: 'I Said Stuff It,'" *Rolling Stone,* 15 November 1969, p. 10.

———, and Ben Fong-Torres. "Hendrix Busted in Toronto," *Rolling Stone,* 31 May 1969, p. 10.

Zappa, Frank. "The Oracle Has It All Psyched Out," *Life,* 28 June 1968, pp. 82ff.

Permissions

"Jimi Hendrix, a fantastic American guitarist . . ." by Chris Welch (31 December 1966) reprinted with permission from *Melody Maker.*

"Hendrix IS Out of This World" by Keith Altham (15 April 1967) reproduced courtesy of *New Musical Express*, London.

"Wild, Man!" by Dawn James appeared in *Rave,* August 1967.

"Who Says Jimi Hendrix Can't Sing? (He Does!)" by Chris Welch (15 April 1967) reprinted with permission from *Melody Maker.*

"Jimi a Hit in Sweden—Refused Hotel Room" (3 June 1967) reprinted with permission from *Melody Maker.*

"Bad Shows Bring Jimi Down" by Norrie Drummond (10 June 1967) reproduced courtesy of *New Musical Express*, London.

"Massive U.S. Campaign to Push Hendrix" (18 March 1967) reproduced courtesy of *New Musical Express*, London.

"The Voice of Experience" from *Newsweek,* 9 October 1967 and ©1967, Newsweek, Inc. All rights reserved. Reprinted by permission.

"I Felt We Were in Danger of Becoming the U.S. Dave Dee" by Alan Walsh (20 July 1968) reprinted with permission from *Melody Maker.*

"Hendrix Busted in Toronto" by Ritchie Yorke and Ben Fong-Torres, from *Rolling Stone* (31 May 1969). By Straight Arrow Publishers, Inc. 1969. All Rights Reserved. Reprinted by Permission.

"Hendrix' One-Year Retirement Plan" from *Rolling Stone* (17 May 1969). By Straight Arrow Publishers, Inc. 1969. All Rights Reserved. Reprinted by Permission.

Index

About the Editor

Chris Potash was pop-music critic for the *Miami Daily News* and the Wilkes-Barre *Times Leader;* he was assistant managing editor of Grove Press, New York, and (later) a bike messenger at UC-Berkeley. He is a published concrete poet.